Praise for Don Box

Essential COM (1998 Addison-Wesley, ISBN: 0-201-63446-5)

"Nobody explains COM better than Don Box."
> —Charlie Kindel, COM Guy, Microsoft Corporation

"Sometimes there are so many good things to say about one book, it's worth saying twice. That's one reason why Don's book has two forewords—it's that good."
> —Grady Booch, author of *Object Solutions: Managing the Object-Oriented Project* and *Object-Oriented Analysis and Design with Applications*

"Don Box makes it possible for mere mortals to join the COM cognoscenti. If you're a C++ COM programmer, buy this book."
> —David Chappell, Principal, Chappell & Associates and author of *Understanding ActiveX and OLE*

"Just as Stroustrup's [*The C++ Programming Language*] is widely considered the definitive reference for C++ for its depth and completeness, so *Essential COM* deserves to be elected the definitive reference for COM due to the same outstanding quality"
> —Davide Marcato, Dr. Dobb's Electronic Review of Computer Books

"Don Box is one of the premier COM gurus, and his *Essential COM* is a great way to develop advanced COM knowledge and illuminate the dark corners . . . the author has a knack for clear explanations with just enough humor to keep things interesting . . . Box keeps everything in perspective."
> —Don Kiely, Book Review at DevX.com

Effective COM, Co-Authored with Keith Brown, Tim Ewald, and Chris Sells
(1999 Addison-Wesley, ISBN: 0-201-37968-6)

"*Effective COM* excels in its succinct style. It presents advanced COM topics in a masterful and hype-free manner, yet without lengthy introductory discussions. It can be recommended for experienced COM programmers and designers who wish to improve their skills by gaining deeper understanding of COM's underlying mechanism."

—Danny Kalev, Book Review at DevX.com

"[If] you are an experienced developer spending hours a day with COM/MTS and C++, or simply a COM programmer with much more theoretical knowledge than practical experience and strong intentions to avoid the typical errors and general misconceptions, you will do yourself a big favor purchasing a copy [of *Effective COM*]."

—Davide Marcato, Dr. Dobb's Electronic Review of Computer Books

"It is easy to see why the authors, individually and as a group, are so highly respected. Reading each COM programming tip is like turning on a lightbulb. The ability of the authors to clearly explain complex problems, and then suggest solutions is what makes this book so useful."

—Ranjiv Sharma, Product Architect, Rights Exchange, Inc.

The DevelopMentor Series
Don Box, Editor

Addison-Wesley has joined forces with DevelopMentor, a premiere developer resources company, to produce a series of technical books written by developers for developers. DevelopMentor boasts a prestigious technical staff that includes some of the world's best-known computer science professionals.

*"Works in **The DevelopMentor Series** will be practical and informative sources on the tools and techniques for applying component-based technologies to real-world, large-scale distributed systems."*
—Don Box

Titles in the Series:

Essential XML
Beyond Markup
Don Box, Aaron Skonnard, and John Lam
0-201-70914-7

Programming Windows Security
Keith Brown
0-201-60442-6

Advanced Visual Basic 6
Power Techniques for Everyday Programs
Matthew Curland
0-201-70712-8

Transactional COM+
Building Scalable Applications
Tim Ewald
0-201-61594-0

Debugging Windows Programs
Strategies, Tools, and Techniques for Visual C++ Programmers
Everett N. McKay and Mike Woodring
0-201-70238-X

Watch for future titles in The DevelopMentor Series.

Essential XML

Beyond Markup

Don Box
Aaron Skonnard
John Lam

Addison-Wesley

Boston • San Francisco • New York • Toronto
Montreal • London • Munich • Paris • Madrid
Capetown • Sydney • Tokyo • Singapore
Mexico City

Copyright © 2000 by Addison-Wesley

The publisher offers discounts on this book when ordered in quantity for special sales. For more information, please contact:

Pearson Education Corporate Sales Division
One Lake Street
Upper Saddle River, NJ 07458
(800) 382-3419
corpsales@pearsontechgroup.com

Visit us on the Web at www.awl.com/cseng/

Library of Congress Control Number: 00-133569

ISBN 0-201-70914-7

Text printed on recycled paper.
1 2 3 4 5 6 7 8 9 10—CRS—04 03 02 01 00
First printing, July 2000

Contents

Preface

XML has replaced Java, Design Patterns, and Object Technology as the software industry's solution to world hunger. The trade press has anointed XML as the universal duct tape for all software integration problems, and the large vendors happily support this vision[1] by integrating XML into everything including database engines, development tools, web browsers, and operating systems. This is especially ironic given the relatively humble origins of XML, which lie squarely in the world of document management systems. Despite these somewhat unglamorous origins, the industry at large is out to recast all things good and honorable in terms of XML whether it makes sense or not. Rather than simply stand on the sidelines questioning the relative nakedness of the emperor du jour, we have written this book largely as an exercise to sort out for ourselves what XML really means to the software practitioner. As Addison-Wesley (and DevelopMentor) were both kind enough to fund our work, the least we can do is let them publish the travelogue to recoup their investment. DevelopMentor has also been kind enough to donate web space for the support page for this book. That page can be found at `http://www.develop.com/books/essentialxml`.

The XML community is a community divided. On one side is the "document" camp; on the other side is the "data" camp. The document-centric view of XML purports that an XML document is an annotated text file that contains markup directives to control the formatting and presentation of the contained text. The data-centric view advocates that XML is but one of many representations of a

---

[1]One could make a convincing argument that the large vendors control the trade press, however, that viewpoint is overly simplistic.

typed value that software agents can use for data interchange and interoperation. The document-centric view assumes that tools like emacs, notepad, or high-priced document management systems will generate XML. This viewpoint emphasizes the syntax of XML and treats the angle bracket as the central theme of XML. The data-centric view assumes that XML is yet another serialization format that will never be manipulated or viewed directly by humans. This viewpoint relegates the syntax of XML to a minor detail that is only important to the small handful of people who write low-level XML parsers. This book falls squarely in this latter camp. That stance may offend some readers; however, it is the authors' strong belief that the ratio of hand-authored XML to software-generated XML is in sharp decline.

XML is a family of layered technologies. This book uses the layering model of XML as its guide and looks at each technology as it relates to the core XML specification: the XML Information Set (Infoset). The Infoset is the most pivotal of all XML specifications, as it describes exactly what an XML document is in syntax-free terms. Most interesting XML specifications and technologies are written in terms of the Infoset. This makes many XML technologies generalizable to applications that do not use the XML 1.0 serialization format, which has extremely interesting implications for the future of XML. The book is organized as follows:

Chapter 1: Beyond Markup

XML is simultaneously an abstract data model and a serialization format. This chapter looks at the relationship between these two roles and presents a detailed overview of the structural model of an XML document as it is described in the XML Information Set (Infoset) specification.

Chapter 2: Programming XML

At the time of this writing, there were two common projections of the Infoset onto programmatic types. The Simple API for XML Version 2 (SAX2) and the Document Object Model Level 2 (DOML2) present completely different models over the same underlying Infoset. This chapter looks at the similarities and differences between the two models. The Apache Xerces and Microsoft XML parsers are used as concrete examples.

Chapter 3: Navigation

XML provides a family of technologies for navigating XML structures and addressing subsets of those structures. This chapter looks at XPath, XPointer, XInclude and XBase as a suite of technologies used to create both intradocument and interdocument relationships.

Chapter 4: Schemas

XML Schemas bring the modern conveniences of running water and electricity to the uncivilized world of pre-schema XML. Prior to the XML Schema language, XML supported structure but not type. Schemas bring a type system to XML that reflects the past 30 years of software engineering practices. This chapter looks at how that type system works and how it is described.

Chapter 5: Transformation

XML has a programming language and that language is the XSL Transformation language (XSLT). This chapter looks at how XSLT joins the ranks of languages such as Perl, Active Server Pages, and Java Server Pages by allowing exemplars of a text file to be adorned with executable instructions.

Chapter 6: Beyond Interface-based Programming

In its rush to attack every software problem with the XML hammer, many XML-based applications are reinventing paradigms and techniques that have already been codified in the world of component integration. This chapter looks at the role of XML as a software integration technology, first by looking at the state-of-the-practice in the pre-XML world, and then looking at how XML can replace large chunks of technology that delivered less than promised.

Appendix A: The XML Information Set (Infoset)

The Infoset is the most important yet least read XML specification. This appendix contains a reprint of the most recent public draft of this specification.

Appendix B: XML 1.0 + Namespaces Productions

The serialization rules and abstract data model rely on a set of productions defined in the *Extensible Markup Language 1.0* and *Namespaces in XML* specifications.

This appendix contains the complete list of productions sorted both by name and by production number.

Appendix C: Example Gallery

The chapters in this book attempt to show only the smallest possible XML or code fragment needed to make the point. This appendix contains larger examples for readers looking for additional context.

Acknowledgements

The authors collectively would like to thank Kristin Erickson, Jacquelyn Doucette, John Wait, Kathy Glidden, and the late[2] Carter Shanklin for shepherding this book through Addison-Wesley. The authors would also like to collectively thank all those who read drafts during the production of this book. These very helpful folk include Bob Beauchemin, Tim Ewald, David Ezell, Dave Hollander, Gopal Kakivaya, David Megginson, Noah Mendelsohn, Chris Sells, and Dan Sullivan. Any errors or flaws that remain are of course the responsibility of the authors (most likely Don).

Don would like to personally thank the always-enthusiastic Aaron Skonnard for initiating the project and acting as spiritual (cheer)leader and John Lam for causing me to look into the blinding white light that is XSLT. This broth was definitely not spoiled by the presence of your culinary expertise.

Thanks to Dave Reed and Greg Hope for roping me into the SOAP project back in March of 1998. I can't believe how much that project has impacted my professional life. Thanks to Bob Atkinson and Mohsen Al-Ghosein of Microsoft for their early dedication to the SOAP cause, and to John Montgomery, Satish Thatte, Andrew Layman, and Henrik Fredrick Neilsen for sneaking SOAP past the 24,000 owner/employees at Microsoft, all of whom wanted to get their fingerprints on the spec.

Special thanks to my friend Gopal Kakivaya, who forced me to rethink my assumptions about XML, COM, and type more times than I can remember. Numerous discussions with Keith Brown, Tim Ewald, Michi Henning, Noah Mendelsohn, Chris Sells and Henry Thompson provided invaluable context for that exploration.

---

[2] OK, so Carter is still walking the earth, just not at Addison-Wesley.

A wet, sloppy thank you to David Baum and his staff, both for providing me with tons of support during an especially difficult time and for letting me hang up the virtual shingle that read "The Law Offices of Donald F. Box" at least for a day. This book would never have been completed if not for the sanctuary (and over-sized bathtub in the Governor's Suite) provided by Roger Evans and Luc Bramlett.

Thanks to Michael Longacre, Joanne Steinhart, and the late Joe Flanigen and Eric Maffei at MSJ for looking the other way as I slipped deadlines during the production of this book. Thanks to the staff at DevelopMentor for ignoring me while I remained dark for month after month and for providing the most supportive working environment I could ever imagine. Special thanks go to Mike Abercrombie, Helga Thomsen, Barbara Box, Maggie Smith, Ron Sumida, Martin Gudgin, Tim Ewald, and Judith Swerling for proving that it takes a village to be Don Box.

Finally, the growing number of Boxes that provide a larger and richer context for all of this have once again proved that there is life beyond the Infoset. I am not worthy of their love and dedication.

Aaron would like to personally thank his wife, Monica, for the patience and support that she willingly gave to this project. I would also like to thank my children, Michelle and Michael, for sacrificing some of their time with Dad. I can't express the joy that each of you bring into my life.

Thanks to my parents, sisters, and in-laws for their endless support and sincere interest in all that I do. Thanks to Kristin Erickson and Addison-Wesley Professional for their hard work and patience. And thanks to everyone at DevelopMentor for your individual contributions toward such an innovative and rewarding environment.

And finally, thanks to my coauthors for their dedication to this project and their never-ending passion. A special thanks to Don Box for his continual guidance and inspiring personality.

John would like to personally thank Aaron for coming up with the original idea for this book, and Don for shaping the story that ultimately became this book. I found that I took far more away from the experience than I put into it. Thanks, guys, for making it such a great experience.

A great big thanks goes out to all of the folks at DevelopMentor, a first-class organization all the way around. Thanks for making it possible for me to do the things that I love to do.

I would like to thank Michael Leneghan for his support and encouragement during and after my transition back to computing. I would not be where I am today without your help. *Gracias.*

I would especially like to thank Professor Ronald Kluger for his mentorship during my tenure in grad school. You taught me how to think critically and write clearly. Your impact is clearly felt throughout the pages of this book. Thanks.

To my parents and my brother, Thomas, who have been with me since the beginning, a heartfelt thanks for taking an interest in my work and in my life. And finally, thanks to Carolyn for her love, support and encouragement over the past 12 years. We made it!

John Lam
Toronto, Ontario
`http://www.iunknown.com`
May 2000

Don Box
Manhattan Beach, California
`http://www.develop.com/dbox`
May 2000

Aaron Skonnard
Layton, Utah
`http://www.skonnard.com`
May 2000

Chapter 1

Beyond Markup

```
struct Element {
wchar_t                          local_name[];
wchar_t                          namespace_URI[];
struct Attribute                 attributes[];
struct NamespaceDeclaration *    declared_namespaces[];
void *                           children[];
} ;
```

Anonymous, 2000

XML is a technology that layers type and structure over information. As Figure 1.1 shows, XML bridges the worlds of application datatypes and units of storage and transmission. To this end, XML can be thought of as a serialization format or transfer syntax. This is certainly one of the primary applications for XML. However, the layering of XML technologies allows the structure and type system of XML to be used independently from the standardized representation used to store XML-based information in files or network messages. This independence allows disparate software agents to interoperate by modeling application boundary crossings in terms of application-specific types, secure in the knowledge that an XML-based representation of these types can be exchanged across language, process, host, and vendor boundaries. It is this feature that has made XML the heir apparent to the component software technologies popularized in the 1990s.

XML is ultimately a set of recommendations published by the World Wide Web Consortium (W3C) that specifies the semantics and syntax of XML and XML-related technologies. Most of the technologies described in this book have achieved recommendation status, which means they are extremely stable and have broad to universal industry support. However, several technologies are still works-in-progress and have not yet been ratified as full recommendations; they are still at the working draft or candidate recommendation stage. Table 1.1 lists the specifications on which this book relies, as well as their status at the time of this writing.

The most critical XML specification is the *XML Information Set (Infoset)* specification. The Infoset models the core abstractions of XML as a set of structural *information items* that have one or more named *properties*. The Infoset model is completely free from the syntactic detail described in the *Extensible Markup Language 1.0* and *Namespaces in XML* specifications.[1] Notions of what is and is not legal syntax (such as the rules of well-formedness and application-defined structural validity) belong exclusively to XML 1.0 + namespaces; the Infoset does not consider documents that are not well-formed or that have failed XML 1.0's application-defined validity constraints. In fact, virtually all parts of XML 1.0 that are used to determine validity are not retained in the Infoset model.

As an example of the relationship between the Infoset and XML 1.0 + namespaces, the XML 1.0 specification describes the serialization format of XML in terms of (potentially named) units of storage called *entities*. The Infoset models an XML 1.0 entity as an *entity information item*. The entity information item has a number of named properties that correspond to aspects of an entity implied by XML 1.0's serialization format. When Infoset property names appear in prose, they are typically written in brackets (e.g., [system identifier]). The Infoset makes explicit the structural model that is implied by the XML 1.0 + Namespaces specifications.

The Infoset considers certain information items and properties to be part of the XML Information Set Core. These items and properties are considered

---

[1] The Namespaces in XML recommendation is an addendum to the original XML 1.0 recommendation. The prenamespace XML 1.0 could more aptly be called the arbitrary markup language, as there was no formalized way to disambiguate element and attribute names on an Internet-wide scale without resorting to ugly hacks.

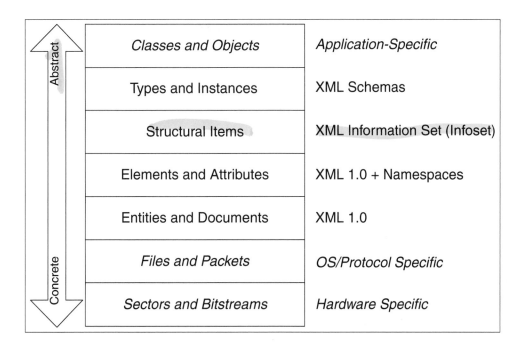

Classes and Objects	*Application-Specific*	
Types and Instances	XML Schemas	
Structural Items	XML Information Set (Infoset)	
Elements and Attributes	XML 1.0 + Namespaces	
Entities and Documents	XML 1.0	
Files and Packets	*OS/Protocol Specific*	
Sectors and Bitstreams	*Hardware Specific*	

Figure 1.1 XML as a better component technology

critical to proper interpretation and must be supported by all XML technologies. To retain fidelity with the underlying serialized representation, the Infoset defines a much broader set of items and properties beyond those in the Infoset core, but these items and properties are considered to be of peripheral importance, and XML technologies are free to simply drop them on the floor. As an example, XML 1.0 supports three mechanisms for adorning content: processing instructions, attributes, and comments. Of these three mechanisms, only processing instructions and attributes are considered part of the Infoset core and must be supported by all XML technologies. Comments, on the other hand, are considered of peripheral interest, and XML processing software is free to discard them without loss of significant information.

It is important to note that the Infoset does not mandate a programmatic interface, however several can be (and have been) inferred. The Infoset also does not mandate the use of XML 1.0's transfer syntax; rather, that format is simply a lowest-common-denominator standard for interchange between heterogeneous

Table 1.1 W3C XML Specifications and Technologies

Specification/URL/Status (as of April 2000)	Description
XML Information Set `http://www.w3.org/TR/xml-infoset` Working Draft in Last Call	A syntax-free description of an abstract XML document.
Extensible Markup Language 1.0 `http://www.w3.org/TR/REC-xml` Recommendation	The core prenamespace transfer syntax of XML 1.0.
Namespaces in XML `http://www.w3.org/TR/REC-xml-names` Recommendation	An addendum to XML 1.0 that specifies how to qualify element and attribute names with unique name-space identifiers.
XML Base (XBase) `http://www.w3.org/TR/xmlbase` Working Draft in Last Call	An addendum to XML 1.0 that specifies how to indicate the base URI to use when calculating relative URI references contained as attribute or element values.
XML Inclusions (XInclude) `http://www.w3.org/TR/xinclude` Working Draft in Development	An addendum to XML 1.0 that provides a non-DTD-based alternative to external parsed general entities.
Document Object Model (DOM) Level 2 `http://www.w3.org/TR/DOM-Level-2` Candidate Recommendation	A set of abstract programmatic interfaces for traversing, manipulating, and creating XML documents.
XML Schema Part 1: Structures `http://www.w3.org/TR/xmlschema-1/` Working Draft in Last Call	An XML-based language for describing XML elements, attributes, and notations in terms of hierarchical types.
XML Schema Part 2: Datatypes `http://www.w3.org/TR/xmlschema-2/` Working Draft in Last Call	A set of built-in textual datatypes (e.g., `float`, `string`) and an XML-based language for defining user-generated textual datatypes.
XML Path Language (XPath) Version 1.0 `http://www.w3.org/TR/xpath` Recommendation	A language for selecting a set of nodes in an XML document.
XML Pointer Language `http://www.w3.org/TR/xptr` Working Draft in Last Call	A language for using XPath expressions as URI fragment identifiers.
XML Linking Language `http://www.w3.org/TR/xlink` Working Draft in Development	A language for representing link relationships between XML documents.
XSL Tranformations (XSLT) Version 1.0 `http://www.w3.org/TR/xslt` Recommendation	A language for expressing transformations from one XML vocabulary to another.

systems. The fact that XML 1.0's transfer syntax is text-based facilitates low-tech solutions based on XML as well as solving the "how do I draw this thing" problem for people who need to mix exposition with examples of XML-based instances in documentation, technical articles, and books like the one you are currently reading. At the time of this writing, several organizations are developing alternative nontextual representations of the XML Infoset. If these representations maintain high fidelity with the Infoset, however, existing systems can continue to interoperate via translation to the canonical text-based format currently in use. In general, this book takes the approach of most XML recommendations and focuses on the information set. It is assumed that readers interested in writing low-level XML parsers will use the *XML 1.0* and *Namespaces in XML* recommendations as the definitive reference on the details of XML's serialized representation.

Document Basics

Entities are the atoms of XML. Entities typically correspond to files or network messages but could potentially be part of any storage medium. To put order around the chaos of multiple entities, XML 1.0 defines a *document* as one or more entities that comprise a single structured data object. The Infoset models an XML 1.0 document as a *document information item,* which, as shown in Figure 1.2, is generally considered the root of the object model defined by the Infoset.

A document information item layers additional structure over the collection of entities in which it was stored. The document information item acts as the root of a tree-oriented graph of element, processing instruction, comment, and character information items. Processing instruction, comment, and character information items act as leaf nodes, and element information items act as internal nodes. The Infoset defines two well-known properties that make this graph explicit. The `[parent]` property references the containing information item, and because the document information item is the root of the graph, it does not have this property. The `[children]` property is the ordered collection of immediate ancestors in the graph, and because the processing instruction, comment, and character information items are leaves of the graph, they do not have this property. Because an element must have a parent and may have children, it has both properties, although the `[children]` property may be empty.

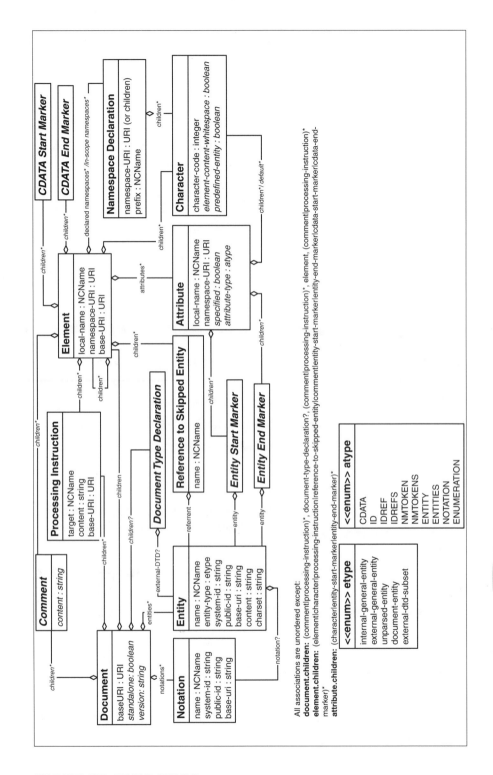

Figure 1.2   UML model of XML Infoset

The workhorse of XML is the element information item, which is the richest data type and in practice the most heavily used (in fact, you cannot have an XML document without at least one element). Every document information item has exactly one element information item in its [children] property. This distinguished element information item is sometimes called the *document* or *root* element. The document's [children] property can contain additional processing instruction and comment information items both before and after the lone element information item. Element information items also have a property named [children] that can contain character information items interleaved with element, comment, and processing instruction information items also supported by the document.

Element information items are fairly adaptable to representing arbitrary data structures, as one simply needs to build an isomorphism between the "native" data structure and a tree-oriented graph of elements and character data. When an element represents an atomic type, the value of that type is encoded as character data. Elements with this content model are referred to as *text-only* elements. When an element represents a structured type, the element typically has no character data children but rather has one or more child elements, one per facet of the structured type. Elements with this content model are referred to as *element-only* elements. For modeling traditional data structures, these two forms are sufficient. However, because of XML's heritage in document management systems, XML allows child elements to be interleaved with character data. This content model is known as mixed content and is shown in Figure 1.3. Mixed content makes sense if one believes that XML is primarily a technology for decorating human-authored text files with formatting directives. However, if one believes that XML is primarily a technology for allowing software agents to share information, the case for mixed content is dubious at best, as the syntactic convenience of mixed content is only more convenient for humans, not for XML processing software. For this reason, XML-based representations of traditional data structures tend to use text-only/element-only content models as shown in Figure 1.4.

Each element information item has an [attributes] property that is an unordered list of uniquely named *attribute information items,* each of which has a [children] property consisting of zero or more characters. Attributes typically act as a set of named properties that annotate the element they are

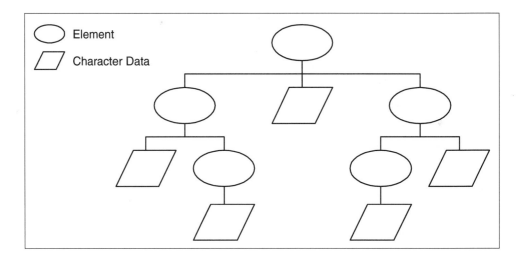

Figure 1.3   Mixed content

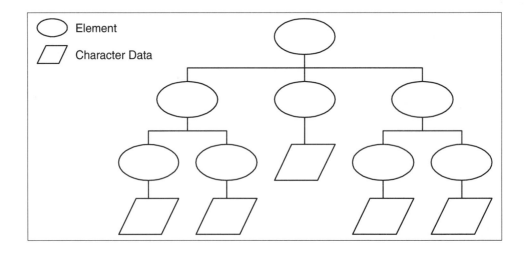

Figure 1.4   Element-only and text-only content

associated with. Unlike an element's `[children]`, the `[attributes]` property is unordered and not considered part of the document content graph.
Because attributes are unordered, accessing an attribute by position makes little
sense. Rather, each attribute of an element is uniquely named to allow unam-
biguous access. Unlike elements, attributes are largely unstructured and cannot

ESSENTIAL XML: BEYOND MARKUP

themselves be annotated with additional attributes, nor can an attribute contain elements, comments, or processing instructions. For this reason, many XML users favor elements over attributes for many situations, as elements are a functional superset of attributes.[2]

Names

Both elements and attributes are named. To ensure that names can be unambiguously interpreted, both element and attribute names use Uniform Resource Identifiers (URI) to ensure naming conflicts do not occur across multiple XML formats. A URI is either a Uniform Resource Name (URN) or a Uniform Resource Locator (URL). The former is a location-independent identifier (like a UUID). The latter embeds location hints into the identifier itself. In either case, when URIs are used to disambiguate names in XML, they are treated as identifiers for an abstract set of names called a *namespace*. There is no requirement that dereferencing a namespace URI will yield anything useful. Rather, namespace URIs are simply opaque identifiers and nothing more. The namespace URI is critical for XML documents that will be exchanged across organizational boundaries, as they identify the context in which the element or attribute has meaning. The namespace URI also disambiguates intradocument name collisions that are inevitable when combining XML constructs from multiple organizations.

All element and attribute names have two components: a local name and a namespace URI. The local name is a sequence of one or more characters that must adhere to the NCName production, which is defined as follows:

```
NCName     ::= (Letter | '_') (NCNameChar)*            [4 xmlns]
NCNameChar ::= Letter | Digit | '.' | '-' | '_'
               | CombiningChar | Extender               [5 xmlns]
```

Broadly speaking, an NCName begins with an alphabetic character or an underscore followed by zero or more alphanumeric characters, periods, hyphens, underscores, or full stops.[3]

---

[2]Prior to XML Schemas, this was not quite true, as only attributes could act as references to unparsed entities or notations. Fortunately, the XML Schema specification removes this (and many other) artificial distinctions between elements and attributes.

[3]Refer to Appendix B for full expansion of all productions of XML 1.0 and Namespaces in XML.

The following is the serialized form of an element information item whose local name is `People` and is not affiliated with any namespace:

```
<People />
```

Because the local name `People` might have somewhat different meaning to various software agents or humans that encounter this XML document, one should exercise caution when using unaffiliated names in XML documents that will be seen by anyone other than the author.

The following is the serialized form of an element information item whose local name is `People` and whose namespace URI is `uuid:1c759aed-b748-475c-ab68-10679700c4f2`:

```
<People xmlns='uuid:1c759aed-b748-475c-ab68-10679700c4f2' />
```

The `xmlns='uri-reference'` namespace declaration binds the URI reference to the *default namespace* of the element. This means that unless otherwise specified, the default namespace URI applies to all child elements. Consider the following serialized element:

```
<People xmlns='uuid:1c759aed-b748-475c-ab68-10679700c4f2' >
  <Person/>
</People>
```

Because there is a default namespace declaration in effect and the `Person` child element does not have an overriding namespace declaration, the namespace URI of the `Person` element is also `uuid:1c759aed-b748-475c-ab68-10679700c4f2`. However, the child element could have explicitly provided its own namespace URI as follows:

```
<People xmlns='uuid:1c759aed-b748-475c-ab68-10679700c4f2' >
  <Person xmlns='http://www.example.net/people/schema/' />
</People>
```

Had the `Person` element also had child elements, they would inherit the default namespace of `http://www.example.net/people/schema/`, unless they explicitly provided a namespace URI of their own.

ESSENTIAL XML: BEYOND MARKUP

To remove the `Person` element from any namespace (in essence, making its local name unaffiliated), one could set the default namespace to the empty string.

```
<People xmlns='uuid:1c759aed-b748-475c-ab68-10679700c4f2' >
  <Person xmlns=" />
</People>
```

Using `xmlns="` indicates that the name `Person` is not affiliated with any namespace.[4]

XML supports using local aliases to namespace URI as a syntactic convenience. Each element contains an unordered list of namespace declarations that map an `NCName`-based prefix to a URI. The following is a serialized namespace declaration:

```
xmlns:myns='uri-reference'
```

The local prefix in this declaration is `myns`, and its format must adhere to the `NCName` production discussed earlier. This alias can be used as a prefix for both element and attribute names, each of which must adhere to the `QName` production:

```
QName     ::= (Prefix ':' )? LocalPart        [6 xmlns]
Prefix    ::= NCName                           [7 xmlns]
LocalPart ::= NCName                           [8 xmlns]
```

If an element name is simply a local name with no prefix, the default namespace declaration in effect is applied (as shown in previous examples). If an attribute name is simply a local name with no prefix, the attribute is not affiliated with any namespace, irrespective of what default namespace may be in effect.[5]

---

[4]This statement reflects the common understanding if not the normative language of the *Namespaces in XML* recommendation.

[5]This unfortunate asymmetry between elements and attributes is an artifact of XML's heritage in document markup, as one of the goals of *Namespaces in XML* was to allow new markup vocabularies to be layered over existing documents. In this scenario, name collisions among markup tags were the primary concern.

Namespace declarations apply to the element they appear in as well as all attributes and child elements. This XML instance

```
<People xmlns='uuid:1c759aed-b748-475c-ab68-10679700c4f2'
        xmlns:ppl='http://www.example.net/people/schema' >
  <ppl:Person />
</People>
```

is logically equivalent to

```
<People xmlns='uuid:1c759aed-b748-475c-ab68-10679700c4f2' >
  <Person xmlns='http://www.example.net/people/schema/' />
</People>
```

as is this.

```
<x:People xmlns:ppl='http://www.example.net/people/schema'
        xmlns:x='uuid:1c759aed-b748-475c-ab68-10679700c4f2' >
  <ppl:Person />
</x:People>
```

In general, the local prefix in use is not considered part of the information set of an element or attribute (only the local name and namespace URI matter). The information set of a given element contains an unordered list of in-scope namespace declarations. This list consists of any namespace declarations explicitly declared by the element as well as any namespace declarations declared in ancestor elements. In the case of a given prefix (or the default namespace) being defined by multiple ancestor elements, the most-descendant declaration masks the declarations of its ancestors. Consider the following XML element:

```
<x:a xmlns:x='http://develop.com' >
  <x:b xmlns:x='http://example.com' >
  <x:c />
  </x:b>
  <x:d />
</x:a>
```

In this example, the namespace URI for elements `a` and `d` is `http://develop.com`, but the namespace URI for elements `b` and `c` is `http://example.com` since the `b` element's namespace declaration redefined the `x` prefix to refer to the latter URI.

Both element names and attribute names have a namespace URI. When the `xmlns` construct is used to set the default namespace of an element, that default only applies to nonprefixed child elements, not to attributes. Attributes that are named using only an `NCName`-based local name are affiliated with no namespace irrespective of the default namespace that may be in effect. The only way to associate an attribute name with a namespace URI is to use a prefixed `QName`. Consider the following serialized element:

```
<a xmlns='http://x.org' xmlns:y='http://y.org'
   b='Hello' y:c='Goodbye' />
```

The `b` attribute is not affiliated with any namespace, and the `c` attribute is affiliated with the `http://y.org` namespace. All attributes on a given element must be uniquely named by a namespace URI/local name pair. That means that the following is a legal XML element:

```
<a xmlns='http://x.org' xmlns:y='http://y.org'
   b='Hello' y:b='Goodbye' />
```

but the following is not:

```
<a xmlns:x='http://z.org' xmlns:y='http://z.org'
   x:b='Hello' y:b='Goodbye' />
```

since the namespace URI and local names of the two `b` attributes match exactly.

Processing Instructions

XML supports inserting tagged text strings into an XML document as out-of-band information. These tagged text strings are called *processing instructions* or PIs. A processing instruction information item has a name [target] and a sequence of zero or more characters [content] that act as the parameters of the instruction. Processing instruction names are never affiliated with a namespace and must conform to the `NCName`[6] production used to define the local part of element and attribute names. Processing instructions are treated as an opaque name/value pair at the information set level. It is up to the consumer to interpret the name and value appropriately.

Processing instructions can appear as `[children]` of either element or document information items. Consider the following serialized XML document:

```
<?xml version='1.0' ?>
<?shoot self in foot?>
<a xmlns='http://hack.com'><?hack goes here?></a>
<?heal?>
```

This document information item contains three child items: a processing instruction information item (`shoot`), the element information item (`a`), and another processing instruction information item (`heal`). The element information item contains one child item, which is the `hack` processing instruction.

Note that the XML declaration on the first line is not a processing instruction even though its syntax might look like one. Rather, the document entity may begin with an XML declaration that indicates which version of XML is assumed (at the time of this writing, "1.0" is the only known version). This version number appears as the `[version]` property of the document information item. To avoid confusing processing instructions with XML declarations, a processing instruction `[target]` can never be the string "`xml`" (or "`XML`").

It is possible to make the argument that all XML needs is elements and that attributes and processing instructions are historical baggage that should be shed like an unneeded tail.[7] Attributes typically play a supporting role to the element, whereas processing instructions typically play a supporting role to the document itself. Attributes act as annotations of the element with which they are associated. Processing instructions are used to inject private, named directives into the

---

[6]Prenamespace XML allowed the target name to contain colons. This capability was deprecated in section 6 of *Namespaces in XML.*

[7]In fact, a group of developers led by Don Park made this argument in the early discussions of the Simple Markup Language (SML), a subset of XML designed to ease the burden on parser implementations. However, during the development of SML, it was discovered that attributes are closer to an opposable thumb than an unneeded tail.

serialized XML character stream. Whereas attributes are closely tied to the element with which they are associated, processing instructions are viewed as being "out-of-band" information and are occasionally used to distort the hierarchical structure of the element graph. It is possible to build entire architectures based on processing instructions. It is possible to ruin entire architectures with them as well, and for that reason their use has fallen out of favor as a mainstream design technique. To that end, the W3C has taken the stance that processing instructions are an architectural deadend, and future W3C efforts are unlikely to leverage them in any significant way. No such stance has been taken on attributes, and it is unlikely that such a stance will be taken in the future.

Entities

The information items discussed so far (document, element, attribute, processing instruction, namespace declaration) all exist outside the realm of physical storage. In general, this is a good thing for most applications that consume XML. However, XML supports composing a single document information item from multiple source files or byte streams for modularity and flexibility. XML makes these underlying units of storage explicit via the notion of *entities*.[8]

Entities are units of storage that contain content or descriptions of content. Entities are often stored as files on disk, but this is not a requirement. For each serialized XML document, there is exactly one *document entity* that acts as the root of the serialization graph used to reconstruct the corresponding document information item. As shown in Figure 1.5, the document information item may consist of information items whose original storage may have originated from one or more external entities that were referenced from the document entity.

Most entities are identified by external identifiers. An *external identifier* is a system identifier and an optional public identifier. The external identifier is defined as follows:

```
ExternalID ::= 'SYSTEM' S SystemLiteral
            | 'PUBLIC' S PubidLiteral S SystemLiteral    [xml 75]
```

---

[8]Entities and DTDs are a holdover from the XML's roots in the documentation world. They are presented here largely for completeness. Their functionality is subsumed by XInclude, XBase, and XML Schemas, especially for software-based applications of XML.

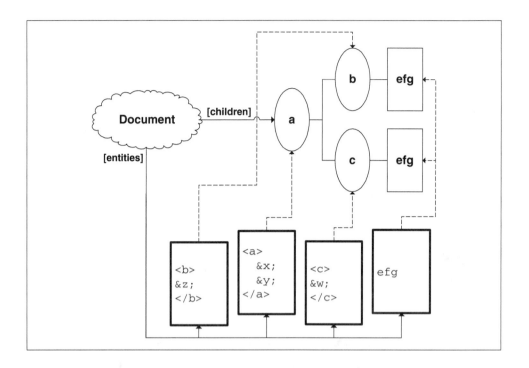

Figure 1.5   Entities and documents

The system identifier is a URI (typically a URL) that can be used to retrieve the entity. The public identifier acts as a location-neutral alternative name for a resource that applications may use to alter the means by which the resource is acquired. Consider the following serialized external identifier:

```
SYSTEM "http://www.develop.com/foo.xml"
```

This identifier contains an absolute URL that identifies the entity located at `http://www.develop.com/foo.xml`. The external identifier

```
PUBLIC "uuid:0ee0ec63-5fb9-436b-bd22-f37464659063"
       "http://www.develop.com/foo.xml"
```

augments the system identifier with a location-independent public identifier. Processing software is free to use location-independent public identifiers that it recognizes to avoid dereferencing the system identifier URI. This is useful for

ESSENTIAL XML: BEYOND MARKUP

processors that wish to cache entity content independent of its location to or precompile a set of well-known entities.

XML supports a rudimentary type mechanism for entities. Document entities are typed using a *document type declaration*. A document type declaration performs several tasks. For one, a document type declaration names the root element of the document by its QName. The following is a minimal XML document with a document type declaration:

```
<?xml version='1.0' ?>
<!DOCTYPE Person >
<Person />
```

The document type declaration can contain a document type definition (DTD). A DTD is an unordered collection of markup declarations. There are four types of markup declarations. Element declarations and attribute list declarations provided a mechanism for primitive typing of elements and attributes and are in the process of being replaced by XML Schemas (which are discussed in detail in Chapter 4). Entity and notation declarations associate named entities and entity types with the current document information item's [entities] and [notations] properties, respectively.

Entity declarations make units of storage available for reference by symbolic name. Entity names (like processing instruction names) are of type NCName and are never affiliated with a namespace. Consider the following serialized XML document:

```
<?xml version='1.0' ?>
<!DOCTYPE Person [
  <!ENTITY a SYSTEM "http://www.develop.com/foo.txt">
]>
<Person />
```

The DTD contains one entity declaration that binds the symbolic name a to the element content stored in the file http://www.develop.com/foo.txt. This entity is a *general parsed* entity, and the corresponding resource must produce a sequence of characters that are legal element content.

General parsed entities can be referenced from within element content using *entity references*. References to general entities are delimited by the characters

'&' and ';' and are replaced with the contents of the referenced entity when a serialized XML document is initially parsed. This replacement happens prior to constructing the Infoset, which means that any serialized elements, processing instructions, or characters that occur in the referenced entity will appear as [children] properties of the element under which the entity reference originally appeared. Consider the following serialized XML document:

```
<?xml version='1.0' ?>
<!DOCTYPE Person [
  <!ENTITY a SYSTEM "http://www.develop.com/foo.txt">
]>
<Person>&a;<red/>&a;</Person>
```

If the corresponding foo.txt file looked like this

```
<?xml version='1.0' encoding='UTF-8' ?>
<green/><blue/>
```

then the Person element information item would have five [children] properties as if it had been serialized as follows:

```
<Person><green/><blue/><red/><green/><blue/></Person>
```

The Infoset allows the use of entity references to be reported via the *entity start marker* and *entity end marker* information items. However, these items are considered of only peripheral concern, and most XML applications do not bother processing them.

General entities bind symbolic names to content. It is also possible to bind symbolic names for replacement within a DTD. This is done using a *parameter* entity declaration, whose serialized form differs only by the presence of the '%' character prior to the entity name. The following is a serialized parameter entity:

```
<!ENTITY % a SYSTEM "http://www.develop.com/foo.txt">
```

Parameter entities are referenced by parameter entity references (which are delimited by '%' and ';' characters). Parameter entity references can appear wherever a markup declaration is allowed.[9] Consider the following serialized XML document:

```
<?xml version='1.0' ?>
<!DOCTYPE Person [
  <!ENTITY % b SYSTEM "http://www.develop.com/bar.txt">
  %b;
]>
<Person>&a;<red/>&a;</Person>
```

Assuming that the `bar.txt` file contained the following

```
<?xml version='1.0' ?>
<!ENTITY a SYSTEM "http://www.develop.com/foo.txt">
```

the resultant document information item would be indistinguishable from the previous example.

The document type declaration supports a distinguished entity that can contain an external subset of the DTD. The markup declarations contained in the external subset are processed after the markup declarations found in the subset contained in document type declaration itself. The following serialized document type declaration

```
<!DOCTYPE Person [
  <!ENTITY c SYSTEM "http://www.develop.com/quux.txt">
  <!ENTITY % b SYSTEM "http://www.develop.com/bar.txt">
  %b;
]>
```

is functionally equivalent to the following

```
<!DOCTYPE Person SYSTEM "http://www.develop.com/bar.txt" [
  <!ENTITY c SYSTEM "http://www.develop.com/quux.txt">
]>
```

---

[9]Parameter entity references can appear *within* a markup declaration provided the declaration appears in an external entity, not the document entity.

The latter is obviously more convenient.

Finally, documents that do not rely on markup declarations from external entities for proper interpretation are said to be *standalone* documents. A standalone document can advertise this in its XML declaration as follows:

```
<?xml version='1.0' standalone='yes' ?>
```

This tells the consumer of the document that no required markup declarations appear in an external DTD subset or an external parameter entity.

Entity declarations that use external identifiers are called *external* entities. It is also possible to define *internal* general or parameter entities using quotation-mark-delimited literal values instead of external identifiers. Internal entities act as "macros" for boilerplate element/attribute content or fragments of markup declarations. Internal entities are fundamentally different from external entities. External general entities contain element content including child elements and processing instructions. In contrast, internal general entities can be referenced from either element or attribute [children]. That means that the following is a legal internal general entity:

```
<!ENTITY legal "This is boilerplate">
```

However, while the following internal general entity is legal

```
<!ENTITY bad "<Hello/>">
```

it cannot be referenced from attribute values because it contains the element delimiter '<'. That stated, internal general entities that do not contain special delimiter characters can be referenced from both element and attribute [children]. For example, given the declaration of the legal entity, the following would be a valid attribute:

```
foo="&legal; text"
```

Had legal been an external entity, this attribute would have not been well-formed and would have caused the containing document to be rejected at deserialization time.

There is a significant difference between internal and external parameter entities as well. External parameter entities can only contain complete markup declarations, comments, and processing instructions. Internal parameter entities can contain partial markup declarations[10] that may be referenced from *within* other markup declarations. Consider the following external DTD subset:

```
<?xml version='1.0' ?>
<!ENTITY %key; "%value;">
```

The general entity declaration uses a parameter entity reference for the entity name. This allows other entities that include this one to define their own name for the following entity:

```
<?xml version='1.0' ?>
<!DOCTYPE a SYSTEM "keyvalue.txt" [
  <!ENTITY % key "Coke">  <!ENTITY % value "Good">
]>
<a>&Coke;</a>
```

After chasing two parameter entities and a general entity, the a element will contain the text Good.

The discussion so far has looked at four of the five varieties of entities, all of which are considered *parsed* entities. The fifth type of entity is the general external unparsed entity (commonly referred to simply as *unparsed entity*). Unparsed entities answer the question "How do I stuff nontextual information into my XML document?" An unparsed entity binds an entity name to externally stored binary data. Unparsed entities are also bound to a *notation*.

The document information item maintains an unordered list of uniquely named notation information items in its [notations] property. Notation information items are used to assign a unique identifier to an entity type (much like MIME types do). A notation declaration maps a locally unique NCName-based notation name to a system and/or public identifier. The following is a notation declaration:

---

[10]This type of internal parameter entity can be declared but not referenced from the document entity's internal DTD subset.

```
<!NOTATION jpeg
        PUBLIC "uuid:e0f83535-d3e2-4751-bbfc-45194f763fd1">
```

The interpretation of the notation's system or public identifier is left to the application. Notations are necessary for declaring an unparsed entity, as the entity declaration must use the NDATA construct to bind a notation name to the entity as follows:

```
<!ENTITY me SYSTEM "http://foo.org/me.jpg" NDATA jpeg>
```

The presence of the NDATA construct informs the consumer that the me entity does not contain valid element content but rather contains information that XML software alone cannot parse. In this case, the notation jpeg is used to identify the type of information using the public identifier uuid:e0f83535-d3e2-4751-bbfc-45194f763fd1. Hopefully, the consumer can use this identifier to properly interpret the information contained in http://foo.org/me.jpg.

Because an unparsed entity does not contain valid XML content, it cannot be referenced using the standard entity reference syntax (for example, &me;). Rather, the only way to reference unparsed entities is using an element or attribute value that was declared as type ENTITY or ENTITIES via an XML Schema or DTD.[11] Consider the following serialized document that uses an attribute list declaration to associate the b and c attributes with types ENTITY and ENTITIES, respectively:

```
<?xml version='1.0' ?>
<!DOCTYPE a [
  <!NOTATION jpeg
        SYSTEM "uuid:e0f83535-d3e2-4751-bbfc-45194f763fd1">
  <!ENTITY me SYSTEM "http://foo.org/me.jpg" NDATA jpeg>
  <!ENTITY you SYSTEM "http://foo.org/you.jpg" NDATA jpeg>
  <!ELEMENT a EMPTY>
  <!ATTLIST a b ENTITY #IMPLIED c ENTITIES #IMPLIED>
]>
<a b='me' c='me me me you' />
```

---

[11]DTDs did not support full-featured element declarations, and therefore only attributes could be used to reference unparsed entities prior to the advent of XML Schemas.

The b attribute refers to the me entity, and the c attribute has three references to the me entity followed by one reference to the you entity.

The document information item has an [entities] property that contains an unordered list of the entity information items that are associated with the document. Because the contents of unparsed entities cannot appear as element content, the [entities] property must contain an entity information item for each unparsed entity declaration. The [entities] property also contains an entity information item for the document entity and (if available) the external DTD subset entity. Because general parsed entities result in replacement via entity references, their presence in the [entities] property is optional.

Types and XML

The previous section illustrated how unparsed entities could be associated with a type using notation declarations. It is also possible to associate elements and attributes with types. The forthcoming XML Schema specification provides a rich type system for both elements and attributes and is discussed in detail in Chapter 4. Prior to XML Schemas, the XML 1.0 recommendation defined a pair of markup declarations to provide rudimentary support for types. Documents that are structurally sound independent of type constraints are considered to be *well-formed*. Well-formed documents whose content complies with the document's type definitions are considered to be *valid* XML documents.

As shown in Table 1.2, element declarations define five general content types for elements (empty, text only, open, mixed, and element only). As shown in Table 1.3, attribute list declarations support ten basic data types for attribute values: one unstructured type (CDATA), six atomic types (NMTOKEN, ID, IDREF, NOTATION, ENTITY, Enumeration), and three list types (NMTOKENS, IDREFS, ENTITIES).

One of the more interesting attribute types is ID. An attribute list declaration can have at most one attribute of type ID. Moreover, all attributes throughout a document of type ID must have unique values. That means that the following serialized XML document is invalid:

```
<?xml version='1.0' ?>
<!DOCTYPE a [
```

```
    <!ELEMENT a (b*)>
    <!ELEMENT b EMPTY>
    <!ATTLIST b c ID #IMPLIED>
]>
<a><b c='x' /><b c='x' /></a>
```

since two ID attributes share the same value.

Attributes of type ID are similar to a primary key in a database. XML also provides the IDREF and IDREFS attribute types, which model DBMS-style referential integrity. The value of an IDREF attribute must correspond to the value of an ID attribute in the same document, or the document is considered to be invalid. An IDREFS attribute contains a whitespace-delimited list of IDREF values, each of which must correspond to the value of an ID attribute in the same document. Consider the following document:

```
<?xml version='1.0' ?>
<!DOCTYPE a [
    <!ELEMENT a (b*)>
    <!ELEMENT b EMPTY>
    <!ATTLIST b c ID #REQUIRED d IDREF #REQUIRED
                 e IDREFS #REQUIRED >
]>
<a><b c='x' d='x' e='x y'/><b c='y'/></a>
```

Table 1.2   Element Content Models

Content Model	Example
Empty: No child elements or character data	`<!ELEMENT qname EMPTY>`
Text Only: Only character data, no child elements	`<!ELEMENT qname #PCDATA>`
Open: Any well-formed XML.	`<!ELEMENT qname ANY>`
Mixed: Only character data, interleaved with zero or more qn1 and qn2 child elements (in any order)	`<!ELEMENT qname (#PCDATA|qn1|qn2)*>`
Element Only: Only the child elements as described by reg-exp with no nonwhitespace characters between child elements	`<!ELEMENT qname (reg-exp)>`

Table 1.3   Attribute Datatypes

Datatype	Description	Production
CDATA	Character data	
NMTOKEN	A name token consisting of one or more alphanumeric characters, periods, hyphens, underscores, or full stops	`(NameChar)+ [7 xml]`
NMTOKENS	Whitespace-delimited list of `NMTOKEN`	`Nmtoken (S Nmtoken)* [8 xml]`
ID	Unique identifier	`Name [5 xml]`
IDREF	Reference to unique identifier	`Name [5 xml]`
IDREFS	Whitespace-delimited list of `IDREF`	`Names [6 xml]`
NOTATION	Reference to notation	`Name [5 xml]`
ENTITY	Reference to an unparsed entity	`Name [5 xml]`
ENTITIES	Whitespace-delimited list of `ENTITY`	`Names [6 xml]`
Enumeration	Choice of one or more `NMTOKEN` values	`'(' S? Nmtoken (S? '|' S? Nmtoken)* S? ')' [59 xml]`

This document is valid since (1) all `ID` attributes have unique values, and (2) all `IDREF` and `IDREFS` values correspond to values in `ID` attributes in the same document.

Serialization Details

The Infoset deals exclusively in the Unicode character set; all strings and characters map onto Unicode code points, which ultimately are just well-known numeric values. For flexibility, XML 1.0's serialization format supports a broad range of non-Unicode encodings. In some scenarios, the encoding scheme in use can be communicated via out-of-band techniques (*e.g.,* a surrounding MIME header). XML 1.0 also supports a more self-contained technique that does not rely on external information. Each parsed entity may begin with a declaration indicating which encoding scheme is in use.

```
<?xml version='1.0' encoding='UTF-8' ?>
```

This declaration is optional if the parsed entity is encoded as UTF-8 or UTF-16. The declaration is mandatory and must be the first sequence of bytes for all other encodings *unless* some other processor-specific means of communicating the encoding scheme is used.

Because some character encoding schemes cannot support the full range of Unicode characters, XML's serialization syntax allows a character reference to be used in place of the desired character. The fact that a character reference was used instead of the literal character is a serialization detail that is completely invisible at the Infoset level.

A character reference is serialized as the reserved character sequence '&#' followed by either the decimal or hexadecimal Unicode code point of the desired character followed by a semicolon. Decimal values are encoded as a string of base-10 digits (0–9). Hexadecimal values are encoded with a leading 'x' followed by a string of base-16 digits (0–F). Consider the following character sequence:

```
Don
```

This sequence could be rewritten using character references as follows:

```
&#68;&#111;&#110;
&#x44;&#x6F;&#x6E;
```

The former sequence uses decimal codes; the latter uses hexadecimal codes. However, the resultant character sequences are the indistinguishable at the Infoset (or API or Schema) level.

Independent of which character encoding is used to serialize an XML document, the following five characters need special treatment: quotation-mark ("), apostrophe ('), ampersand (&), less-than (<), and greater-than (>). One can always use the corresponding character references.

```
&#34; <!-- quotation mark -->
&#39; <!-- apostrophe -->
&#38; <!-- ampersand -->
&#60; <!-- less than -->
&#62; <!-- greater than -->
```

XML also supports the following five built-in internal entities to make hand authoring XML documents easier.

```
&quot;  <!-- quotation mark -->
&apos;  <!-- apostrophe -->
&amp;   <!-- ampersand -->
&lt;    <!-- less than -->
&gt;    <!-- greater than -->
```

That means that the following two character sequences are functionally identical:

```
(x &#38; y) &#60; &#34;z&#39; &#62; w
(x &amp; y) &lt; &quot;z&apos; &gt; w
```

Both correspond to the following raw character sequence

```
(x & y) < 'z' > w
```

that is illegal as element or attribute content.

The ampersand and less-than can never appear in a serialized XML document except as the initial character of a character (or entity) reference or an element tag respectively. The quotation mark and apostrophe can appear in the raw anywhere except inside an attribute value that uses that character as its surrounding delimiter. That means that the following is illegal:

```
<a b="I said "hi" to you" c='Don't stop' />
```

But the following is not:

```
<a b='I said "hi" to you' c="Don't stop" />
```

The quot and apos entities must be used when an attribute value contains both quotation marks and apostrophes.

```
<a b='I said "hi" to you so don&apos;t stop' />
```

Note that in this example, the quotation marks around hi were perfectly legal.

To help facilitate manual creation of XML documents, XML 1.0's serialization format supports an escape mechanism to allow the five special characters to appear in their raw form without special treatment. If the character sequence `<![CDATA[` is encountered in element content, all subsequent characters are assumed to be character data and not markup characters. This interpretation stops when the character sequence `]]>` is encountered. The following is a demonstration of its use:

```
<a><![CDATA[(x & y) < "z" > w]]></a>
```

The use of `<![CDATA[` is considered peripheral to the underlying information set of the document, and XML processing software is not required to report its use.

Whitespace characters are given special treatment in XML 1.0's serialization format. In particular, XML takes a rather UNIX-like stance on CR versus LF treatment. Line breaks are always normalized to a single LF (`&#xA;`) independent of whether the original parsed entity contained a CR, CR/LF, or LF. Whitespace in general is handled differently based on where it occurs. Whitespace inside of element tags used to separate attributes and namespace declarations is never maintained at the Infoset level. Leading and trailing whitespace in attributes and text-only elements is discarded when the type is known to be something other than CDATA/string. For list types (e.g., NMTOKENS), whitespace between list items is normalized to a single space character (`&#x20;`). Whitespace handling between elements is a bit more complicated.

In general, whitespace between child elements is preserved unless (1) the parent element's content model is element only, or (2) the `xml:space` attribute is used to override the default. Consider the following serialized XML document:

```
<?xml version='1.0' ?>
<!DOCTYPE a [
  <!ELEMENT a ANY>
  <!ELEMENT b (#PCDATA|a)*>
  <!ELEMENT c (a*)>
  <!ELEMENT d (a*)>
]>
```

```
<a>
  <b>
    <a/>       <a/>
  </b>
  <c>
    <a/>       <a/>
  </c>
  <d xml:space='preserve'>
    <a/>       <a/>
  </d>
</a>
```

The whitespace between b's child elements is significant because b's element declaration states that it is of mixed content. The whitespace between d's child elements is significant due to the use of the xml:space attribute. However, because
c's content model is element only and the xml:space attribute is not in use, XML
processing software can safely ignore the whitespace between elements.

Where Are We?

XML layers type and structure over information. An XML document combines
one or more serialized entities to form a single data object that is treated as a
whole. The XML document is then decomposed into one or more named elements, each of which consists of an unordered sequence of uniquely named
attributes and an ordered sequence of character data, child elements, and processing instructions. The *XML Information Set* specification puts shape around
these abstractions and the *XML 1.0* and *Namespaces in XML* specifications
define the concrete transfer syntax. The next chapter will look at how the *XML
Information Set* is exposed to software agents via programmatic interfaces.

Chapter 2

Programming XML

```
printf("<%s %s=\"%s\"/>\n", elemName, attName, attVal);
```

Anonymous, 1998

The previous chapter described the XML Information Set, which is the normative definition of an XML document's abstract data model. The chapter presented a variety of example XML documents and document fragments in their serialized form as part of the discussion of various Infoset information items. One reason this approach was used was to avoid the complete alienation of readers already familiar with XML's serialization format. The primary reason, however, was to demonstrate that there is an isomorphic translation between the data model of the Infoset and the serialization format known as XML 1.0 + namespaces.

This chapter builds on this translation and describes two common techniques for translating between the Infoset and some format suitable for use by computer programs. These two common techniques are based on taking the abstractions of the Infoset and projecting them onto an object model that allows programmers to work in terms of the abstract information items, not the angle brackets and character references of XML's serialization format. These two common techniques are known as the Simple API for XML (SAX) and the Document Object Model (DOM).

Both SAX and DOM are a set of abstract programmatic interfaces that model the XML information set. The SAX and DOM approaches differ in two fundamental ways. First, the DOM is a W3C Candidate Recommendation and carries with it the weight of the W3C (this is both good and bad). In contrast, SAX is a *de facto* standard developed by a group of developers on the XML-DEV mailing list and supervised by David Megginson.[1] The lack of "official" endorsement of SAX has not prevented most major XML products from supporting SAX and DOM as peer technologies.

The more important distinction between SAX and DOM is the differences between their basic technical approaches. SAX is a set of streaming interfaces that decompose the Infoset of an XML document into a linear sequence of well-known method calls. DOM is a set of traversal interfaces that decompose the Infoset of an XML document into a hierarchal tree of generic objects/nodes. DOM is best suited to applications that need to retain an XML document in memory for generic traversal or manipulation. SAX-based applications typically have no need to retain a generic view of the XML Infoset in memory.[2] Fortunately, since both SAX and DOM are isomorphisms of the Infoset, one can typically mix the two with very little trouble (in fact, many DOM-based implementations are built in terms of an underlying SAX-based code base).

Simple API For XML Version 2 (SAX2)

SAX is a set of abstract programmatic interfaces that project the Infoset of an XML document onto a stream of well-known method calls. At the time of this writing, version 2 of SAX was in beta form and will likely become finalized by the time this book is published. Version 1 of SAX was standardized prior to namespaces or the Infoset and requires proprietary extensions to be useful for modern XML applications. For that reason, this book ignores version 1 of SAX and uses the term SAX as a synonym for SAX2.[3] At the time of this writing, SAX had only been defined for the Java programming language. However, efforts to map SAX to C++, Perl, Python, and COM were all in various stages of development. Figure 2.1 presents the UML model of the SAX2 interface suite.

---

[1]XML-DEV is hosted at http://www.xml.org/xml-dev/ at the time of this writing. The SAX specification is available at http://www.megginson.com/SAX.

[2]The distinction between SAX and DOM is similar to the distinction between read-only, forward-only firehose-mode database cursors and static database cursors that allow full traversal and updates.

[3]SAX2 provides two adapter classes that allow SAX1 and SAX2 software to interoperate.

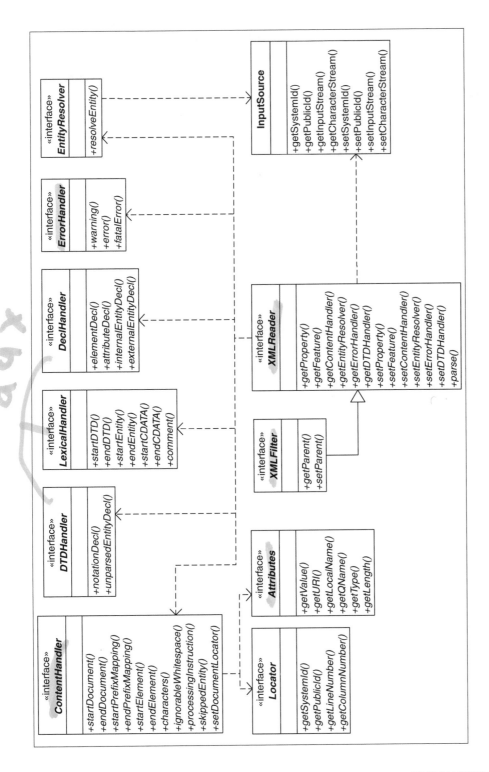

Figure 2.1   The UML model of the SAX2 interface suite.

The primary interface of SAX is `ContentHandler`. The `ContentHandler` interface models most of the information set core as an ordered sequence of method calls. The remaining information set items are modeled by the `DTDHandler`, `DeclHandler` and `LexicalHandler` interfaces, which are described later in this chapter. The following is the Java version of `ContentHandler`:

```java
package org.xml.sax;
public interface ContentHandler {
// signals the beginning/end of a document
  void startDocument () throws SAXException;
  void endDocument() throws SAXException;

// signals the beginning/end of an element
  void startElement(String namespaceURI, String localName,
                    String qName, Attributes atts)
        throws SAXException;
  void endElement(String namespaceURI, String localName,
                  String qName) throws SAXException;

// signals a namespace declaration entering/leaving scope
  void startPrefixMapping(String prefix, String uri)
        throws SAXException;
  void endPrefixMapping(String prefix) throws SAXException;

// signals character data in element content
  void characters(char ch[], int start, int length)
        throws SAXException;

// signals ignorable whitespace in element content
  void ignorableWhitespace(char ch[], int start, int length)
                    throws SAXException;

// signals a processing instruction
  void processingInstruction(String target, String data)
        throws SAXException;
// signals a skipped entity reference
  void skippedEntity (String name) throws SAXException;

// supplies context information about the caller
  void setDocumentLocator (Locator locator);
}
```

This interface is implemented by code that wishes to "receive" an XML document and consumed by code that wishes to "send" an XML document. A component that emits serialized XML would implement `ContentHandler`. A component that parses serialized XML would consume `ContentHandler`. Since the typical application both consumes and emits XML documents, an application programmer will likely wind up both implementing and consuming this interface.

The protocol of the `ContentHandler` interface implies that a certain amount of context information will be retained between method calls. In particular, for information items that have a `[children]` property (for example, document and element information items), a given information item will be represented by at least two method invocations, one signaling the "beginning" of the item and another signaling the "end." Any intermediate method invocations that may occur between these two signals correspond to `[children]` property of the "current" information item. For example, a document information item will be represented by a call to `startDocument` followed by a call to `endDocument`. In between these two calls, there will be at least one `startElement`/`endElement` pair representing the lone element information item in the document's `[children]` property. There may also be calls to `ContentHandler.processingInstruction` (or `LexicalHandler.comment`) representing additional information items that are also in the document's `[children]` property. Implementations of `ContentHandler` are expected to retain some notion of context in order to properly interpret the method invocations issued by the caller.

The most heavily utilized methods of `ContentHandler` are `startElement` and `endElement`. The `startElement` method signals the beginning of a new element information item. The `endElement` method signals the ending of the current element information item. All methods invoked between `startElement`/`endElement` correspond to the `[children]` property of the corresponding element information item. Both methods have a similar set of parameters.

```
void startElement(String namespaceURI,
                  String localName,
                  String qName,
                  Attributes atts) throws SAXException;
```

```
void endElement(   String namespaceURI,
                   String localName,
                   String qName) throws SAXException;
```

The namespaceURI and localName parameters correspond directly to the [namespace URI] and [local name] Infoset properties. The atts parameter corresponds to the [attributes] property. Finally, the qName parameter corresponds to the QName of the element. Depending on which SAX features are supported by the caller, this parameter may simply be the empty string. The configuration of SAX features is discussed later in this chapter, but the default behavior is to *not* report the QName of the element.

Consider the following Java code that consumes a ContentHandler interface:

```
void emit(org.xml.sax.ContentHandler handler)
            throws org.xml.sax.SAXException {
  org.xml.sax.Attributes a =
                  new org.xml.sax.helpers.AttributesImpl();
  handler.startElement("", "period", "", a);
    handler.startElement("", "artist", "", a);
    handler.endElement("", "artist", "");
    handler.startElement("", "artist", "", a);
    handler.endElement("", "artist", "");
  handler.endElement("", "period", "");
}
```

This set of method invocations corresponds directly to the following XML fragment:

```
<period xmlns=""><artist/><artist/></period>
```

In fact, one could easily imagine a simple implementation of ContentHandler that emitted XML as its methods are invoked.

```
class Emitter implements org.xml.sax.ContentHandler {
  CharacterStream out;
  public void startElement(String namespaceURI,
              String localName, String qName,
```

```
                    org.xml.sax.Attributes atts) {
     out.write("<" + localName
                + " xmlns=\"" + namespaceURI + "\">");
   }
   public void endElement(String namespaceURI,
                String localName, String qName) {
     out.write("<" + localName + ">");
   }
 // other ContentHandler methods elided for clarity
 }
```

Note that this overly simplistic implementation makes no attempt to collapse start and end tags for empty elements, nor does it do anything reasonable with namespace declarations or prefixes.[4]

It is difficult to look at the `ContentHandler` interface without also looking at one of the interfaces that it relies on: `Attributes`. The `Attributes` interface models the `[attributes]` property of an element information item. It exposes an element's attributes as an unordered property bag that can be traversed by name or position. The following is the Java version of `Attributes`:

```
package org.xml.sax;
public interface Attributes {
// return the number of attributes in the list
   int getLength ();
// look up an attribute's Namespace URI, local name or raw
// XML 1.0 name by index
   String getURI (int index);
   String getLocalName (int index);
   String getQName (int index);
// look up an attribute's index by Namespace or raw name
   int getIndex (String uri, String localPart);
   int getIndex (String qName);
// Look up an attribute's value
   String getValue (String uri, String localName);
   String getValue (int index);
```

---

[4]As this chapter was being finalized, David Megginson floated the XMLWriter class that provides a complete implementation of a SAX2-based serializer.

```
      String getValue (String qName);
// Look up an attribute's type
   String getType (String uri, String localName);
   String getType (int index);
   String getType (String qName);
 }
```

For convenience, the Java version of SAX provides a default implementation of this interface (`AttributesImpl`) that allows populating the collection via the following method:

```
public void addAttribute(String uri, String localName,
                    String qName, String type, String value);
```

The following Java code fragment demonstrates how to create an attribute collection that contains three attributes:

```
org.xml.sax.Attributes create( ) {
  org.xml.sax.helpers.AttributesImpl atts =
                  new org.xml.sax.helpers.AttributesImpl( );
  atts.addAttribute("", "a", "", "CDATA", "Hello, World");
  atts.addAttribute("", "b", "", "NMTOKEN", "Hello");
  atts.addAttribute("http://www.w3.org/1999/xlink", "href",
                      "", "CDATA", "#foo");
  return (org.xml.sax.Attributes)atts;
}
```

Note that in this example, the `qName` parameter is the empty string. This is consistent with the default behavior of `ContentHandler`.

Implementations of `ContentHandler.startElement` receive an `Attributes` implementation as the last parameter. This is the one chance that the `ContentHandler` implementation gets to see the attribute names, values, and types. The following `startElement` handler prints out the value of the `href` attribute that is qualified by the XLink namespace URI:

```
void startElement(String namespaceURI, String localName,
                    String qName, Attributes atts) {
// lookup attribute for this element
```

```
String val = atts.getValue("http://www.w3.org/1999/xlink",
                           "href");
// test for presence and act accordingly
  if (val != null)
    System.out.println("Link to " + val);
  else
    System.out.println("No link attribute present");
}
```

Attributes can also be accessed by position, but because the [attributes] Infoset property is an unordered collection, the actual order in which the attributes appear is insignificant.

SAX treats namespace declarations as distinct facets of an element information item. Because XML documents are increasingly using the QName datatype in element and attribute content, the actual namespace prefix-to-URI mappings that are in scope needs to be known by the ContentHandler implementation. Acknowledging the fact that namespace declarations and attributes are distinct Infoset information items, SAX models namespace declarations as a distinct pair of ContentHandler methods and does *not* deliver them as part of the Attributes collection at startElement-time. The startPrefixMapping method is called just prior to the startElement and corresponds to the namespace declarations of the element about to be processed. Once all of the element content has been processed, the endPrefixMapping method is called *after* issuing the endElement method call. Consider the following serialized element information item:

```
<artist
    xmlns='uri-one'
    xmlns:two='uri-two'
    xmlns:three='uri-three'
/>
```

This element information item corresponds to the following sequence of Java method invocations:

```
void emit2(org.xml.sax.ContentHandler handler)
        throws org.xml.sax.SAXException {
```

```
        org.xml.sax.Attributes a =
                      new org.xml.sax.helpers.AttributesImpl();
  // indicate namespace declarations coming into scope
    handler.startPrefixMapping("", "uri-one");
    handler.startPrefixMapping("two", "uri-two");
    handler.startPrefixMapping("three", "uri-three");
  // indicate element start and finish
    handler.startElement("uri-one", "artist", "", a);
    handler.endElement("uri-one", "artist", "");
  // indicate namespace declarations leaving scope
    handler.endPrefixMapping("three");
    handler.endPrefixMapping("two");
    handler.endPrefixMapping("");
  }
```

Note that the protocol of ContentHandler does not require the start-PrefixMapping/endPrefixMapping calls to occur in the same order (or reverse order). The only ordering requirement is that all startPrefixMapping calls occur immediately prior to the corresponding startElement call and that all endPrefixMapping calls occur immediately after the corresponding endElement call.

To lighten the load of ContentHandler implementers, SAX provides a built-in class called NamespaceSupport that provides most of the default processing one would need to properly deal with QNames in attribute/element content. The following is the public interface to NamespaceSupport:

```
package org.xml.sax.helpers;
public class NamespaceSupport {
// The XML Namespace URI as a constant
  public final static String XMLNS =
                    "http://www.w3.org/XML/1998/namespace";
// reset this NamespaceSupport object for reuse
  public void reset( );
// enter/leave a new Namespace scope
  public void pushContext( );
  public void popContext( );
// add a namespace declaration to the current scope
  public boolean declarePrefix(String prefix, String uri)
```

```
// Process a raw XML 1.0 name.
  public String [] processName(String qName,
                      String parts[], boolean isAttribute);
// resolve prefix against in-scope namespaces
    public String getURI(String prefix);
// return all in-scope namespace prefixes
    public java.util.Enumeration getPrefixes( );
// return prefixes declared specifically in current scope
    public java.util.Enumeration getDeclaredPrefixes( );
}
```

The NamespaceSupport class keeps a stack of namespace declaration scopes. Calling pushContext starts a new scope; calling popContext reverts back to the previous scope. Assuming that each namespace declaration has been inserted using declarePrefix, the getURI method will return the name-space URI that corresponds to a given NCName-based prefix.

ContentHandler implementations typically use the NamespaceSupport class as follows:

```
class MyHandler implements org.xml.sax.ContentHandler {
  org.xml.sax.helpers.NamespaceSupport ns =
                new org.xml.sax.helpers.NamespaceSupport( );
  public void startPrefixMapping(String prefix, String uri){
    ns.pushContext( );
    ns.declarePrefix(prefix, uri);
  }
  public void endPrefixMapping(String prefix, String uri) {
    ns.popContext( );
  }
}
```

Given this implementation of startPrefixMapping/endPrefixMapping, one can now look up the correct mapping of a namespace prefix by calling the getURI method. Additionally, the processName method can be used to crack a QName into its constituent components.

```
String[] ss = new String[3];
ss = processName("two:LName", ss, false);
```

This would result in the following three-tuple if called against the namespace declarations from the `artist` element shown earlier in this chapter.

```
{ "uri-two", "LName", "two:LName" }
```

If called using the string "LName", one would have gotten

```
{ "uri-one", "LName", "LName" }
```

assuming the `isAttribute` parameter was false (note that the default name-space of the `artist` element was `uri-one`). Had the `isAttribute` parameter been set to true, the `QName` would have been interpreted according to the rules of attribute names, which means that a name with no prefix belongs to no namespace and thus would have yielded the following three-tuple:

```
{ "", "LName", "LName" }
```

Note that the first string is the empty string.

The discussion so far has focused on the basic structure of a document's elements and has ignored the content model of each element. SAX defines four additional `ContentHandler` methods that are used to signal the presence of nonelement [children] facets of the current element. The simplest of these methods is the `processingInstruction` method.

```
void processingInstruction(String target, String data)
               throws SAXException;
```

Consider the following serialized processing instruction:

```
<?hack Magnum PI?>
```

This PI would be conveyed in SAX as follows:

```
void emit3(org.xml.sax.ContentHandler handler)
           throws org.xml.sax.SAXException {
  handler.processingInstruction("hack",
                                  "Magnum PI");
}
```

As processing instructions are also valid [children] of the document information item, calls to processingInstruction may occur prior to the first startElement and after the final endElement. However, all processingInstruction and startElement calls will be surrounded by a pair of calls to startDocument and endDocument that signal the beginning and end of the document information item.

For elements whose content model is mixed or text only, the characters method must be called to convey the character data that appears as element content. For elements whose content model is known to be element only, any interleaving whitespace between child elements may be delivered using the ignorableWhitespace method.[5] Both methods take an array of characters as a parameter. An initial offset and length is provided to indicate which subset of the array contains the actual content. Consider the following element information item:

```
<x xmlns='uri-one'>Hello, World</x>
```

The following Java code shows the corresponding SAX ContentHandler call sequence:

```
void emit4(org.xml.sax.ContentHandler handler)
          throws org.xml.sax.SAXException {
  org.xml.sax.Attributes a =
               new org.xml.sax.helpers.AttributesImpl();
  handler.startElement("uri-one", "x", "", a);
    char[] rgch = "Hello, World".toCharArray();
    handler.characters(rgch, 0, rgch.length);
  handler.endElement("uri-one", "x", "");
}
```

The offset and length parameters are Java-isms that allow Java-based XML parsers to avoid excessive memory movement.

---

[5]This assumes the caller knows the expected content model of the current element either via a DTD, an XML Schema, or some other technique.

The final [children]-related method is skippedEntity, whose signature looks like the following:

```
void skippedEntity(String name) throws SAXException;
```

This method corresponds to the reference to a skipped entity information item as a child of the current element. It signals the presence of an entity reference that will not be expanded by the caller. This method exists primarily due to a loophole in the XML 1.0 specification that allows nonvalidating parsers to skip external parsed entities.

Because SAX is commonly used to interface with XML parsers, it is occasionally useful for a ContentHandler implementation to discover exactly what portion of which document the parser is currently working on. To support this functionally, SAX defines the Locator interface, which is typically implemented by SAX-aware parsers to allow implementations of ContentHandler to discover exactly where the current method corresponds to in the underlying serialized form. The following is the Java version of Locator:

```
package org.xml.sax;
public interface Locator {
  String getPublicId( );
  String getSystemId( );
  int getLineNumber( );
  int getColumnNumber( );
}
```

For convenience, the Java version of SAX provides a default implementation of this interface (LocatorImpl) that has four corresponding "setter" methods to allow setting of the various location properties. SAX parsers make this interface available to ContentHandler implementations by calling the setDocumentLocator method prior to calling any other ContentHandler methods.

Auxiliary SAX Interfaces

The ContentHandler interface models 100 percent of the Infoset needed by 95 percent of the world's XML applications. The needs of the remaining 5 percent are addressed by three auxiliary interfaces: LexicalHandler, DTDHandler, and DeclHandler. LexicalHandler models peripheral

ESSENTIAL XML: BEYOND MARKUP

Infoset-isms such as `<!CDATA[` boundaries; `DTDHandler` models notations and unparsed entities; and `DeclHandler` models markup and entity declarations from DTDs. If your application does not need to deal with these aspects of XML, feel free to ignore these interfaces (and this section of the chapter).

The `LexicalHandler` models Infoset information items that are not required for proper interpretation. None of these items are part of the Infoset core. Rather, they are of peripheral interest mainly for parties that wish to retain/reconstruct the original serialized form of a document. The following is the Java version of `LexicalHandler`:

```
package org.xml.sax.ext;
public interface LexicalHandler {
// signal beginning/end of DTD
   void startDTD(String name, String publicId,
                 String systemId)
       throws SAXException;
   void endDTD() throws SAXException;
// signal beginning/end of general entity reference
   void startEntity(String name) throws SAXException;
   void endEntity(String name) throws SAXException;
// signal beginning/end of <![CDATA[ section
   void startCDATA() throws SAXException;
   void endCDATA() throws SAXException;
// signal presence of <!-- comment -->
   void comment(char ch[], int start, int length)
       throws SAXException;
}
```

The `comment` method is the easiest to grasp. The `comment` method corresponds to a comment information item and conveys the character data of the comment. Because SAX works at the Infoset level, the `<!--` and `-->` delimiters are not delivered.

The `startCDATA`/`endCDATA` methods are used to indicate that the intervening `ContentHandler.characters` methods are contained in a `<!CDATA[` section. For example, this Java code

```
void emit6(org.xml.sax.ContentHandler ch,
           org.xml.sax.LexicalHandler lh) {
```

```
    char[] ch = "John".toCharArray();
    ch.characters(ch, 0, ch.length);
    lh.startCDATA();
    ch.characters(ch, 0, ch.length);
    ch.characters(ch, 0, ch.length);
    lh.endCDATA();
    ch.characters(ch, 0, ch.length);
}
```

corresponds to the following serialized XML:

```
John<!CDATA[JohnJohn]]>John
```

Had the receiver not implemented `LexicalHandler`, this XML would have been indistinguishable from the following:

```
JohnJohnJohnJohn
```

In general, most applications prefer to ignore <!CDATA[usage, but for applications looking to retain the original form of a serialized document, this particular detail is likely to be important.

The `startEntity`/`endEntity` methods are used to indicate that the intervening `ContentHandler` methods happened as the result of a parsed entity reference, not literal content. For example, the Java code

```
void emit7(org.xml.sax.ContentHandler ch,
           org.xml.sax.LexicalHandler lh) {
  char[] ch = "John".toCharArray();
  ch.characters(ch, 0, ch.length);
  lh.startEntity('jj');
  ch.characters(ch, 0, ch.length);
  ch.characters(ch, 0, ch.length);
  lh.endEntity('jj');
  ch.characters(ch, 0, ch.length);
}
```

corresponds to the following serialized XML

```
John&jj;John
```

assuming the following entity declaration had appeared elsewhere

```
<!ENTITY jj "JohnJohn">
```

Had the receiver not implemented `LexicalHandler`, this XML would have been indistinguishable from the following

```
JohnJohnJohnJohn
```

which again is typically what almost all applications care about. Like `startCDATA`/`endCDATA`, these methods exist primarily to retain fidelity with serialized XML documents, not for mainstream XML applications.

Finally, the document type (`DOCTYPE`) declaration is modeled by the `startDTD`/`endDTD` methods. These methods convey the `QName` of the expected document element and the system and public identifiers of the external DTD subset. Consider the following Java code:

```
void emit8(org.xml.sax.LexicalHandler handler) {
   handler.startDTD("foo:bar", "-//DevelopMentor//fb//EN",
                 "http://foo.bar.com");
   handler.endDTD();
}
```

This code corresponds to the following serialized `DOCTYPE` declaration:

```
<!DOCTYPE foo:bar PUBLIC '-//DevelopMentor//fb//EN'
                      'http://foo.bar.com' >
```

Note that there are no `LexicalHandler` methods that model the contents of the document type definition. Rather, that is the role played by `DTDHandler` and `DeclHandler`.

SAX uses two interfaces to model the contents of a DTD, largely due to the history of the Infoset. At the time of SAX2's development, the Infoset did not address parsed entity declarations, attribute list declarations, or element declarations. However, the Infoset's document information item has always had two core properties (`[notations]` and `[entities]`) that are not addressed by

`ContentHandler`. These two properties are modeled by the `DTDHandler` interface. The following is the Java version of `DTDHandler`:

```
package org.xml.sax;
public interface DTDHandler {
  void notationDecl(String name, String publicId,
                                 String systemId)
          throws SAXException;
  void unparsedEntityDecl(String name, String publicId,
                      String systemId, String notationName)
          throws SAXException;
}
```

Consider the following Java code fragment:

```
void emit5(org.xml.sax.DTDHandler handler) {
  handler.notationDecl("wav", "-//DevelopMentor//fb//EN",
                       null);
  handler.notationDecl("au", null, "http://mp9.com/au");
  handler.unparsedEntityDecl("woosh", "",
                             "http://foo.com", "wav");
  handler.unparsedEntityDecl("wooosh", "-//DM//foooo//EN",
                             "http://fooo.com", "au");
}
```

This corresponds to the following DTD declarations:

```
<!NOTATION wav PUBLIC '-//DevelopMentor//fb//EN' >
<!NOTATION au  SYSTEM 'http://mp9.com/au' >
<!ENTITY woosh SYSTEM 'http://foo.com' NDATA wav>
<!ENTITY wooosh PUBLIC '-//DM//foooo//EN'
                       'http://fooo.com' NDATA au>
```

It is important to note that the caller is responsible for fully resolving the URI in the system identifier prior to invoking `notationDecl` or `unparsedEntityDecl`.

In addition to notation and unparsed entity declarations, SAX supports the remaining DTD-isms via the `DeclHandler` interface. The following is the Java version of `DeclHandler`:

```
package org.xml.sax.ext;
public interface DeclHandler {
// signal an ELEMENT declaration
  void elementDecl(String name, String model)
        throws SAXException;
// signal one attribute from an ATTLIST declaration
  void attributeDecl(String eName, String aName,
            String type, String valueDefault, String value)
        throws SAXException;
// signal an internal parsed general ENTITY declaration
  void internalEntityDecl(String name, String value)
        throws SAXException;
// signal an external parsed general ENTITY declaration
  void externalEntityDecl(String name, String publicId,
                          String systemId)
        throws SAXException;
}
```

The four methods of `DeclHandler` correspond to a DTD-style element declaration, attribute list declaration, internal parsed entity declaration, and external parsed entity declaration. Of these four methods, only `attributeDecl` warrants any real discussion, as its mapping to a DTD-style `ATTLIST` declaration is not a one-to-one mapping. Rather, an `attributeDecl` invocation corresponds to only one attribute from an attribute list declaration. For example, consider the following serialized attribute list declaration:

```
<!ATTLIST foo bar    CDATA #REQUIRED
              baz    NMTOKEN "foobar"
              quux   IDREF #IMPLIED
              quuux IDREFS #FIXED "hey joe"
>
```

This would correspond to the following Java code:

```
void emit9(org.xml.sax.DeclHandler handler) {
  handler.attributeDecl("foo", "bar",
                        "CDATA", "#REQUIRED", null);
  handler.attributeDecl("foo", "baz",
                        "NMTOKEN", null, "foobar");
```

```
        handler.attributeDecl("foo", "quux",
                              "IDREF", "#IMPLIED", null);
        handler.attributeDecl("foo", "quuux",
                              "IDREFS", "#FIXED", "hey joe");
    }
```

Assuming that the receiver of the document implements both `DeclHandler` and `LexicalHandler`, all calls to `DeclHandler` methods must occur after a call to `LexicalHandler.startDTD` and prior to a call to `LexicalHandler.endDTD`.

SAX and I/O

SAX provides a fair amount of flexibility with respect to I/O handling of serialized XML documents. Wherever SAX expects I/O to occur, the `InputSource` utility class is used as an extended wrapper around the native I/O stream model (which in the case of Java is `java.io.InputStream` for byte-oriented I/O and `java.io.Reader` for character-oriented I/O). The following is the Java definition of `InputSource`:

```
package org.xml.sax;
public class InputSource {
// fields and method implementations elided for clarity
    public InputSource();
    public InputSource(String systemId);
    public InputSource(InputStream byteStream);
    public InputSource(Reader characterStream);

    public void setPublicId(String publicId);
    public String getPublicId();

    public void setSystemId(String systemId);
    public String getSystemId();

    public void setByteStream(InputStream byteStream);
    public InputStream getByteStream();

    public void setEncoding(String encoding);
    public String getEncoding();

    public void setCharacterStream(Reader characterStream);
    public Reader getCharacterStream();
}
```

Note that the primary enhancement that `InputSource` provides over native Java I/O types is that `InputSource` allows the character encoding, public, and system identifiers to be associated with the stream. When presented with an `InputSource`, a SAX-based parser will first attempt to acquire a character stream using `getCharacterStream`. If that method returns null, the parser will then attempt to acquire a byte stream using `getByteStream`. If that method also returns null, then the parser will use the URI returned by `getSystemId`.

The `getSystemId` method is important even when character or byte streams are used, as it provides the `[base URI]` property that is used to normalize relative URIs contained in the serialized stream. For that reason, it is critical that applications set this property even when they are providing their own byte/character streams. Consider the following code:

```
org.xml.sax.InputSource getMyXML(String url) {
    java.net.URL u = new java.net.URL(url);
    java.net.UrlConnection conn = u.openConnection();
    java.io.InputStream in = conn.getInputStream();
    return new org.xml.sax.InputSource(in);
}
```

Because this code fragment does not set the system identifier property of the `InputSource` object, any relative URIs contained in the document cannot be correctly resolved. The correct version of this code fragment is as follows:

```
org.xml.sax.InputSource getMyXML(String url) {
    java.net.URL u = new java.net.URL(url);
    java.net.UrlConnection conn = u.openConnection();
    java.io.InputStream in = conn.getInputStream();
    org.xml.sax.InputSource source =
            new org.xml.sax.InputSource(in);
    source.setSystemId(url);
    return source;
}
```

This version provides the consumer with the `[base URI]` Infoset property, ensuring that any relative URLs in the document can be resolved.

There are two common locations where `InputSource` is used. The most common is when bootstrapping an XML parser. This usage is discussed in a subsequent section. The more interesting application of `InputSource` is the `EntityResolver` interface. The `EntityResolver` is an extensibility interface that implementations of `ContentHandler` *et al.* can implement to provide for custom resolution of external entities. By default, when an external entity needs to be resolved, the system identifier can be used as a URI that is easily dereferenced using well-known techniques. However, if an implementation of `EntityResolver` has been provided to complement the `ContentHandler` implementation, the `EntityResolver`'s `resolveEntity` method will be called first, giving the implementation an opportunity to provide its own `InputSource` for a given public/system identifier pair. The Java definition of `EntityResolver` is extremely simple.

```
package org.xml.sax;
public interface EntityResolver {
// return null to indicate systemId should be used as URI
   InputSource resolveEntity(String publicId,
                             String systemId)
       throws SAXException, java.io.IOException;
}
```

If the implementation of `resolveEntity` returns a non-null `InputSource` reference, that object's character/byte stream (or systemId) must be used. If a null reference is returned, the default behavior of dereferencing the systemId as a URI will be used.

Consider the following implementation of `EntityResolver` that prevents all FTP-based access by throwing an exception:

```
import org.xml.sax.*;
class Resolver1 implements EntityResolver {
  public InputSource resolveEntity(String pub, String sys)
                          throws SAXException {
    if (sys.toUpperCase().startsWith("FTP"))
      throw new SAXException("FTP not allowed");
    return null; // default processing
  }
}
```

The following implementation of EntityResolver redirects all requests destined for one vendor to the boilerplate XML document from another:

```
import org.xml.sax.*;
class Resolver1 implements EntityResolver {
  public InputSource resolveEntity(String pub, String sys)
                         throws SAXException {
    InputSource result = null;
    if (sys.toLowerCase().startsWith("http://www.sun.com"))
      result = new InputSource("http://redhat.com/bp.xml");
    return result;
  }
}
```

It is also possible to provide alternative character or byte streams simply by returning an InputSource that contains the appropriate Reader or InputStream.

SAX Error Handling

Most SAX interface methods throw SAXException. SAXException extends java.lang.Exception and adds one fundamental feature, which is the ability to piggyback an arbitrary exception inside of a SAXException. This allows implementations to propagate non-SAX-related exceptions across SAX interface method boundaries. Consider the following implementation of ContentHandler.characters:

```
void characters(char[] ch, int offset, int length)
                     throws org.xml.sax.SAXException {
  try {
    this.out.write(ch, offset, length);
  }
  catch (java.io.IOException ex) {
    throw new org.xml.sax.SAXException(ex);
  }
}
```

This implementation embeds a java.io.IOException inside the SAXException that it is required to throw. Callers can then scrape out the exception by calling the SAXException.getException method as follows:

```
void emit11(org.xml.sax.ContentHandler handler) {
  try {
    char[] rgch = "Hello".toCharArray();
    handler.characters(rgch, 0, rgch.length);
  }
  catch(org.xml.sax.SAXException sex) {
    java.lang.Exception ex = sex.getException();
    if (ex == null) // no embedded exception
      logerror("SAXException thrown");
    else
      logerror(ex.getClass().getName() + "thrown");
  }
}
```

SAXException is functionally identical to java.lang.Exception beyond this feature of embedding a nested exception.

As shown in Figure 2.2, there are three extended exception types in SAX beyond SAXException. Of these three types, the most commonly used is SAXParseException. SAXParseException is used to indicate a processing error while deserializing an XML document. In addition to indicating that the exception was parse-related, SAXParseException exposes the four properties supported by Locator: system identifier, public identifier, line number, and column number.

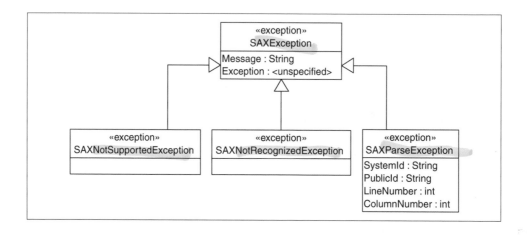

Figure 2.2   SAX2 exceptions

Exceptions of type `SAXException` are generally thrown by `Content Handler` implementations and caught by `ContentHandler` consumers. For many scenarios, this is reasonable, as the `ContentHandler` implementation typically can perform application-specific validation and communicate constraint violations by throwing exceptions from `startElement` and friends. However, there are scenarios where the consumer of `ContentHandler` wishes to abort the stream of method invocations due to a caller-side error. The most common scenario is of course when an XML parser who is calling your `ContentHandler` implementation needs to report a parse error detected in the underlying serialized XML document. To support reporting error information in that direction, SAX defines the `ErrorHandler` interface, whose Java version is shown here:

```
package org.xml.sax;
public interface ErrorHandler {
  void warning(SAXParseException exception)
                  throws SAXException;
  void error(SAXParseException exception)
                  throws SAXException;
  void fatalError(SAXParseException exception)
                  throws SAXException;
}
```

This interface is typically implemented alongside `ContentHandler` when interfacing with an XML parser.

Section 1.2 of the XML 1.0 recommendation details two forms of processing errors: errors and fatal errors. The `error` and `fatalError` methods will be called in response to these two conditions, respectively. Fatal errors are either violations of XML's well-formedness rules (1.2), encountering an unrecognized character encoding (4.3.3), or certain illegal uses of entity or character references (4.4.4). Nonfatal errors are typically violations of validity constraints imposed by element and attribute list declarations (3.2.1) and XML version mismatches (2.8). Exceptional conditions that are less serious than error or fatal error are reported via the `warning` method. In all cases the parser will provide a `SAXParseException` that indicates where the parse error occurred. Provided the `ErrorHandler` implementation does not throw an exception, the parser will continue processing after a warning or error. A parser *may* continue processing after a `fatalError`, but any subsequent `ContentHandler` invocations are of questionable use.

The Glue of SAX: XMLReader

SAX defines the `XMLReader` interface to tie together many of the interfaces discussed so far. This interface is typically implemented by XML parsers but can be implemented by anyone who needs to tie together implementations of the various handler interfaces whose stream of method invocations represent an XML document information item. The `XMLReader` interface has three families of methods: handler methods, configuration methods, and parse methods. The handler methods consist of four get/set method pairs that allow implementations of `ContentHandler`, `DTDHandler`, `ErrorHandler`, and `EntityResolver` to be tied together to interpret a single document information item.

```
package org.xml.sax;
public interface XMLReader {
  void            setContentHandler(ContentHandler handler);
  ContentHandler  getContentHandler();
  void            setDTDHandler(DTDHandler handler);
  DTDHandler      getDTDHandler();
  void            setEntityResolver(EntityResolver resolver);
  EntityResolver  getEntityResolver();
  void            setErrorHandler(ErrorHandler handler);
  ErrorHandler    getErrorHandler();
        :                   :
```

Note that there are no `XMLReader` methods that correspond to `DeclHandler` or `LexicalHandler`. Rather, these two interfaces are dealt with by the second group of methods that focus on configuration.

`XMLReader` has four configuration methods: two that deal with *properties* and two that deal with *features*. Properties are uniquely named values that can be associated with an `XMLReader` instance. Features can be viewed as configuration-specific boolean properties that are used to turn specific processing features on or off.

SAX2 predefines a set of well-known properties and features, which are listed in Tables 2.1 and 2.2. To support extensibility, properties and features are *enable/disable*

Table 2.1   SAX2 Features

Feature	True
namespaces	Perform namespace processing.
namespace-prefixes	Report the original prefixed names and attributes used for Namespace declarations.
string-interning	All element names, prefixes, attribute names, Namespace URIs, and local names are internal ized using java.lang.String.intern.
external-general-entities	Include external general (text) entities.
external-parameter-entities	Include external parameter entities and the external DTD subset.
validation	Report all validation errors (implies *external-general-entities* and *external-parameter-entities*).

Note: Feature IDs prefixed with *http://xml.org/sax/features/*.

per instance

Table 2.2   SAX2 Properties

Property	Description [Type]
dom-node	The DOM node currently being visited, if SAX is being used as a DOM iterator. If the parser recognizes and supports this property but is not currently visiting a DOM node, return null. [DOM Node—Read Only]
Xml-string	Get the string of characters associated with the current event. If the parser recognizes and supports this property but is not currently parsing text, it should return null. [String—Read Only]
lexical-handler	An optional extension handler for lexical events like comments.
declaration-handler	An optional extension handler for DTD-related events other than notations and unparsed entities.

Note: Property IDs prefixed with *http://xml.org/sax/properties/*.

named by URIs. If the `XMLReader` implementation recognizes the property/feature name but does not support it, it must throw a `SAXNotSupported Exception`. If the `XMLReader` implementation does not recognize the property/feature name to begin with, it must throw a `SAXNotRecognized Exception`. The four configuration methods are defined as follows:

```
package org.xml.sax;
public interface XMLReader {
        :               :
   Object  getProperty(String name)
              throws SAXNotRecognizedException,
                     SAXNotSupportedException;
   void    setProperty(String name, Object value)
              throws SAXNotRecognizedException,
                     SAXNotSupportedException;
   boolean getFeature(String name)
              throws SAXNotRecognizedException,
                     SAXNotSupportedException;
   void    setFeature(String name, boolean value)
              throws SAXNotRecognizedException,
                     SAXNotSupportedException;
        :               :
}
```

The concrete type of a property value is property-specific. Because features are used to turn processing features on or off, the type of a feature is hardwired to `boolean`.

Note that two of the predefined properties are the `DeclHandler` and `LexicalHandler`. The following code associates a `DeclHandler` with an `XMLReader` implementation:

```
boolean bind(org.xml.sax.XMLReader reader,
             org.xml.sax.DeclHandler handler) {
  boolean result = false;
  try {
    reader.setProperty(
        "http://xml.org/sax/properties/declaration-handler",
        handler);
    result = true;
  }
```

ESSENTIAL XML: BEYOND MARKUP

```
    catch (org.xml.sax.SAXException sex) {   }
    return result;
}
```

And the following code retrieves the `LexicalHandler` associated with an `XMLReader`:

```
org.xml.sax.LexicalHandler get(org.xml.sax.XMLReader read) {
  org.xml.sax.LexicalHandler result = null;
  try {
    Object prop = reader.getProperty(
        "http://xml.org/sax/properties/lexical-handler");
    result = (org.xml.sax.LexicalHandler)prop;
  }
  catch (org.xml.sax.SAXException sex) {   }
  return result;
}
```

Note that neither of these code fragments distinguish between unrecognized properties and recognized but unsupported properties.

Because `XMLReader` is often implemented by XML parsers, it exposes an overloaded pair of `parse` methods.

```
package org.xml.sax;
public interface XMLReader {
      :               :
  void parse(String systemId)
          throws SAXException, java.io.IOException;
  void parse(InputSource source)
          throws SAXException, java.io.IOException;
}
```

The following code fragment demonstrates using the Apache xerces parser to parse an XML document against a caller-provided `ContentHandler`:

```
boolean parseIt(org.xml.sax.ContentHandler handler) {
  boolean result = false;
  try {
    org.xml.sax.XMLReader reader;
    reader = new org.apache.xerces.parsers.SAXParser();
```

```
        reader.setContentHandler(handler);
        reader.parse("http://www.develop.com/dbox/home.xml");
        result = true;
      }
    catch (Exception ex) { }
    return result;
  }
```

Note that a call to the `String-based` `parse` method

```
reader.parse("foo.xml");
```

is equivalent to calling the `InputSource-based` `parse` method as follows:

```
reader.parse(new org.xml.sax.InputSource("foo.xml"));
```

The former is obviously more convenient.

Most SAX interfaces are amenable to pipeline-style processing, where an implementation of, say, `ContentHandler` can intercept certain information items it recognizes but pass along unrecognized information items to a downstream processor that also implements `ContentHandler`. SAX makes this model concrete via its `XMLFilter` interface. `XMLFilter` extends the `XMLReader` interface by adding two methods, one to discover the upstream `XMLReader` implementation and one to set it. The following is the definition of `XMLFilter`:

```
package org.xml.sax;
interface XMLFilter extends XMLReader {
  XMLReader getParent();
  void      setParent(XMLReader parent);
}
```

As shown in Figure 2.3, this interface allows several independent processing components to be chained together with UNIX pipes. To make writing filters easier, SAX provides the `XMLFilterImpl` helper class that provides default implementations of most methods of the following interfaces: `XMLFilter`, `EntityResolver`, `DTDHandler`, `ContentHandler`, and `ErrorHandler`. The implementations of the last four interfaces simply forward the calls to the corresponding objects registered via the `setXXXHandler` methods.

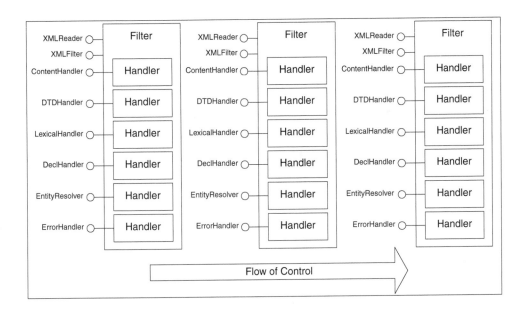

Figure 2.3   SAX2 pipelines

As this chapter has shown, SAX is a streaming interface that is designed around a serial stream of method invocations that convey the information items contained in an XML document. For applications that can act upon a document a chunk at a time, this style of interface is ideal, as there is no need to retain the original information items once they have been conveyed via the appropriate handler method. For resource-sensitive applications (e.g., low-memory devices, high-throughput server applications), this is arguably the only way an XML document can be conveyed in memory. However, applications that need to convey an XML document *en masse* often find SAX bothersome at best and impossible to use at worst. For these applications, the Document Object Model is more appropriate.

The Document Object Model

The Document Object Model (DOM) is a set of abstract interfaces that model the XML Infoset. The DOM Level 1 specification was designed prior to the Namespaces in XML recommendation and is not considered in this chapter. The DOM Level 2 specification is currently a W3C Candidate Recommendation and has already gained support from commercial and open-source XML processing software. For that reason, when this book refers to "the DOM," it is referring to DOM Level 2 or greater.

Like SAX, the DOM operates at the Infoset level and is devoid of angle brackets or character references. Additionally, the DOM is defined entirely in terms of abstract interfaces; implementations are free to implement these interfaces in any manner they choose. However, unlike streaming interfaces such as SAX, the DOM supports in-memory traversal, navigation, and modification of an abstract XML document. While the DOM currently does not mandate I/O functionality, most (if not all) implementations of the DOM interfaces support reading and/or writing XML 1.0 + Namespaces documents.

The DOM specification defines interfaces using the OMG's Interface Definition Language (IDL). IDL is a programming language-neutral language for defining programmatic types. To reduce the dependencies on external specifications,[6] the DOM also defines two language mappings: Java and ECMAScript (the standardized version of Javascript/JScript). The primary difference between these two bindings relates to the handling of field accessors. For IDL interfaces that have attributes (OMG IDL attributes, not XML attributes), the ECMAScript language binding maps the attribute to a property. For example, the `Node` interface has an attribute named `nodeValue`.

```
interface Node {
    attribute DOMString nodeValue;
        :            :              :
```

Accessing `nodeValue` from ECMAScript is fairly trivial.

```
node.nodeValue = "Hello, World";
```

The Java language binding maps IDL attributes to `getXXX/setXXX` methods, so the Java equivalent to the previous statement would look like this.

```
node.setNodeValue("Hello, World");
```

IDL `readonly` attributes of course do not have a `setXXX` method.

---

[6]This statement is overly polite. The OMG language bindings for many programming languages are unwieldy and overly baroque due to a variety of factors that are outside the scope of this book. It is unfortunate that one cannot count on a portable C++ definition of the DOM for that reason.

The Object Model

The DOM is a projection of the XML Infoset. The object model of the DOM represents the Infoset as a tree-structured graph of nodes. The DOM specifies several aspects of this graph, including the interfaces that must be supported by each node, the syntax/semantics of the each node interface, and the relationships between the different node types. The DOM does not, however, mandate how the underlying code is structured or what algorithms or data structures are used to maintain the internal form of the underlying information items.

Figure 2.4 shows the UML model of the DOM. The focal point of the DOM is the Node interface, which acts as the base interface for all node types. Table 2.3 shows the various node types and their corresponding Infoset information item where applicable. The fact that virtually everything is a node makes traversal code extremely uniform, as a standard set of methods is available no matter where one is in the object model. However, each node supports an extended interface type that exposes information item-specific functionality in a type-safe

Table 2.3   DOM Nodes and the Infoset

DOM Node	Infoset Information Item
Document	Document Information Item
DocumentFragment	N/A
DocumentType	Document Type Declaration Information Item
EntityReference	Entity Start/End Marker Information Items
Element	Element Information Item
Attr	Attribute Information Item
ProcessingInstruction	Processing Instruction Information Item
Comment	Comment Information Item
Text	Sequence of Character Information Items
CDATASection	CDATA Start/End Marker Information Items
Entity	Entity Information Item
Notation	Notation Information Item

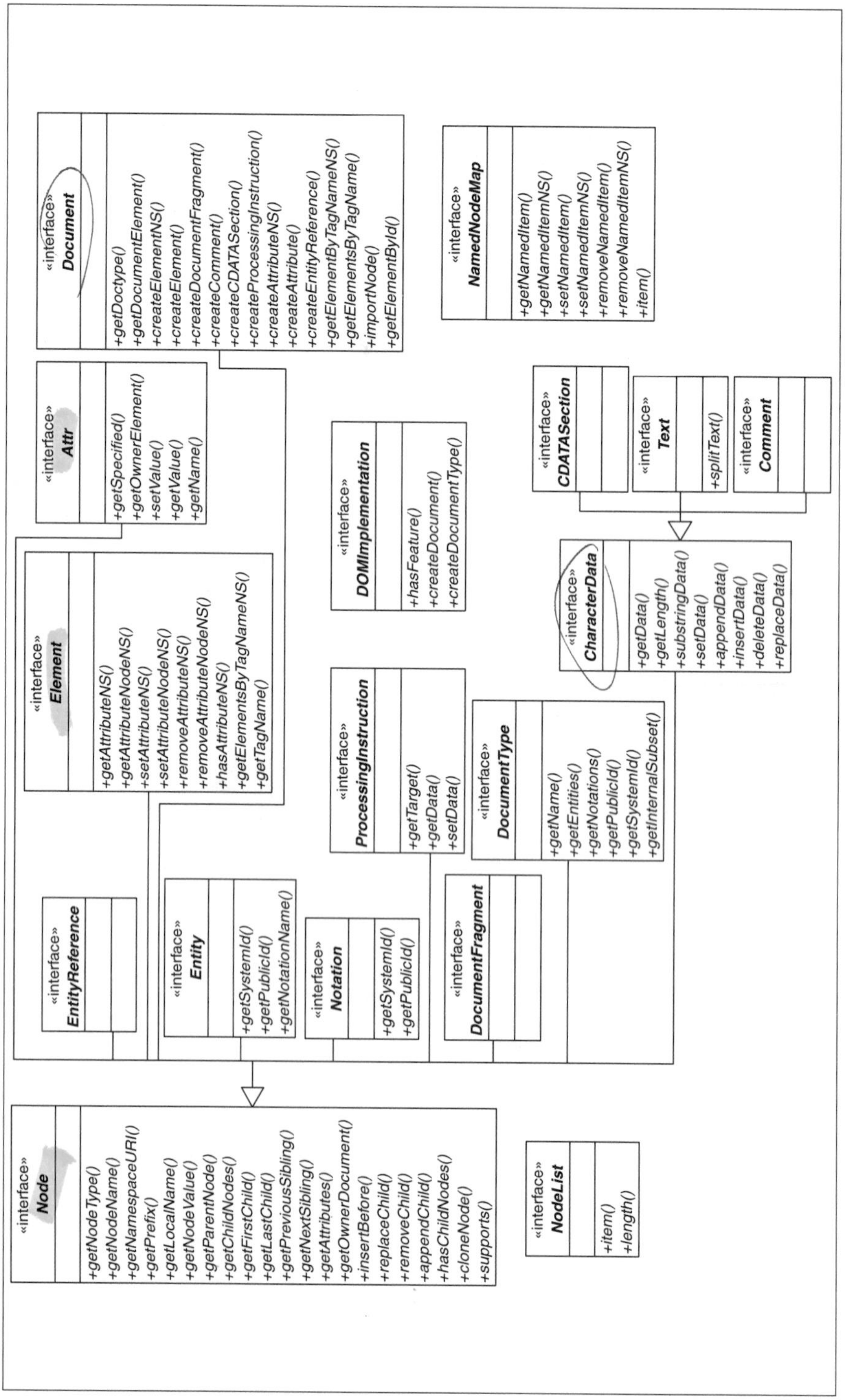

Figure 2.4 DOM interfaces

ESSENTIAL XML: BEYOND MARKUP

interface type that exposes information item-specific functionality in a type-safe manner.

To see how the DOM object model reflects the Infoset, consider the following serialized XML document:

```
<?xml version="1.0"?>
<?order alpha ascending?>
<art xmlns='http://www.art.org/schemas/art'>
  <period name="Renaissance">
    <artist>Leonardo da Vinci</artist>
    <artist>Michelangelo</artist>
    <artist>Donatello</artist>
  </period>
  <!-- insert period here -->
</art>
```

Figure 2.5 shows what happens when this XML document is projected onto the DOM. Notice that the topmost node in the DOM structure corresponds to the document information item and is of type `Document`. The `Document` node has two child nodes that correspond to the document information item's

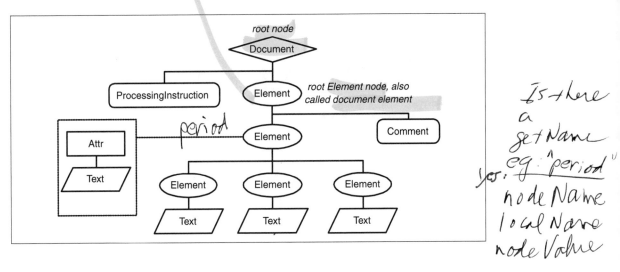

Figure 2.5   The DOM and art

[children] property: a `ProcessingInstruction` node[7] and an `Element` node. The `Element` node is the distinguished document element and has two child nodes corresponding to the element information item's [children] property: one `Element` node and one `Comment` node. That `Element` node has three `Element` nodes as children, again corresponding to the [children] Infoset property.

As just described, there is a striking similarity between the node-based model of the DOM and the Infoset. Where the DOM's node-based model departs from the Infoset is in its treatment of character information items. The Infoset treats each character in element content as a distinct information item. This is reasonable for an abstract model, but the performance impact of using an object per character would render the DOM completely unusable. For that reason, the DOM aggregates adjacent character information items into a single node of type `Text`. It is also interesting to note that the `nodeValue` property of the parent `Element` nodes is always null. Rather, to access the character data [children] from an `Element` node, one must first access the `Text` node that is the child of the element. The `nodeValue` of that node will contain a string of characters reflecting the element content.

The DOM and Factories

The DOM relies on a fairly stylized resource management strategy. Because the DOM consists solely of abstract interfaces and has no concrete classes, there is no class one can simply call `new` on to create new nodes. Rather, the DOM expects that all objects (except for one) are created indirectly via well-known factory methods that are exposed on several DOM interfaces. Of course, this still leaves a bootstrapping problem, as one must have an object reference in order to call a DOM-specified factory method. This is where the `DOMImplementation` interface comes in.

Each implementation of the DOM interfaces must provide an object that implements `DOMImplementation`. This object acts as a rendezvous point for

---

[7]At least one DOM implementation (MSXML 2.x) erroneously makes the XML declaration available as a `ProcessingInstruction` node.

all component-wide functionality. The `DOMImplementation` interface is defined as follows:

```
interface DOMImplementation {
  boolean        hasFeature(in DOMString feature,
                            in DOMString version);
  DocumentType createDocumentType(
                   in DOMString qualifiedName,
                   in DOMString publicId,
                   in DOMString systemId) raises(DOMException);
  Document       createDocument(
                   in DOMString namespaceURI,
                   in DOMString qualifiedName,
                   in DocumentType doctype)
                        raises(DOMException);
};
```

How one acquires an initial reference to this interface is proprietary to each implementation. The following illustrates the Apache xerces-specific technique:

```
org.w3c.dom.DOMImplementation loadDOM() {
   return new org.apache.xerces.dom.DOMImplementationImpl();
}
```

Note that in Java, all core DOM interfaces are in the `org.w3c.dom` package.

Given an implementation of `DOMImplementation`, one can create nodes of type `Document` and of type `DocumentType` (which corresponds to the DTD of a document information item). Consider the following Java code:

```
org.w3c.dom.Document create() {
  org.w3c.dom.DOMImplementation impl = loadDOM();
  org.w3c.dom.DocumentType dtd = impl.createDocumentType(
        "foo:bar", "-//FooBar//", "foo.dtd");
  return impl.createDocument("http://foo.com/schema/",
                             "foo:bar", dtd);
}
```

This function returns a `Document` node that corresponds to the following serialized document:

```
<?xml version='1.0' ?>
<!DOCTYPE foo:bar PUBLIC "-//FooBar//" "foo.dtd">
<foo:bar xmlns:foo='http://foo.com/schema/" />
```

Note that at the time of this writing, the W3C DOM specification provided no standard mechanism for translating a DOM `Document` to or from a serialized XML document. However, most implementations provide a proprietary mechanism for doing this.

The `DOMImplementation` interface provides factory methods for `Document` and `DocumentType` nodes. The factory methods for most of the remaining node types are on the `Document` interface itself.

```
interface Document : Node {
   Element  createElementNS(in DOMString namespaceURI,
                             in DOMString qualifiedName);[8]
   Attr     createAttributeNS(in DOMString namespaceURI,
                               in DOMString qualifiedName);
   DocumentFragment    createDocumentFragment();
   Text                createTextNode(in DOMString data);
   Comment             createComment(in DOMString data);
   CDATASection        createCDATASection(in DOMString data);
   ProcessingInstruction createProcessingInstruction(
        in DOMString target, in DOMString data);
   EntityReference     createEntityReference(
                            in DOMString name);
   Node                importNode(in Node importedNode,
                                  in boolean deep);
   // remaining methods elided for clarity
};
```

As an example, this Java code

```
void addComment(org.w3c.dom.Document document) {
  org.w3c.dom.Comment comment;
  comment = document.createComment("Hello, world");
```

---

[8]The DOM Level 1 `createElement` and `createAttribute` methods are depreciated due to their lack of namespace support.

```
      document.appendChild(comment);
   }
```

would append a comment node containing the text "Hello, world" to the given document.

When a new node is created by a `Document`, that node can only be inserted into that document. That means that the results of running the following code are undefined:

```
void evilCode(Document doc1, Document doc2) {
   Node node = doc1.createComment("Hello, world");
   doc2.appendChild(node); // this will fail!
}
```

To support using nodes created by foreign `Document` objects, the `Document` interface provides `importNode` method.

```
Node importNode(in Node importedNode, in boolean deep);
```

This method should be called on the target `Document` that will accept the node into its hierarchy. The following is the correct version of the previous illegal code fragment:

```
void niceCode(Document doc1, Document doc2) {
   Node node = doc1.createComment("Hello, world");
   Node safe = doc2.importNode(node, true);
   doc2.appendChild(safe); // this will succeed!
}
```

`Document.importNode` is the only method in the DOM core that accepts a cross-document node reference.

It is always possible to find the `Document` with which a node is associated via the `Node.ownerDocument` attribute.

```
interface Node {
   readonly attribute Document ownerDocument;
      :           :           :
```

Similarly, it is always possible to find the `DOMImplementation` with which a Document node is associated via the `Document.implementation` attribute.

```
interface Node {
    readonly attribute DOMImplementation implementation;
        :            :              :
```

These two attributes ensure that given any node in a document, one can safely create related nodes using the corresponding `Document` and `DOM Implementation` objects.

The Node Interface

The primary purpose of the `Node` interface is to define the base functionality for all node types. It defines the set of attributes, methods, and constants that must be available on any node within the DOM hierarchy. This makes it possible to traverse a DOM hierarchy in a uniform fashion strictly using the `Node` interface without having to downcast to more specific interface types. The more specific interfaces are available when necessary to access features that only make sense for a given node type.

One of the tradeoffs of a fairly general base interface like `Node` is that some of its operations do not apply to all of the node types. The DOM working group made a conscious decision to not factor the `Node` interface to the smallest common subset. Rather, the DOM working group tried to balance the benefits of type safety with the convenience and uniformity of a single model-wide interface. This compromising of type-safety means that some errors may not be detected until runtime rather than at compile-time.

For generality, the DOM does not rely on the use of runtime type identification (RTTI) in the target programming language. Rather, the `nodeType` attribute is used to test a node for compatibility with a derived interface (for example, `Element`, `Document`). The `Node` interface also defines a group of symbolic constants that correspond to the different node types.

```
interface Node {
    readonly attribute unsigned short nodeType;
    const unsigned short ELEMENT_NODE                = 1;
```

```
const unsigned short ATTRIBUTE_NODE                      = 2;
const unsigned short TEXT_NODE                           = 3;
const unsigned short CDATA_SECTION_NODE                  = 4;
const unsigned short ENTITY_REFERENCE_NODE               = 5;
const unsigned short ENTITY_NODE                         = 6;
const unsigned short PROCESSING_INSTRUCTION_NODE         = 7;
const unsigned short COMMENT_NODE                        = 8;
const unsigned short DOCUMENT_NODE                       = 9;
const unsigned short DOCUMENT_TYPE_NODE                  = 10;
const unsigned short DOCUMENT_FRAGMENT_NODE              = 11;
const unsigned short NOTATION_NODE                       = 12;
    :              :                    :
};
```

The `nodeType` attribute acts as a poor man's RTTI mechanism. For example, the Java function

```
boolean isElement(org.w3c.dom.Node n) {
  return n.getNodeType() == org.w3c.dom.Node.ELEMENT_NODE;
}
```

Better

is functionally equivalent to

```
boolean isElement(org.w3c.dom.Node n) {
  return n instanceof org.w3c.dom.Element;
}
```

The advantage of the latter is that it is integrated into the type system of the language. The advantage of the former is that it works consistently even in typeless languages (such as ECMAScript) where RTTI is impractical. Additionally, the former approach provides implementations with more flexibility with respect to factoring which concrete classes implement which interfaces, and for that reason one should always use the former style of test to ensure portability.

Many node types support names. These names are exposed via the `Node.nodeName` property, and for node types such as `Processing-Instruction` or `Entity`, this is sufficient. However, because both element and attribute names can be affiliated with a namespace URI, the `Node` interface also contains attributes for retrieving namespace information.

```
interface Node {
   readonly attribute DOMString         nodeName;
   readonly attribute DOMString         namespaceURI;
            attribute DOMString         prefix;
   readonly attribute DOMString         localName;
        :              :           :                    :
}
```

The `Node.nodeName` attribute always returns the `QName` based on the qualified name of the element or attribute information item. More importantly, the `Node` interface makes the `[namespace URI]` and `[local name]` Infoset properties available via the `Node.namespaceURI` and `Node.localName` attributes. For convenience, the actual prefix used in the `QName` is available via the `Node.prefix` attribute. Since only element and attribute names may be affiliated with a namespace, these namespace-specific attributes return null for all other node types.

There are several node types that don't have an obvious name (for example, `Document`, `Text`, or `Comment` nodes). The DOM specification defines fixed values that must be used for the `Node.nodeName` of these node types. For example, the `Node.nodeName` attribute for `Document` nodes always evaluates to "#document". For text nodes the attribute must evaluate to "#text", for comment nodes "#comment," and so on.

A node's value is accessed generically via the `Node.nodeValue` attribute. Certain node types can have values, whereas others cannot. For example, `Element` nodes only have children and their `nodeValue` is always `null`. In contrast, for `Text` nodes, the `nodeValue` attribute evaluates to the character data content of the text node. Table 2.4 lists the `nodeName`/`nodeValue` values for each of the possible node types. Figure 2.6 shows the `nodeName` and `nodeValue` values for each node in the DOM hierarchy shown earlier in this section.

Both `nodeType` and `nodeName` are read-only properties. Because of this, there is no way to change a node's name once it has been created. While this does simplify DOM implementations, there are still situations where this type of functionality is necessary (such as with an XML editor). If you need to change a node's name on the fly, you're required to create a completely new node and copy the node's value as appropriate.

ESSENTIAL XML: BEYOND MARKUP

examples

Table 2.4 DOM Node Types, Names and Values

NodeType	#	nodeName	nodeValue
Element	1	Tag name	Null
Attr	2	Name of attribute	value of attribute
Text	3	#text	Content of the text node
CDATASection	4	#cdata-section	Content of the CDATA section
EntityReference	5	Name of entity referenced	Null
Entity	6	Entity name	Null
ProcessingInstruction	7	Target	Entire content excluding the target
Comment	8	#comment	Content of the comment
Document	9	#document	Null
DocumentType	10	Document type name	Null
DocumentFragment	11	#document-fragment	Null
Notation	12	Notation name	Null

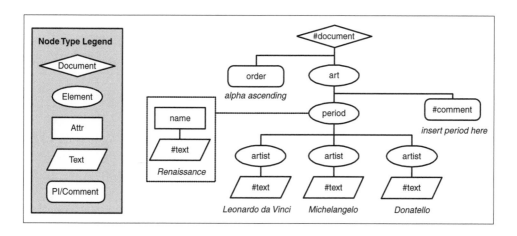

Figure 2.6   Node types, names, and values

Parents and Children

The node relationships of the DOM are a direct manifestation of the [parent]/
[children] relationships of the Infoset. The Node interface provides a set of
attributes and methods that correspond to these two Infoset properties.

```
interface Node {
    readonly attribute Node         parentNode;
    readonly attribute Node         firstChild;
    readonly attribute Node         lastChild;
    readonly attribute Node         previousSibling;
    readonly attribute Node         nextSibling;
    readonly attribute NodeList      childNodes;
    boolean                         hasChildNodes();
    readonly attribute Document      ownerDocument;
        :               :                    :
};
```

Figure 2.7 illustrates how these attributes relate to a given node in a document.
Due to the Node interface's generality, some aspects of this interface may not
be applicable for all node types. For example, the document information item
does not have a [parent] property. For that reason, the Node.parentNode
attribute will always evaluate to null for nodes of type Document. Similarly,

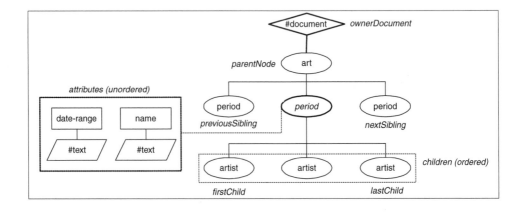

Figure 2.7   **The Node interface's [parent]/[children] properties**

since processing instruction information items do not have a [children] property, the Node.firstChild and Node.lastChild attribute of ProcessingInstruction nodes will always evaluate to null.

The Node interface was designed to make document traversal uniform and simple. For example, the following Java method performs a depth-first traversal of the given node:

cf: linked list

```
void traverseTree(Node current) {
    myProcessNode(current);
    for (Node child = current.getFirstChild(); child != null;
        child = child.getNextSibling() )
        traverseTree(child);
}
```

myProcessNode use nodeName nodeValue nodetype

This depth-first traversal corresponds exactly to the document-order of [children] properties in the Infoset. The following Java method performs the traversal in reverse-document-order:

```
void traverseTreeReverse(Node current) {
    for (Node child = current.getLastChild(); child != null;
        child = child.getPreviousSibling() )
        traverseTreeReverse(child);
    myProcessNode(current);
}
```

Note that both of these examples use a sequential access pattern much like that imposed by a linked-list. It is also possible to use a more array-like random-access pattern using the NodeList interface.

The DOM defines the NodeList interface to provide random access to an ordered collection of nodes. The NodeList interface is defined as follows:

```
interface NodeList {
    Node item(in unsigned long index);
    readonly attribute unsigned long    length;
};
```

7

cf: array

The [children] property of the current node can be accessed using the NodeList interface via the Node.childNodes attribute. The traverseTree method shown earlier can be rewritten as follows:

```
void traverseTree(Node current) {
   myProcessNode(current);
   NodeList children = current.getChildNodes();
   for (int i = 0; i < children.getLength(); i++)
      traverseTree(children.item(i));
}
```

The traverseTreeReverse can also be rewritten using the NodeList interface

```
void traverseTreeReverse(Node current) {
  NodeList children = current.getChildNodes();
  for (int i = children.getLength() - 1; i >= 0; i--)
    traverseTreeReverse(children.item(i));
  myProcessNode(current);
}
```

For these two examples, the difference is largely stylistic. However, if random access to the *ith* child node is desired, then the NodeList approach will likely be considerably faster.[9]

Independent of the [parent]/[children] relationship, DOM nodes always belong to a particular Document. As soon as a new node is created through one of the Document's factory methods, that node is automatically associated with the Document that created it. This association cannot be changed and is made explicit via the node's ownerDocument attribute.

```
void create(org.w3c.dom.Document doc) {
 Node n = doc.createElementNS("http://books.org", "author");
 assert(n.ownerDocument == doc);
}
```

---

[9]Although different implementations of the DOM may or may not be able to provide faster access using this technique.

Note that the value of the `Node.ownerDocument` attribute cannot be changed and will be the same for all nodes within a document.

The `Node` interface also provides a set of methods for manipulating the DOM hierarchy. These methods enforce the type constraints of the [children] properties. For example, one can use these methods to add a `Text` node child to an `Element` node but not to a `Document` node. The definition of these manipulation methods is as follows:

```
interface Node {
    Node insertBefore(in Node newChild,  in Node refChild)
    Node appendChild(in Node newChild)
    Node removeChild(in Node oldChild)
    Node replaceChild(in Node newChild,  in Node oldChild)
    Node cloneNode(in boolean deep);
    ...
};
```

Both the `Node.insertBefore` and `Node.appendChild` methods are used to add nodes to the hierarchy.

`Node.appendChild` simply adds the new child to the end of the list of children, whereas `Node.insertBefore` allows you to specify where the new node should appear in the sequence of children. Both methods return the node that was inserted. For example, the following code adds a new `artist` element node to the end of `period`'s children:

```
import org.w3c.dom.*;
void addNewArtist(Document doc, Node period) {
    Node newChild = doc.createElementNS(
        "http://www.art.org/schemas/art", "artist");
    Node insertedNode = period.appendChild(newChild);
    assert(newChild == insertedNode);
    assert(insertedNode == period.getLastChild());
}
```

The `Node.insertBefore` accepts an additional object reference as a parameter. This reference indicates the node that the insertion should precede. If this parameter is `null`, `Node.insertBefore` behaves exactly like

`Node.appendChild`. Consider the following code that uses both insertion techniques:

```
import org.w3c.dom.*;
void addTwoPeriods(Document doc, Node art) {
   Node newChild1 = doc.createElementNS(
       "http://www.art.org/schemas/art", "period");
   art.appendChild(newChild1);
   Node newChild2 = doc.createElementNS(
       "http://www.art.org/schemas/art", "period");
   Node pos = period.getFirstChild().getNextSibling();
   Node insertedNode = art.insertBefore(newChild2, pos);
   assert(newChild2 == insertedNode);
   assert(insertedNode == period.getChildNodes().item(1));
}
```

Figure 2.8 shows the results of this code.

Whereas the DOM's `Node.nodeType` reinvents RTTI to distinguish node types, the DOM leverages the native programming system's notion of object identity. To this end, a given instance of `Node` can only appear once in a document hierarchy. When calling `Node.insertBefore` or `Node.appendChild`, if the node to be inserted already appears elsewhere in the DOM hierarchy, it will automatically be removed from its current location before being inserted to a new location. For example, consider the following Java code:

```
import org.w3c.dom.*;
void doubleIt(Document doc, Node parent) {
   Node child = doc.createElementNS("", "child");
   parent.appendChild(child);
   parent.insertBefore(child, parent.getFirstChild());
}
```

Because a given node object can only appear once in a document hierarchy, this code winds up inserting exactly one `Element` node at the beginning of the list of child nodes of `parent`. The work done by the call to `Node.appendChild` is undone by the call to `Node.insertBefore` that "reinserts" the same node.

ESSENTIAL XML: BEYOND MARKUP

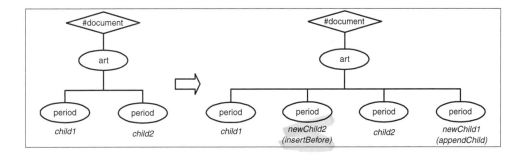

Figure 2.8   Node.appendChild and Node.insertBefore

In addition to inserting nodes into a list of child nodes, it is is also possible to remove or replace a node via `Node.removeChild` and `Node.replaceChild` methods respectively. Consider the following Java code:

```java
import org.w3c.dom.*;
void figureNine(Document doc, Node art) {
  Node newChild = doc.createElementNS(
      "http://www.art.org/schemas/art", "period");
  art.replaceChild(newChild, art.getFirstChild());
  art.removeChild(art.getLastChild());
}
```

The results of this code are shown in Figure 2.9. Note that the resources held by the node that is replaced or removed are not necessarily destroyed at removal-time.

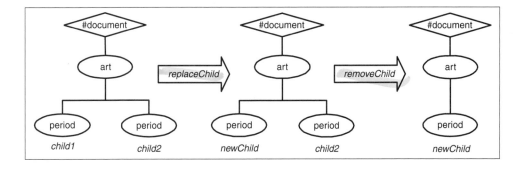

Figure 2.9   Node.replaceChild and Node.removeChild

It is interesting to note that the `Node.replaceChild` method simply combines insertion and removal in a single operation. For example, this Java method

```java
import org.w3c.dom.*;
void swap(Node parent, Node oldChild, Node newChild) {
  parent.insertBefore(newChild, oldChild);
  parent.removeChild(oldChild);
}
```

could be replaced with

```java
import org.w3c.dom.*;
void swap(Node parent, Node oldChild, Node newChild) {
  parent.replaceChild(newChild, oldChild);
}
```

The latter is obviously more convenient and maintainable.

Finally, the `Node.cloneNode` method provides a way to copy a node and optionally all of its ancestor nodes. The newly created clone node is not attached to any document hierarchy and does not have a parent until it is inserted using one of the methods described above. The new node will be an exact copy of original node, plus if the `deep` parameter is `true`, `Node.cloneNode` will recursively copy all child nodes as well. If the node happens to be an `Element` node, `Node.cloneNode` will also copy all of the attribute information items associated with the element. The following example copies a `period` element and all of its children and attributes and then inserts it into the hiearchy:

```java
import org.w3c.dom.*;
void cloneLastPeriod(Node art) {
  Node clone = art.getLastChild().cloneNode(true);
  art.appendChild(clone);
}
```

As shown in Figure 2.10, this simple method call can do a lot of work.

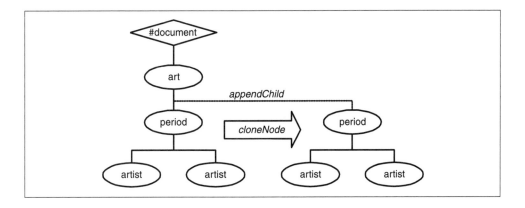

Figure 2.10   Node.cloneNode

The various parent/child attributes of the `Node` interface are considered live in the face of updates. Additionally, the object returned by `childNodes` doesn't represent a static snapshot of the child nodes but rather a dynamic cursor over the current collection of children. Any changes to the underlying content is automatically visible in all outstanding `NodeList` references as shown here.

```
NodeList nl = period.getChildNodes();
// nl.getLength() == 3
Node newNode = doc.createElement("author");
period.appendChild(newNode);
// nl.getLength() == 4
```

Notice that after inserting a new author node under `period`, the changes are automatically visible to the outstanding `NodeList` reference, `nl`, without any additional intervention.

Because `NodeList`s are live, care needs to be taken when dealing with them in certain situations. For example, take a look at the following code that attempts to remove all nodes from a `NodeList`:

```
NodeList nl = node.getChildNodes();
for (int i = 0; i < nl.getLength(); i++) {
```

```
        node.removeChild(nl.item(i));
    }
```

This code doesn't work as expected because the `NodeList` is live. If there were 5 nodes in the list, it's only going to remove nodes 1, 3, and 5. Every time a node is removed, the `NodeList`'s length changes along with each node index. To handle this type of operation properly, it's better to delete from the front of the list until the list is empty.

```
NodeList nl = node.getChildNodes();
while (nl.getLength() > 0) {
    node.removeChild(nl.item(0));
}
```

Of course, this code could have also been written using `Node.firstChild`.

The `parentNode` value is also dynamic in the face of node manipulation. For example, upon creation via `createElementNS`, a new element's `parentNode` attribute will be `null`. However, once it has been inserted into a document's hierarchy, the element's `parentNode` attribute will be adjusted accordingly.

```
Node n = doc.createElementNS("http://books.org", "author");
// n.parentNode == null
doc.appendChild(n); // insert the node
// n.parentNode == doc
```

All nodes except for `Document`, `DocumentFragment`, `Attr`, `Entity`, and `Notation` nodes will have a non-null parent node when they exist within the hierarchy.

Nonhierarchical Nodes

There are a few structural Infoset properties that do not fit into the `[parent]`/`[children]` relationships of the Infoset. These include the `[attributes]` property of an element information item as well as the `[notations]` and `[entities]` properties of a document information item. Each of these properties exposes a collection of information items as an unordered collection that is accessed by name. To model this sort of collection, the DOM defines the `NamedNodeMap` interface.

```
interface NamedNodeMap {
  Node item(in unsigned long index);
  readonly attribute unsigned long    length;
  Node getNamedItemNS(in DOMString namespaceURI,
                      in DOMString localName);
  Node getNamedItem(in DOMString name);
  Node setNamedItemNS(in Node arg) raises(DOMException);
  Node setNamedItem(in Node arg)    raises(DOMException);
  Node removeNamedItemNS(in DOMString namespaceURI,
                         in DOMString localName)
                            raises(DOMException);
  Node removeNamedItem(in DOMString name)
                            raises(DOMException);
};
```

Note that this interface provides both positional and named access via its `item` and `getNamedItem` methods, respectively. The `NamedNodeMap` interface is used to access attribute, entity, and notation information items. Since attribute information items use namespaces, but entity and notation information items do not, the three "NamedItem" methods come in two forms—one that works in terms of namespace URI + local name and one that works in terms of just name. The former style is for attributes, and the latter form is for entities and notations.

The [attributes] Infoset property is exposed via the `attributes` attribute on the `Node` interface.

```
interface Node {
  readonly attribute NamedNodeMap attributes;
     :          :            :                 :
};
```

The following code adds an attribute to the provided element:

```
import org.w3c.dom.*;
void annotate(Node elem) {
  Document document = elem.getOwnerDocument();
```

```
Node attr = document.createAttributeNS(
                    "http://foo.com/names", "note");
attr.setNodeValue("Hello, world");
NamedNodeMap attrs = elem.getAttributes();
attrs.setNamedItemNS(attr);
}
```

Because the `attributes` attribute is only valid for `Element` nodes, this code will fail miserably for non-`Element` nodes.

The `[notations]` and `[entities]` Infoset properties are exposed via the `notations` and `entities` attributes of the `DocumentType` interface.

```
interface DocumentType : Node {
  readonly attribute NamedNodeMap entities;
  readonly attribute NamedNodeMap notations;
};
```

The `DocumentType` node is available as an attribute of the `Document` interface.

```
interface Document : Node {
  readonly attribute DocumentType doctype;
     :              :              :              :
};
```

Given these interface definitions, the following Java code returns the entity named `bob` that is related to a node's document:

```
import org.w3c.dom.*;
Node getBob(Node someNode) {
  Document document = someNode.getOwnerDocument();
  DocumentType doctype = document.getDoctype();
  if (doctype == null) return null;
  NamedNodeMap entities = doctype.getEntities();
  return entities.getNamedItem("bob");
}
```

Note that the node returned by this function also implements the `Entity` interface to provide access to the `[system identifier]`, `[public identifier]`, and `[notation]` Infoset properties.

Text Nodes

The ensure interoperability, the DOM defines a standard data type for representing character data in a source document. The DOM defines the `DOMString` as a sequence of 16-bit units (encoded using UTF-16) for this purpose.[10] The DOM also defines a generic `CharacterData` interface deriving from `Node` that encapsulates `DOMString` and provides behavior for inserting, appending, replacing, and deleting the `DOMString`'s value. All other DOM interfaces that deal directly with character data extend the `CharacterData` interface, which itself extends `Node`.

The `CharacterData` interface provides basic string manipulation operations. The `CharacterData` interface is never implemented by itself; it is always implemented in tandem with an extended interface. The `Text` interface is the most common extended interface, and it is used to model collections of character information items that appear as in an element information item's `[children]` property. Consider the following XML document:

```
<foo>The <bar>quick</bar> brown <bar>fox <baz>jumped</baz>
over <baz>the</baz> lazy</bar> dog</foo>
```

When this document is loaded into the DOM, contiguous text not separated by markup will be contained within a `Text` node as shown in Figure 2.11.

The text of an element is considered *normalized* when it contains no two adjacent `Text` nodes, as was shown above. In general, deserializing an XML document into a DOM will yield normalized elements. However, when new `Text` nodes are inserted into the hierarchy, one can wind up with a denormalized element. While completely legal, various XML technologies have a difficult time handling denormalized elements. XPath, for example, depends on a normalized document tree structure to behave properly. Performing an XPath traversal against a document with denormalized elements would yield unexpected results. This can be prevented using the `Node.normalize` method,

---

[10]As stated in the DOM specification, DOM implementations are required to encode `DOMString`'s using UTF-16 because of its widespread industry practice. However, because XML's character set is technically UCS, a single numeric character reference in a source document may in some cases correspond to two 16-bit units in a `DOMString`.

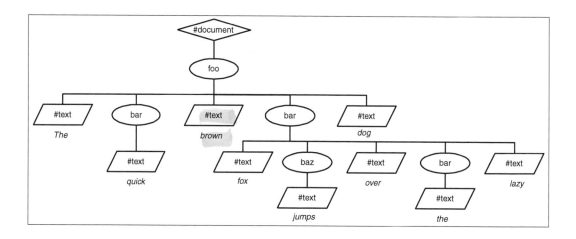

Figure 2.11   Text nodes

which recursively normalizes all ancestor `Text` nodes. Consider the following Java code:

```
import org.w3c.dom.*;
void appendText(Document doc, Node elem) {
  int nChildren = elem.getChildNodes().getLength();
  Node text1 = doc.createTextNode("hello ");
  Node text2 = doc.createTextNode("world");
  elem.appendChild(text1);
  elem.appendChild(text2);
  text2.splitText(2);
  assert(elem.getChildNodes().getLength() == nChildren + 3);
  elem.normalize();
  assert(elem.getChildNodes().getLength() == nChildren + 1);
}
```

As shown in Figure 2.12, after the call to `Text.splitText`, there are three new `Text` node children. However, after the call to `Node.normalize`, the three adjacent `Text` nodes are folded into a single node containing the string "hello, world".

The DOM defines two other `CharacterData`-related interfaces: `Comment` and `CDATASection`. The `Comment` interface (and corresponding concrete node type) extends `CharacterData` and is used to represent comment information

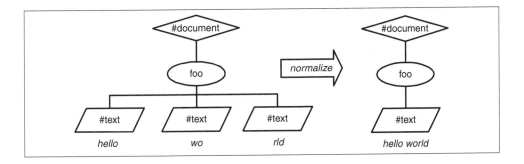

Figure 2.12 Text node normalization

items. The CDATASection interface (and corresponding concrete node type) extends Text and is used to signal the presence of CDATA start and end information items. Neither of these interfaces adds any operations beyond those present in their base interfaces.

Element and Attribute Nodes

The Element and Attr node types correspond to the Infoset's element and attribute information items, respectively. The [children] and [parent] Infoset properties of the element information item are exposed via the standard Node methods, and no additional functionality is needed to address these properties. The parent of an Attr node is always null, but the associated Element node is available via the Attr.ownerElement attribute. The [children] property of the attribute information item is available via both Node.nodeValue and via the Text and EntityReference children of the Attr node.

The primary extensions that Element provides are to address the [attributes] Infoset property, which is always treated as distinct from the [children] property. As mentioned previously, the [attributes] property is available via the Node.attributes read-only attribute. As a convenience, the Element interface also defines Attr-specific methods that mirror the more generic NamedNodeMap methods.

```
interface Element : Node {
    DOMString getAttributeNS(in DOMString namespaceURI,
                             in DOMString localName);
```

```
Node        getAttributeNodeNS(in DOMString namespaceURI,
                              in DOMString localName);
void        setAttributeNS(in DOMString namespaceURI,
              in DOMString qualifiedName, in DOMString value)
                                        raises(DOMException);
Attr        setAttributeNodeNS(in Attr attr)
                                        raises(DOMException);
void        removeAttributeNS(in DOMString namespaceURI,
                              in DOMString localName)
                                        raises(DOMException);
Attr        removeAttributeNode(in Attr attr)
                                        raises(DOMException);
   :             :                           :
};
```

The prenamespace versions of these methods are elided for clarity.

The attribute-specific `Element` methods are functionally identical to using the `NamedNodeMap` exposed via the `Node.attributes` attribute. This simple Java function

```
import org.w3c.dom.*;
void setIt(Element elem) {
  elem.setAttributeNS("http://x.com/ns", "x:hi", "earth");
}
```

could be written using generic `Node`-isms as follows

```
import org.w3c.dom.*;
void setIt(Node elem) {
  Document doc = elem.getOwnerDocument();
  Node attr = doc.createAttributeNS("http://x.com/ns",
                                    "x:hi");
  Node text = doc.createTextNode("earth");
  attr.appendChild(text);
  elem.getAttributes().setNamedItemNS(attr);
}
```

The former is obviously worth the downcast.

Note that the `getAttribute` methods use an `NCName`-based local name but the `setAttributeNS` method uses a `QName`-based qualified name. This provides control over the namespace prefix that is used to qualify the attribute name. Recall that nonprefixed attribute names are not affiliated with any namespace URI. For that reason, when passing a nonempty namespace URI to `setAttributeNS`, a namespace prefix must be selected. Additionally, because the DOM does not treat namespace declaration information items as first-class citizens, the burden is on the developer for managing which prefixes are associated with each namespace URI.

There is one other method available on the `Element` interface that has nothing to do with attributes *per se* but shares the model of retrieving things by name. This method is `getElementsByTagNameNS`.

```
interface Element : Node {
   NodeList getElementsByTagNameNS(in DOMString namespaceURI,
                                   in DOMString localname);

       :              :                    :
}
```

As shown in Figure 2.13, `Element.getElementsByTagNameNS` returns all descendant elements of the specified name as a `NodeList` in the order they would have been encountered doing a preorder (left to right, depth first) traversal. Additionally, one can pass the "*" wildcard to either parameter, telling

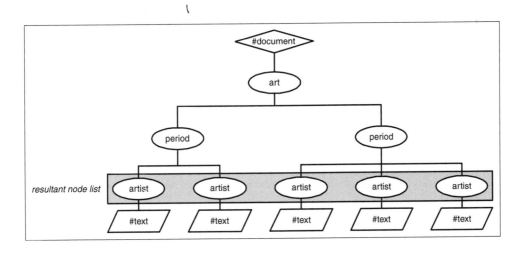

Figure 2.13   Element.getElementsByTagNameNS in action

`Element.getElementsByTagNameNS` to ignore either namespace affiliation or local name (or both). `Element.getElementsByTagNameNS` is the most sophisticated node retrieval mechanism that is specified by the DOM core. There are separate XML initiatives, such as XPath and XPointer, that define more sophisticated navigation techniques.

Document, Document Type, and Entity Nodes

The `Document` node represents a document information item in addition to acting as the factory for new nodes. The `DocumentType` node has no direct Infoset equivalent, but it is where the document information item's `[entities]` and `[notations]` properties are accessed. Like the Infoset `[entities]` property, the `DocumentType` interface's `entities` attribute never contains parameter entities. Unlike the Infoset `[entities]` property, the `DocumentType` interface's `entities` attribute does not contain the document entity. However, the `DocumentType` interface does expose the external identifier (and optionally the contents) of the external DTD subset.

The `Document` node has two related nodes that are given special status: One is the distinguished `[children]` node that represents the root element of the document; the other is the node that represents the document type declaration of the document. The root element of the document is exposed via the normal child node accessors as well as via the `Document.documentElement` attribute. The document type declaration node is *not* a child node and is only accessible via the `Document.doctype` attribute.

```
interface Document : Node {
  readonly attribute Element documentElement;
  readonly attribute DocumentType doctype;
     :              :             :
}
```

The `Document` interface also provides two convenience methods for navigating to child `Element` nodes.

```
interface Document : Node {
  Element  getElementById(in DOMString elementID);
```

```
    NodeList getElementsByTagNameNS(in DOMString namespaceURI,
                                    in DOMString localName);

}
```

The `Document.getElementById` method finds the element that is uniquely identified by an `ID` attribute with the value specified as the method parameter. The `Document.getElementsByTagNameNS` method is identical to the same-named method exposed by the `Element` interface. The primary distinction is that because it appears on the parent of all elements in the document, it may return the root element of the document. Calling `Element.getElementsByTagNameNS` will never return the root element of the document, as it only returns descendant nodes.

The `DocumentType` node exposes two `NamedNodeMaps`, one for the document's `[entities]` and one for `[notations]`. These maps contain nodes that implement the `Entity` and `Notation` interfaces, respectively. Both interfaces expose the `[system identifier]` and `[public identifier]` Infoset properties. The `Entity` interface also exposes the `[notation]` property as a string. For both node/interface types, the `[name]` property is accessed via the generic `Node.nodeName` attribute. The actual content of the entity is exposed as child nodes.

The DOM takes an unorthodox approach to handling references to entities in element content. Rather than inject distinct nodes for the entity start and end marker information items, the DOM inserts an intermediate node between the parent element and the replacement content. This node implements the `EntityReference` interface and has child nodes that correspond to the replacement content. `EntityReference` nodes make it somewhat more complicated to process a DOM hierarchy since there may be `EntityReference` nodes sprinkled throughout. Because of this, some DOM implementations provide a mechanism for automatically expanding entity references in the DOM hierarchy to remove all `EntityReference` nodes. While this simplifies the programming model, it defeats possible implementation-specific optimizations that result from otherwise lazy evaluation (see Figure 2.14).

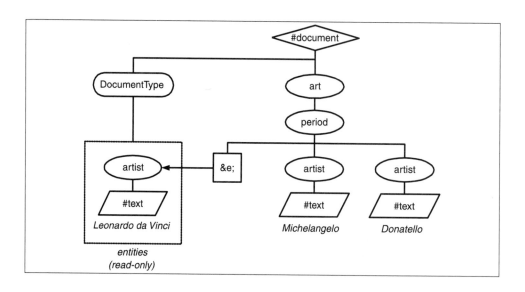

Figure 2.14   Entity references and the DOM

Bulk Insertion Using Document Fragment

The DocumentFragment node is a very lightweight version of the Element object meant for DOM cut and paste operations. A DocumentFragment node is a generic container for other nodes that can be inserted as a group somewhere else in the hierarchy. The DocumentFragment node must implement the DocumentFragment interface, which is a marker interface that extends Node but adds no new methods. The key to the DocumentFragment node type is how other methods treat it when it is passed as a parameter. Consider the following Java code:

```
import org.w3c.dom.*;
void dupEm(Document doc) {
  DocumentFragment frag = doc.createDocumentFragment();
  NodeList authors = doc.getElementsByTagNameNS("urn:bru",
                                                "author");
  frag.appendChild(authors.item(0));
  frag.appendChild(authors.item(2));
  doc.getDocumentElement().appendChild(frag);
}
```

When `frag` is passed to `appendChild`, the implementation knows to "skip" the node being passed as an argument and instead enumerates its child nodes, appending each of them in turn. The following pseudocode shows how this is done:

```
void appendChild(Node node) {
    if (node.getNodeType() != Node.DOCUMENT_FRAGMENT_NODE)
        this.realAppendChild(node);
    else {
        for (Node child = node.getFirstChild(); child != null;
                child = child.getNextSibling()) {
            this.realAppendChild(child);
        }
    }
}
```

Note that due to this special treatment, `DocumentFragment` nodes never appear in a document's parent/children hierarchy.

DOM Error Handling

Error handling throughout the DOM is handled through a combination of return values and exceptions. All exceptions thrown by DOM methods must be compatible with the `DOMException` type, which contains a single member named `code`. The DOM also specifies a list of `ExceptionCode` values and constant names that must be used by all DOM implementations. The DOM specification outlines which `ExceptionCode` values can be thrown for a given method and when they should be used. The following Java code fragment illustrates how to catch a `DOMException` thrown by the `createElementNS` method of the `Document` interface:

```
Document doc = new Document();
try {
    Element el = doc.createElementNS("urn:foo-bar", "foo");
}
catch(DOMException e) {
    System.out.println(e.code);
}
```

Certain DOM implementations may automatically map these `ExceptionCode` values to string descriptions that can be displayed to the user. For example, a given implementation's exception object might allow you to write code that looks like this.

```
Document doc = new Document();
try {
    Element el = doc.createElementNS("urn:foo-bar", "foo");
}
catch(DOMException e) {
    System.out.println(e.getDescription());
    e.printStackTrace(System.out);
}
```

Remember that `getDescription` and `printStackTrace`, in this case, are implementation specific and may not be available across different DOM implementations. The only standard member of `DOMException` is `code`.

Because certain programming languages and component technologies don't support the standard notion of exceptions (as in Java or C++), the DOM specification leaves the overall exception handling requirements somewhat open. In other words, the specification is flexible in terms of what is required of a conforming DOM implementation. Language bindings that cannot properly deal with exceptions can alternatively use native error reporting mechanisms that map to the `ExceptionCode` values. DOM implementations may also raise other proprietary exceptions necessary for the implementation's language binding that are not specifically defined in the DOM specification.

Implementation vs Interface

The discussion so far has focused on DOM Level 2 core functionality. The DOM working group defines a base set of functionality that all implementations must fulfill. The DOM working group has also defined interfaces that model peripheral functionality that implementations can elect to implement or not implement as they see fit. Rather than use the well-known component development techniques[11] for

---

[11]One of the tenets of component software is the importance of typed contracts between components. The DOM Level 2 plays fast and loose with the weight of these contracts. In particular, the DOM working group has no reservation about modifying interface definitions after they are published, weakening the typed contract of the DOM specification. Fortunately, the SAX interfaces do not suffer from this lax management policy.

interface discovery, the DOM working group instead relies on a hard-coded method (`DOMImplementation.hasFeature`) to determine whether a given implementation supports some feature. `DOMImplementation.hasFeature` allows you to query for specific versions of DOM feature support. The following Java code tests if the DOM implementation supports the DOM Level 2 XML Core functionality and drops back to using DOM Level 1 XML Core features otherwise:

```
if (domimp.hasFeature("XML", "2.0")) {
   // supports DOM Level 2 XML Core
}
else if (domimp.hasFeature("XML", "1.0")) {
   // otherwise give up or revert to DOM Level 1 XML Core
}
```

DOM Level 2 adds several chapters to the specification that formalize additional (optional) DOM features such as CSS, Events, Range, Stylesheets, Traversal, and Views. To test whether a DOM implementation supports one of these features, use the appropriate feature string along with a version string of "2.0". See Table 2.5 for a list of all the possible DOM features and available feature versions at publication time.

The DOM is notorious for lacking explicit mechanisms for translating between serialized XML documents and DOM hierarchies. While future versions of the DOM may address this need, each XML parser must now define its own proprietary interface for performing I/O operations. For example, the Apache Software Foundation's Xerces-J parser uses a SAX-based parser to load an XML document into the DOM structure as shown here.

```
try {
   org.apache.xerces.parsers.DOMParser parser =
                 new org.apache.xerces.parsers.DOMParser();
   parser.parse("http://www.develop.com/book.xml");
   org.w3c.dom.Document doc = parser.getDocument();
   // use DOM Document here...
}
catch(SAXException e) {
}
catch(IOException e) {
}
```

Table 2.5 DOM Implementation Features

DOM Feature	Feature Name	Known Versions
XML	`"XML"`	`"1.0"`, `"2.0"`
HTML	`"HTML"`	`"1.0"`, `"2.0"`
CSS	`"CSS"`	`"2.0"`
CSS Extended Interfaces	`"CSS2"`	`"2.0"`
Events	`"Events"`	`"2.0"`
User Interface Events	`"UIEvents"`	`"2.0"`
Mouse Events	`"MouseEvents"`	`"2.0"`
Mutation Events	`"MutationEvents"`	`"2.0"`
HTML Events	`"HTMLEvents"`	`"2.0"`
Range	`"Range"`	`"2.0"`
StyleSheets	`"StyleSheets"`	`"2.0"`
Traversal	`"Traversal"`	`"2.0"`
Views	`"Views"`	`"2.0"`

Xerces-J also provides a few implementation-specific features to tweak the DOM behavior. The `http://apache.org/xml/features/dom/defer-node-expansion` feature makes it possible to defer node expansion until the DOM tree is traversed. The `http://apache.org/xml/features/dom/create-entity-ref-nodes` feature controls whether or not entity reference nodes show up in the DOM tree. Aside from these implementation-specific features and the proprietary serialization mechanism described above, Xerces-J completely adheres to the DOM Level 2 Core API.

Another commonly used XML processor is Microsoft's MSXML 3.0. MSXML 3.0 is a COM-based implementation of the DOM Level 2 feature set. MSXML's COM language binding prefixes all DOM interface names with `IXMLDOM`. For example, the `Node` interface in MSXML is called `IXMLDOMNode`. The ECMAScript bindings are mostly compatible with the DOM Level 2 specification at the time of this writing. In terms of serialization, MSXML adds `load`, `loadXML`, and `save` methods to the `Document` interface. The `loadXML` method expects the serialized XML stream to be passed as a literal string. The `load` and `save` methods expect either a system identifier or an `IStream` interface to the actual data. The following ECMAScript demonstrates the MSXML parser:

```
var doc = new ActiveXObject("msxml.domdocument")
doc.async = false
doc.validateOnParse = false
if (doc.load("http://www.awl.com/book.xml"))
  myHandler(doc, doc.documentElement);
else
    error(doc.parseError.reason);
end if
// load another document
doc.loadXML("<book><authors></authors></book>");
```

This example also illustrates several other MSXML-specific extensions. The `async` property is used to control asynchronous loading of the XML document. If `async` is not explicitly set to `false`, the Document will load asynchronously.[12] The `validateOnParse` property controls document validation against a DTD or XML Data Reduced schema definition. Finally, the `parseError` property makes it easy to figure out what went wrong if loading fails. MSXML provides several other proprietary extensions that are commonly used by programmers today, including `xml`, `text`, `async`, `readyState`, `preserveWhiteSpace`, `nodeTypedValue`, and `nodeTypeString` properties.

DOM Traversal

DOM Level 2 defines an optional DOM feature referred to as DOM Traversal. DOM implementations can be tested for DOM Traversal support through the `DOMImplementation.hasFeature` method. Although DOM traversal can be accomplished through the `Node` and `NodeList` interfaces, the DOM WG decided it was beneficial to define standard traversal interfaces that simplify the process.

---

[12]When using asynchronous behavior, it's usually necessary to also use the `readystate`, `onreadystatechange`, and `ondataavailable` MSXML extensions for asynchronous callbacks.

DOM Traversal defines two types of node traversal mechanisms: `Node Iterator`s and `TreeWalker`s. `NodeIterator` traverses a *list* of nodes (much like the `NodeList` interface), whereas `TreeWalker` traverses a *tree* of nodes (much like the `Node` interface). The `NodeIterator` interface has two traversal methods, `nextNode` and `previousNode`, for moving back and forth through a list of nodes. The `TreeWalker` interface, on the other hand, contains the same traversal functionality as the `Node` interface (such as `firstChild`, `lastChild`, `nextSibling`, `previousSibling`, `nextNode`, `previous Node`, and so on) for moving throughout a tree hierarchy.

The `DocumentTraversal` interface is used to create `NodeIterator` and `TreeWalker` instances through the corresponding `createXXX` methods. `Document` implementations supporting DOM Traversal will also implement the `DocumentTraversal` interface.

```
package org.w3c.dom.traversal;
interface DocumentTraversal {
  NodeIterator   createNodeIterator(in Node root,
                   in unsigned long whatToShow,
                   in NodeFilter filter,
                   in boolean entityReferenceExpansion);
  TreeWalker     createTreeWalker(in Node root,
                   in unsigned long whatToShow,
                   in NodeFilter filter,
                   in boolean entityReferenceExpansion)
                         raises(DOMException);
};
```

The main benefit that these traversal mechanisms have over using the standard `Node`/`NodeList` interfaces relates to filtering. When creating `NodeIterator`s and `TreeWalker`s, one can specify a bitmask (`whatToShow`) indicating which node types are desired. For example, the following code demonstrates how to create a `NodeIterator` that only traverses `Text` and `Comment` nodes:

```
import org.w3c.dom.traversal.NodeIterator;
import org.w3c.dom.traversal.NodeFilter;
import org.w3c.dom.traversal.DocumentTraversal;
import org.w3c.dom.Document;
```

```
NodeIterator getTextAndComments(Document doc) {
   try {
     DocumentTraversal dt = (DocumentTraversal)doc;
     return dt.createNodeIterator(doc,
         NodeFilter.SHOW_TEXT | NodeFilter.SHOW_COMMENT,
         null, true);
   } catch (ClassCastException ex) {
     return null; // traversal not supported
   }
}
```

Applications can also write custom filters that extend the NodeFilter interface. The NodeFilter interface contains one method, acceptNode, which will be called during the traversal process to let the application decide whether to include/exclude a given node from the traversal. The following class, MyFilter, only includes nodes with a name of "author".

```
class MyFilter implements NodeFilter {
   public short acceptNode(Node p1) {
   if (p1.getNodeName() == "author")          X    .equals("author")
      return NodeFilter.FILTER_ACCEPT;
   else
      return NodeFilter.FILTER_SKIP;
   }
}
```

An instance of MyFilter can be passed to the createXXX methods of DocumentTraversal to further qualify the node subset as shown here.

```
NodeIterator iter = dt.createNodeIterator(rootNode,
              NodeFilter.SHOW_ALL, new MyFilter(), true);
Node n = iter.nextNode();
while (n != null) {
   // do something here with "author" nodes
   n = iter.nextNode();
}
```

DOM Traversal filters make it possible to create customized and reusable traversal components that simplify the process of walking a DOM tree and locating specific DOM nodes.

Where Are We?

The Infoset is a nice idea, but it is barely useful if software cannot be written against it. Fortunately, there are two widely accepted programmatic interfaces based on the Infoset that allow documents to be manipulated and [de]serialized at the Infoset level, not at the character-stream/markup level. The Simple API for XML (SAX) is a streaming interface that models a document information item as a stream of well-known method invocations. The Document Object Model (DOM) models a document information item as a hierarchical set of nodes that are instances of Infoset-like abstract types. Both styles of interfaces are likely to survive for some time, as they serve completely different purposes.

Chapter 3

Navigation

`http://www.xmlhack.com/read.php?item=190`

Anonymous, 1995

The Infoset describes the abstract model of an XML document based largely on its logical structure. The Infoset's definition implies intrinsic hierarchical relationships (e.g., parent, child, descendant) between the information items of a given document. These intrinsic relationships can assist in formally addressing subsets of a document (e.g., 'give me the all child elements named `bob` whose `id` attribute is not `id-xyz`'). Where the Infoset stops short is in defining a uniform syntax for addressing and identifying these subsets.

In the absence of such syntax, it's impossible for an attribute or element to reference another portion of the same document in a uniform manner (`ID`/`IDREF` has only limited utility in this role). While an application program can traverse a DOM structure to harvest the desired subset of DOM nodes, this is not a generalizable technique that can be captured as an attribute value or as element content. Instead, what is needed is a simple text-based addressing language that captures the traversal of a document in a programming language-neutral fashion.

This does not mean that such an addressing language would be useless to programmers. Adoption of a uniform addressing language can simplify application code tremendously. Instead of writing tedious traversal and extraction routines, developers can encapsulate those details within opaque addressing expressions and let the underlying XML processor do the heavy lifting. This approach has several distinct advantages over a simpler programming model. For one, these addressing expressions can be loaded/read dynamically and do not have to be "baked into" the application, in essence acting as "script" for identifying pieces of an XML document. Second, the reduction in application code that results from hoisting the common traversal code into a shared library can potentially yield performance results due to both reduced working set size as well as opportunistic nonlinear traversal inside the parser/processor.

The W3C-sanctioned language for addressing subsets of an XML document is called the *XML Path Language 1.0 (XPath)*. XPath allows for *intradocument* expressions that identify subsets *within* a single document. The *XML Pointer Language (XPointer)* is the W3C specification for addressing subsets of an external XML document, in essence adding *interdocument* addressing support for XPath. There are a number of XML technologies that rely on one or both of these specifications including XML Inclusions (XInclude), XML Linking Language (XLink), XSL Transforms (XSLT), and XML Schemas.

XPath Basics

XPath got its name from its use of *path-based* syntax for traversing a document's Infoset. XPath syntax is very similar to those used to traverse file systems or other hierarchical structures. The following is an example of an XPath expression that locates all `model` elements that are children of `guitar` elements, which are themselves children of the root node `guitars` in some arbitrary XML document:

```
/guitars/guitar/model
```

XPath defines its own data model in parallel with the Infoset. This data model is based on a tree of nodes. As shown in Table 3.1, XPath defines seven node types that can be part of an XPath tree. The node-based tree-model of XPath has obvious parallels to the `[parent]`/`[children]` model of the Infoset.

The properties of each XPath node can be viewed in terms of corresponding Infoset information item properties. For example, the children of the root node[1]

---

[1]The XPath root node is conceptually the same as the DOCUMENT_NODE (#document) in the DOM.

ESSENTIAL XML: BEYOND MARKUP

Table 3.1 XPath Tree-Model to Infoset Mapping

XPath Node Type	Infoset Information Item
Root Node	Document Information Item
Element Node	Element Information Item
Attribute Node	Attribute Information Item
Text Node	Sequence of Character Information Items
Processing Instruction Node	Processing Instruction Information Item
Comment Node	Comment Information Item
Namespace Node	Namespace Declaration Information Item

map to the document information item's `[children]` property. Consistent with the Infoset, the root node can only have three types of child nodes: element, processing instruction, and comment nodes. As another example, the attributes of an element node map to the element information item's `[attributes]` property and therefore aren't considered children of an element node. For details on XPath's data model and properties, consult Section 5 of the XPath specification.

Understanding the XPath data model and its relationship to the Infoset is the key to understanding XPath expressions. To help clarify what the XPath tree-model looks like, consider the following XML document:

```
<?xml version='1.0'?>
<?play guitar-jingle welcome.wav?>
<guitars xmlns='urn:schemas-develop-com:music'>
   <guitar type='Electric'>
      <model>Strat</model>
      <model>Tele</model>
      <model>Les Paul</model>
   </guitar>
</guitars>
<!-- end of guitars -->
```

As shown in Figure 3.1, the XPath tree-model for this document contains all seven node types defined by XPath. Notice that the root node has three children:

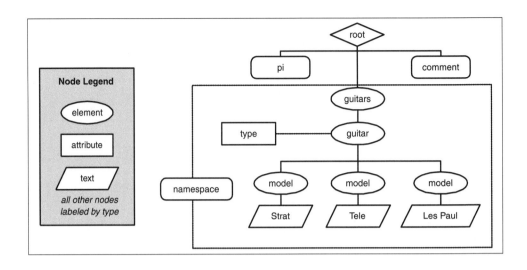

Figure 3.1   XPath information model

a processing instruction node, an element node, and a comment node. The `guitars` node contains a namespace node, which is in-scope for all descendant nodes. The `guitar` node has an attribute node (`type`) along with three `model` child nodes, each of which has a child text node.

While XPath does not rely on a particular processor or API, there are several XML processors available at the time of this writing that support XPath. Some of these processors allow developers to perform XPath queries through implementation-specific mechanisms. For example, developers using Microsoft's MSXML Version 2.6 or greater can use the `selectNodes` and `selectSingleNode` methods (available on the `IXMLDOMNode` interface) to perform XPath queries against the document currently loaded in memory. The following Javascript code demonstrates how to use the `selectNodes` method:

```
var dom = new ActiveXObject("MSXML.DOMDocument");
dom.setProperty("SelectionLanguage", "XPath");
if (dom.load("guitars.xml")) {
    var sel = dom.selectNodes("/guitars/guitar/model");
    for (i=0; i<sel.length; i++)
        UseThisNode(sel.item(i));
}
```

ESSENTIAL XML: BEYOND MARKUP

This example finds all of the `model` elements that are children of the `guitar` element that are themselves children of the `guitars` element under the root node. In this case, it's not terribly difficult to accomplish the same task manually using either the SAX or DOM APIs, but as the XPath expressions become more complex, the benefits of pushing the traversal code into the XML processor become greater. There are several other XML processors besides MSXML that provide similar functionality to the example shown here.

Besides basic API processing, XPath is also used by the XSLT 1.0 specification to assist in XML document transformations. XSLT uses XPath to identify subsets of a source document that will be translated into portions of the output document as shown here.

```
<xsl:template match='guitar/model'>
    <modelo> <xsl:value-of select='text()'/></modelo>
</xsl:template>
```

This example translates the name of selected `model` elements into their Spanish counterparts in the resulting document. As discussed in detail in Chapter 5, XPath is used in XSLT `select` attributes to identify subsets of a document. A subset of the XPath is also used in XSLT `match` attributes when defining template rules.

XPath Expressions

The most fundamental concept of XPath is the expression. An XPath expression evaluates to a value that must be of type `string`, `boolean`, `number`, and `node-set` (an ordered collection of nodes). XPath defines rules for coercing from any of the four types to a `string`, `boolean`, or `number`. Under certain scenarios, the coercion happens silently, based on how or where the expression is evaluated. Under other scenarios, the coercion must be made explicit by using a coercion function. Coercion between `string`, `boolean`, and `number` is fairly intuitive. Coercion from `node-set` to the other three types is not.

When a `node-set` is coerced to a `boolean`, the result is true if the `node-set` is nonempty, false if the node-set is empty. When a `node-set` is coerced to a `number`, the `node-set` is first converted to a `string` and then converted to a `number` according to standard IEEE-style string-to-number conversion. Converting a `node-set` to a string is the interesting part of this conversion. The XPath specification defines how to evaluate the `string-value` for each node type. For example, the `string-value` of the root and all element nodes is the concatenation of all descendant text nodes in document order. The `string-value` of an attribute node is the attribute's normalized value. The `string-value` of a text node is the node's character data. Table 3.2 describes how the `string-value` is evaluated for each node type.

The most important type of XPath expression is called a *location path*. Just like file system paths, location path expressions can be either *absolute* or *relative*. Absolute location paths begin with a forward slash (`/`) and specify that navigation should begin at the root node in the tree-model.

```
/guitars/guitar/model
```

A relative location path expression does not begin with a forward slash and specifies that navigation should begin at the node where the location path is applied. The following expression is an example of a relative location path:

```
guitar/model
```

If this location path were applied to the root `guitars` element, it would produce the same result as the previous absolute expression. The following code illustrates

Table 3.2 XPath Node String-Values

Node Type	String-Value
Root Node	Concatenation of all descendant text nodes
Element Node	Concatenation of all descendant text nodes
Attribute Node	Normalized attribute value
Text Node	Character data
Processing Instruction Node	Character data following the PI target
Comment Node	Character data within comment delimiters
Namespace Node	Namespace URI

how to apply the relative location path shown above directly to the `guitars` element using the MSXML `selectNodes` method:

```
var dom = new ActiveXObject("MSXML.DOMDocument");
dom.setProperty("SelectionLanguage", "XPath");
if (dom.load("guitars.xml")) {
    var gts = dom.documentElement; // get guitars element
    // apply relative location path to guitars element
    var sel = gts.selectNodes("guitar/model");
    for (i=0; i<sel.length; i++)
        UseThisNode(sel.item(i));
}
```

Location paths can be written in two forms: *verbose* or *abbreviated*. Verbose expressions are considered the primary view of the XPath language syntax, but many developers use abbreviated expressions because they save space and are easier to write. The examples shown so far in this chapter have all used the abbreviated syntax by leaving out the axis identifier. That stated, the remainder of this chapter will focus on the verbose form, as certain features are not accessible using the abbreviated form.

A location path can be broken down into one or more *location steps* separated by forward slashes. The location steps in an XPath expression are interpreted from left to right. Each location step identifies nodes in the tree-model relative to the preceding location step. Each location step consists of three parts: an *axis identifier,* a *node test,* and zero or more *predicates*. The general form of a location step is as follows:

```
axis-identifier::node-test[predicate1][predicate2]
```

Note that the axis identifier is separated from the node test with two colons (`::`) and that each predicate expression is enclosed within square brackets (`[ ]`). Figure 3.2 shows the decomposition of an XPath expression and its constituent location steps.

An XPath expression is evaluated relative to a context node and produces a resultant `node-set`. Each location step in the XPath expression produces a

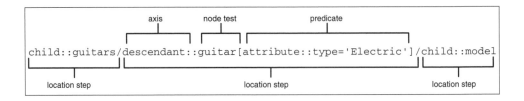

Figure 3.2   Location path and location step parts

node-set that in turn acts as the context node-set for the location step to the right. The context node-set for the first location step is either the root node (for absolute expressions) or the node where the expression was applied (for relative expressions). The node-set that is produced by the last location step is the final result of the overall XPath expression.

Listing 1 shows the Java pseudocode for evaluating an XPath expression. The evaluateXPathExpression function takes a location path expression as a String argument (exp) along with the current node (current) in the tree-model to support relative expressions. Notice that the function first checks the initial character of the expression to determine whether the location path is absolute or relative in order to set up the initial context node-set properly. The function then breaks the location path into its constituent location steps and begins processing them one at a time by calling applyStep with the current context node-set. The applyStep function returns a result node-set, which then becomes the current context node-set for the next location step (the next iteration of the top-level for loop). The node-set returned by the last location step becomes the result node-set for the expression.

Listing 1:   XPath Expression Evaluation Pseudocode

```
NodeSet evaluateXPathExpression(String exp, Node current) {
   NodeSet contextSet = new NodeSet();
   if (exp.charAt(0) == '/') // absolute
      contextSet.Add(current.getOwnerDocument());
   else                       // relative
      contextSet.Add(current);
   // break location path expression into location steps
   LocationStep[] steps = tokenizePathIntoSteps(exp);
```

ESSENTIAL XML: BEYOND MARKUP

```
      // apply each location step to the context node-set and
      // reset the context node-set with the resulting node-set
      for (int i = 0; i < steps.length; i++) {
         contextSet = applyStep(steps[i], contextSet);
      }
      return contextSet;
   }

   NodeSet applyStep(LocationStep step, NodeSet input) {
      NodeSet output = new NodeSet();
      for (int i = 0; i < input.length; i++) {
         NodeSet temp = selectAxisNodes(input.item(i),
                                        step.axis);
         temp = filterByNodeTest(temp, step.nodeTest);
         for (int j=0; j <step.predicates.length; j++)
            temp = filterByPredicate(temp,step.predicates[j]);
         output.AddNodes(temp);
      }
      return output;
   }
```

The applyStep function takes a location step (step) and the context node-set (input). The location step is applied to each node in input in left-to-right order. When the location step is applied against a given node, it first identifies an initial node-set (temp) based on the axis identifier. This node-set is then filtered first by the node test and then by each of the predicates, one at a time. The nodes left in temp after filtering are added to the result node-set for the entire location step. This process is then repeated for each node in input. After the location step has been applied to each node in input, the resulting node-set (output) is returned for the location step. This node-set returned by applyStep becomes the context node-set for the next location step in the expression.

For example, consider the following XPath expression that consists of four location steps:

```
/child::guitars/child::guitar/child::model/child::*
```

Figure 3.3 illustrates the nodes that are identified when this expression is evaluated.

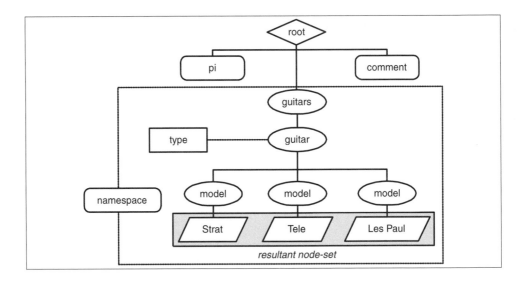

Figure 3.3   Simple XPath expression

Two or more location path expressions can also be combined together through the | operator to union their resulting node-sets. For example, the following XPath expression identifies all of the foo, bar, and baz child elements of the context node:

```
child::foo | child::bar | child::baz
```

The location path evaluation process is the most fundamental concept of the XPath language. Most of the remainder of this chapter will focus on various aspects of location path evaluation.

Axis

The first part of a location step is referred to as the axis identifier. XPath defines several node relationships relative to the context node(s). The set of nodes referred to by such a relationship is referred to as a node *axis*. Axes are used in location steps to specify the initial node-set that the rest of the location step (the node test and predicates) filters through. Table 3.3 lists all of the axes defined by XPath and descriptions of the nodes they identify. Each of the axes identifies a set of nodes relative to the context node. For example, consider the following XML document:

```
<?xml version='1.0'?>
<A>
  <B>
    <C/>
    <D>
      <E>
        <F/>
      </E>
      <G/>
    </D>
    <H/>
    <I>
      <J/>
      <K/>
    </I>
  </B>
  <L>
    <M/>
  </L>
</A>
```

Table 3.3   XPath Axes

Axis Name	Direction	Principle Node Type	Description
self	N/A	Element	Identifies the context node
child	Forward	Element	Identifies the children of the context node
parent	Forward	Element	Identifies the parent of the context node if there is one
descendant	Forward	Element	Identifies the descendants of the context node. A descendant is a child or a child of a child and so on; thus, the descendant axis never contains attribute or namespace nodes
descendant-or-self	Forward	Element	Identifies the context node and the descendant axis

(continued)

Table 3.3 (*continued*)

Axis Name	Direction	Principle Node Type	Description
ancestor	Reverse	Element	Identifies the ancestors of the context node. The ancestors of the context node consist of the parent of the context node and the parent's parent and so on; thus, the ancestor axis will always include the root node, unless the context node is the root node.
ancestor-or-self	Reverse	Element	Identifies the context node and the ancestor axis
following	Forward	Element	Identifies all nodes in the same document as the context node that are after the context node in document order, excluding any descendants and excluding attribute nodes and namespace nodes
following-sibling	Forward	Element	Identifies all the following siblings of the context node. If the context node is an attribute node or namespace node, the following-sibling axis is empty.
preceding	Reverse	Element	Identifies all nodes in the same document as the context node that are before the context node in document order, excluding any ancestors and excluding attribute nodes and namespace nodes
preceding-sibling	Reverse	Element	Identifies all the preceding siblings of the context node. If the context node is an attribute node or namespace node, the preceding-sibling axis is empty.
attribute	N/A	Attribute	Identifies the attributes of the context node. The axis will be empty unless the context node is an element.
namespace	N/A	Namespace	Identifies the namespace nodes of the context node. The axis will be empty unless the context node is an element.

Assuming that D is the context node, it's simple to determine the set of nodes identified by each of the XPath axes as shown in Figure 3.4.

The self axis identifies the context node, in this case D. The parent axis identifies the context node's parent node, in this case B. The child axis identifies

ESSENTIAL XML: BEYOND MARKUP

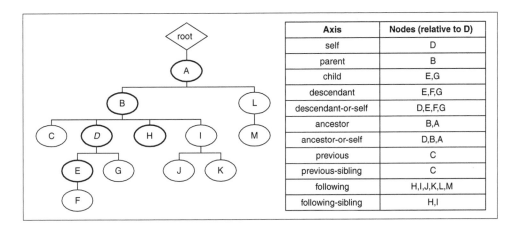

Figure 3.4　Axes

the context node's immediate children, E and G. The `descendant` axis identifies all descendant nodes of the context node, in this case E, F, and G. The `descendant-or-self` axis works the same way, but it also includes the context node. The `ancestor` axis identifies all ancestor nodes of the context node, in this case A and B. The `ancestor-or-self` axis works the same way, but it also includes the context node.

The `preceding` axis identifies all nodes that come before the context node in document order excluding ancestor nodes, in this case C. The `preceding-sibling` axis works the same way, but it is restricted to sibling nodes. The `following` axis identifies all nodes that come after the context node in document order excluding descendants, in this case H, I, J, K, L, and M. The `following-sibling` axis works the same way, but it is restricted to sibling nodes. As Figure 3.5 shows, the `self`, `ancestor`, `descendant`, `following`, and `preceding` axes completely partition the document with no overlap.

As Table 3.3 illustrates, every axis has a principle node type. For the 11 axes discussed so far, the principle node type is element node. These axes may contain nodes of other types, but the principle node type is element. The principle node type of the `attribute` axis is attribute node, and the principle node type of the `namespace` axis is namespace node. The principle node type of an axis is important, as node tests that are performed by name will only result in nodes of the principle node type. For example, the XPath expression

```
/child::bob
```

will only return nodes of type element, since element is the principle node type of the `child` axis. Any processing instruction or text nodes are ignored for this axis.

As shown in Table 3.3, every axis has a specified direction and is either a *forward axis* or a *reverse axis*. A forward axis always identifies the context node or nodes that come after it in document order. A reverse axis always identifies the context node or nodes that come before it in document order. Although the `self` axis seems to be caught in the middle, it will never contain more than one node, so it doesn't really matter how it's classified. According to these definitions, `ancestor[-or-self]` and `preceding[-sibling]` are considered reverse axes, and all others are considered forward axes. The direction of the axis is important when building more sophisticated predicate expressions. In particular, the often-used `position` function takes into account the direction of the current axis.

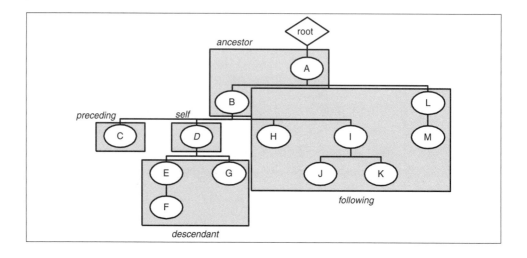

Figure 3.5   Axis partitions

Node Tests

The purpose of the location step's node test is to further refine the initial `node-set` identified by the axis identifier. A node test can filter nodes from the axis `node-set` *by name* or *by type*. The most common node tests select nodes by name. For example, the following location step has a node test of `model`:

```
descendant::model
```

This location step identifies all nodes that are descendants of the context node and *from those nodes* identifies nodes with a name equal to `model`. When identifying nodes by name, the node in question must not only match the supplied name but also the axis's principle node type. If there were text, processing instruction, comment, attribute, or namespace nodes with a name of model, they would not be selected by this location step because they don't match the principle node type of the `descendant` axis, which is element node.

The wildcard character (`*`) may be used to select all nodes from the axis that are of the axis's principle node type. For example, consider the following location step:

```
child::*
```

This example identifies all child element nodes of the context node. Now consider this location step:

```
attribute::*
```

Since the principle node type of the `attribute` axis is attribute, this example identifies all attribute nodes of the context node.

Now look at the following location path that consists of two location steps, one whose axis is `descendant` followed by a location step whose axis is `attribute`:

```
/descendant::guitar/attribute::type
```

This expression identifies the set of nodes shown in Figure 3.6. Note that because the last location step had an `attribute` axis and a node test by name, the resultant node set consisted solely of attribute nodes.

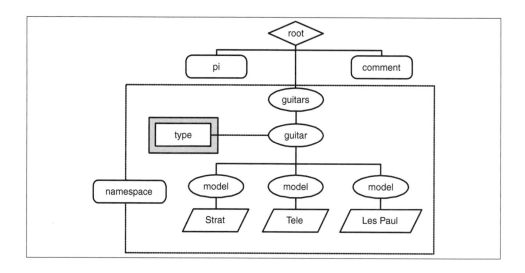

Figure 3.6   Node test by name

Element and attribute node tests use `QNames` rather differently. Non-prefixed names are never affiliated with a namespace. Prefixed names are resolved using the namespace declarations that are part of the XPath evaluation context. Consider the following expression.

```
child::g:model
```

This example identifies all `model` child elements that belong to the namespace identified by `g`. You can also use the wildcard character in combination with namespace prefix matches.

```
child::g:*
```

This example identifies all child element nodes that have belong to the namespace identified by `g`.[2] Consider the following XML document that uses a namespace declaration:

---

[2]The "Predicates" section of this chapter covers how to identify nodes by the actual namespace identifier (namespace URI).

```
<?mypi?><guitars xmlns='http://guitars.com'>
  <g:guitar xmlns:g='urn:edison.org' type='electric'>
    <g:model>Strat</g:model><g:model>Tele</g:model>
    <g:model>Les Paul</g:model>
  <g:guitar>
</guitars><!-- uhhhhh -->
```

When this location path is evaluated

```
/descendant::g:*
```

the nodes shown in Figure 3.7 are identified.[3] Note that this node test is true for all elements whose namespace URI is the same as the URI identified by the specified prefix.

Node tests can filter by type as well as by name. Since attribute and namespace axes each have their own dedicated node types, further filtering by node type isn't necessary for these two axes. However, all other axes (e.g., child,

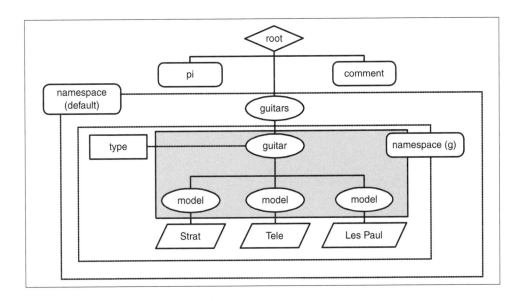

Figure 3.7   Node test by namespace prefix

---

[3]Note that at the time of this writing, several popular XPath implementations had conformance issues surrounding namespace handling.

descendant, etc.) can return a variety of node types, so filtering by node type adds some flexibility. XPath provides the node test expressions listed in Table 3.4 for filtering by node type.

For example, the following location path identifies all child text nodes of the context node:

```
child::text()
```

The following location path identifies all comment nodes anywhere in the document:

```
/descendant-or-self::comment()
```

Processing instruction nodes can be filtered two ways. The generic approach identifies all processing instruction nodes in the specified axis.

```
child::processing-instruction()
```

The `processing-instruction()` expression can also take a parameter to identify only the processing instructions with the specified target. For example, the following location path finds all processing instructions in the document with a target name of `hack` (e.g., `<?hack on this?>`):

```
/descendant-or-self::processing-instruction('hack')
```

Table 3.4   Node Tests by Type

Node Test by Type	Description
`text()`	Identifies all text nodes
`comment()`	Identifies all comment nodes
`processing-instruction(target?)`	Identifies all processing instruction nodes that match the (optionally) specified target string
`node()`	Identifies all nodes regardless of type

The `node()` node test expression identifies all nodes regardless of type. The following example location path identifies all nodes in the document hierarchy regardless of type:

```
/descendant-or-self::node()
```

This expression identifies all element, text, comment, and processing instruction nodes from the root down. It doesn't identify attribute or namespace nodes, however, because they are not contained by the `descendant-or-self` axis.

Predicates

Predicates make it possible to further filter the `node-set` identified by the axis identifier and node test.[4] A predicate is a `boolean` expression that is tested on every node in the context `node-set`. If the predicate evaluates to true for a given node, the node remains in the context `node-set`. If the predicate evaluates to false, the node is discarded. For example, consider the following location path:

```
/descendant::guitar[child::model/child::text() = 'Strat']
```

The axis and node test identifies all `guitar` element nodes that are descendants of the root node. The predicate expression `[child::model/child::text() = 'Strat']` is evaluated against each node in the context `node-set`. If a given `guitar` node has a child `model` node that has a child text node equal to `'Strat'`, it remains in the `node-set`, otherwise it's removed.

Whenever nodes are compared to `string` literals in a predicate expression, the `string-value` of the node is automatically evaluated for the comparison (see Table 3.2). Because of this, the previous example can be rewritten as follows to produce the same results:

```
/descendant::guitar[child::model = 'Strat']
```

---

[4]The axis identifier and node test can also be viewed as predicate expressions. An axis identifier is a static predicate that evaluates to true for nodes that belong to the specified axis. The node test is a dynamic predicate that evaluates to true when a given node matches the specified name or type. In fact, the location step `child::model` is equivalent to `child::*[name() = 'model']`.

Recall that the `string-value` of an element node is the concatenation of all descendant text nodes. Since in this case you can assume there is only a single text node under `model`, when `child::model` is evaluated as part of the `string` comparison, it produces the same `string` that is returned from `child::model/child::text()`.

As a more complete example, the following location path expression identifies the two `model` nodes that have child text nodes consisting of `'Strat'` in Figure 3.8:

```
/child::guitars/child::guitar/child::model[child::text() =
'Strat']
```

Location steps can have zero or more predicates. When no predicate exists, the axis identifier and node test identify the result `node-set`. When there are multiple predicates, they are evaluated in order left to right. After the first predicate is applied, a new `node-set` is produced. The next predicate is then evaluated against the `node-set` produced by the previous predicate and so on. This is repeated for each predicate that exists in the location step.

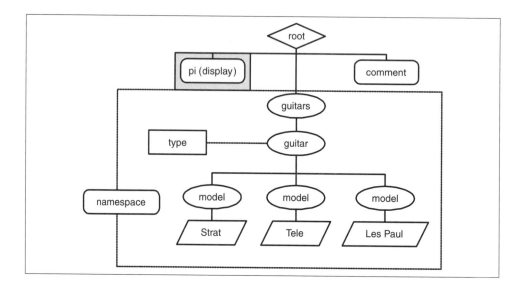

Figure 3.8   Predicate filtering

For example, the following location path identifies all child element nodes of the root node that have a child text node equal to 'Strat' *and* that have an ID attribute whose value is greater than 100:

```
/child::*[child::text() = 'Strat'][attribute::ID > 100]⁵
```

Furthermore, since predicates are part of the location step, a given location path can have several predicates throughout the different steps of the expression, as shown here.

```
/child::*[attribute::type = 'Electric']/child::*
[attribute::ID > 100]
```

These examples illustrate that XPath predicates support standard comparison operators like equals (=) and greater than (>). In fact, all standard comparison operators are supported, including the following:

```
=   !=   <   <=   >   >=
```

For example, by changing the last example slightly, the following expression now identifies all child element nodes that don't have a child text node equal to 'Strat' and that have an ID attribute less than or equal to 100:[6]

```
/child::*[child::text() != 'Strat'][attribute::ID <= 100]
```

Note that four of the comparison operators use the < and > characters, which must be escaped using entity references or CDATA sections when used in actual XML documents.

A single predicate may also contain multiple boolean expressions combined with the standard boolean and/or operators. For example, the last example that used two predicates could be combined into one as follows:

```
/child::*[child::text() != 'Strat' and attribute::ID <= 100]
```

---

[5]Note that the entity reference.> must be used if this expression appears in the content of an XML document.

[6]The string-value of attribute::ID is converted to a number before the comparison occurs.

Using the `boolean and` operator produces the same result as two separate predicates. Using the `boolean or` operator, however, produces a different result. In this case, the location path identifies all child element nodes of the root that either don't have a child text node equal to `'Strat'` *or* that have an `ID` attribute less than 100.

```
/child::*[child::text() != 'Strat' or attribute::ID <= 100]
```

In this case, there is no way to produce the same result using multiple predicate expressions.

Besides comparison and `boolean` expressions, predicates support a standard set of mathematical operators for dealing with numeric values. The mathematical expressions that are supported are addition (+), subtraction (-), multiplication (*), division (`div`), and modulo division (`mod`). When these mathematical operators are used on nodes, the `string-value` of the node is converted to a `number` prior to evaluation. For example, consider the following relatively simple XML document

```
<Invoices>
   <Invoice id='inv1'>
      <Item1>10</Item1Item2>15</Item2>
   </Invoice>
   <Invoice id='inv2'>
      <Item1>5</Item1Item2>7</Item2>
   </Invoice>
</Invoices>
```

and the corresponding XPath expression

```
/descendant::Invoice[(child::Item1 + child::Item2) > 20]
```

This expression only identifies the first `Invoice` element node (`inv1`) because the sum of its child `Item1` and `Item2` element content is greater than `20`. Notice the use of parentheses to control operator precedence.

Most of the predicate examples shown so far have contained additional location paths within the predicate expression. For instance, in the previous example, both `child::Item1` and `child::Item2` are also location path expressions. Because these location paths are relative, they are evaluated against the current context node. In this case, `child::Item1` and `child::Item2` will be evaluated against the `Invoice` element node returned by the node test of the location step. The location path expressions contained within predicates can be arbitrarily complex. Additionally, location path expressions contained within predicates can be relative (to the result of the node test or preceding predicate) or absolute. See Appendix C for additional examples of XPath expressions and predicates.

XPath Functions

The examples in the previous section illustrated the basics of building predicate expressions as part of a location step. In order to build more advanced XPath expressions, one must take advantage of the XPath function library. XPath defines several types of functions that may be used within location paths (mostly within predicates) that are required to build more advanced expressions. These functions are divided into the following four groups:

- Node-set
- String
- Boolean
- Numeric/Mathematic

Of these four groups, the `node-set` functions are the most commonly used. Each of the functions in the `node-set` group interacts in some way with a `node-set`. Table 3.5 contains a list of available `node-set` functions and their brief descriptions. When used in predicate expressions, most of the `node-set` functions interact with the context `node-set` selected by the axis identifier and node test, but some of them can take an explicit `node-set` parameter.

The behavior of the `position` function depends entirely on the *direction* of the axis used in the expression (refer to Table 3.3 for direction details). The `position` function returns the position of the current context node within the context `node-set` relative to the axis direction. All positions are 1-based. For

Table 3.5   Node-set Functions

Function	Description
number position()	Returns the position within the current node-set
number last()	Returns the size of the current node-set
number count(node-set)	Returns the number of nodes in the argument node-set
node-set id(object)	Identifies nodes based on their unique ID (requires XML Schema or DTD)
string local-name(*node-set?*)	Returns the local part of the node's QName
string namespace-uri(*node-set?*)	Returns the namespace URI associated with the node
string name(*node-set?*)	Returns the node's Qname

example, the following location path identifies all model element nodes that are the first child of their parent guitar element in document order:

```
/descendant-or-self::guitar/child::model[position() = 1]
```

On the other hand, this location path identifies the first ancestor node of the context node in reverse document order, which in this case happens to be the same as the context node's parent:

```
ancestor::*[position() = 1]
```

The last function can be used in conjunction with the position function to identify the last node in the node-set. The following location path returns the last model child node of the context node:

```
child::model[position() = last()]
```

The count function is useful for selecting nodes by node-set size. The count function is different from position and last in that it takes a node-set as a parameter. The node-set can also be specified using another location path expression. For instance, the following location path identifies all `guitar` child element nodes that have exactly three `model` element child nodes:

```
child::guitar[count(child::model) = 3]
```

Developers can also use the `id` function to identify nodes by unique ID, provided the source document explicitly declares attributes of type `ID` using either an XML Schema or DTD. For example, the following expression identifies all of the `model` child element nodes of the `guitar` element node that has a unique ID attribute of `'g1'`:

```
id('g1')/child::model
```

Although DOM Level 2 introduced the `getElementById` method to provide similar functionality, the `id` function is more flexible because it also takes a space-delimited list of `ID` strings. The expression

```
id('g1 g2 g3')
```

identifies the nodes with a unique ID of g1, g2, and g3, respectively. The `id` function may also take a `node-set` parameter instead of a `string`. For instance, the following location path identifies the `model` element nodes referenced by the `models` attribute (which is of type `IDREFS`) of the specified context node:

```
id(child::guitar[position()=1]/attribute::models)
```

In the case where a `node-set` is passed to the `id` function, the result is the union of applying the `id` function to each node in the `node-set`. For another example, consider the following XML document:

```
<?xml version='1.0' ?>
<!DOCTYPE guitars [
  <!ELEMENT guitars (guitar+, guitarrefs)>
  <!ELEMENT guitar EMPTY>
  <!ATTLIST guitar id ID #REQUIRED>
  <!ELEMENT guitarrefs (guitarref+)>
  <!ELEMENT guitarref (#PCDATA)>
]>
```

```
<guitars>
   <guitar id='100'/> <!-- id is of type ID -->
   <guitar id='101'/>
   <guitar id='102'/>
   <guitarrefs>
      <guitarref>100</guitarref>
      <guitarref>101</guitarref>
   </guitarrefs>
</guitars>
```

The following expression identifies the set of `guitarref` element nodes and passes that `node-set` to the `id` function:

```
id(/descendant-or-self::guitarref/child::text())
```

This expression identifies all the nodes that are referenced by any `guitarref` node anywhere in the document. In this case, the expression identifies the following `guitar` element nodes from the above document fragment:

```
<guitar id='100'/>
<guitar id='101'/>
```

Expressions that use the `id` function with parameterized `node-set`s makes it straightforward to leverage intradocument ID relationships even in the absence of IDREF-based attributes.

The last three `node-set` functions shown in Table 3.5 return node name information. The `local-name` function returns the local name of the specified node's QName. The `namespace-uri` function returns the namespace URI associated with the specified node. And finally, the `name` function returns the full QName of the specified node. All three of these functions take an optional `node-set` parameter. If a `node-set` is supplied to the function, the function operates on the node within the set that is first in document order. If the parameter is omitted, the function operates on the current context node. For example, consider the following XML document:

```
<f:foo xmlns:f='urn:foobarbaz'>
   <f:bar/>
```

```
    <f:baz/>
  </f:foo>
```

Omitting the `node-set` parameter tests the context node for a given name. For instance, the following location path identifies all element nodes within the document that have a local name of `'bar'`:

```
/descendant-or-self::*[local-name() = 'bar']
```

The `namespace-uri` function is useful for finding all nodes that belong to a given namespace identifier. The following example identifies all element nodes within the document that have a namespace URI of `'urn:foobarbaz'`:

```
/descendant-or-self::*[namespace-uri() = 'urn:foobarbaz']
```

Finally, the `name` function is useful for comparing QNames as illustrated by this example:[7]

```
/descendant-or-self::*[name() = 'f:foo']
```

All of these examples omitted the `node-set` parameter, which makes the functions operate on the current context node. In certain situations, however, it's useful to pass a `node-set` to one of the name functions. When a `node-set` is supplied the function operates on the first node within the set. For instance, the following expression

```
/descendant-or-self::*[local-name(child::*) = 'bar']
```

identifies all element nodes in the document that have a first child element named `bar`. As shown here, the `node-set` functions make it possible to build more powerful expressions that leverage information contained in the underlying `node-set`.

XPath also offers a group of functions for manipulating `strings` within location path expressions, as shown in Table 3.6. The `string` functions add

---

[7]This is equivalent to the following expression: `/descendant-or-self::f:foo`.

Table 3.6 String Functions

Function	Description
string string *(object?)*	Converts an object to a `string`
string concat *(string, string, string*)*	Returns the concatenation of the arguments
boolean starts-with *(string, string)*	Returns true if the first `string` starts with the second
boolean contains *(string, string)*	Returns true if the first `string` contains the second
string substring-before *(string, string)*	Returns the `substring` from the first argument that precedes the first occurrence of the second argument
string substring-after *(string, string)*	Returns the `substring` from the first argument that follows the first occurrence of the second argument
string substring *(string, number, number?)*	Returns the `substring` of the first argument starting at the position specified in the second argument with length specified in the third argument
number string-length *(string?)*	Returns the number of characters in the `string`
string normalize-space *(string?)*	Returns the argument `string` with whitespace normalized
string translate *(string, string, string)*	Returns the first argument `string` with occurrences of characters in the second argument `string` replaced by the character at the corresponding position in the third argument `string`

flexibility to predicate expressions by making it possible to further filter nodes based on string or substring values that can be generated on the fly using the contents of the document.

The most fundamental of the `string` functions is the `string` function, which converts an object to a `string`. In many situations this function is used implicitly during XPath expression evaluation. Although all of the `string` functions are useful in certain situations, the most commonly used functions are `concat`, `starts-with`, `contains`, and `string-length`.

The `concat` function returns the concatenation of all the arguments. This function is useful when searching for a sequence of text node values. For example, consider the following document fragment:

```
<foos>
    <foo id='foo1'>
        <bar>hello </bar>
        <baz>world</baz>
    </foo>
    <foo id='foo2'>
        <bar>goodbye </bar>
        <baz>world</baz>
    </foo>
</foos>
```

The following location path expression identifies all descendant `foo` element nodes whose first and second descendant text nodes concatenated together equal `'hello world'` (assuming no whitespace text nodes):

```
/descendant::foo[concat(descendant::text()[position()=1],
descendant::text()[position()=2]) = 'hello world']
```

In this case, the expression returns the first `foo` element. More interestingly, the `concat` function can be used to test the combined values of distinct node-sets throughout the document (as opposed to comparing against a literal string like `'hello world'`).

The `starts-with` and `contains` functions are useful for matching against certain substrings within the expression. For example, to find all `foo` element nodes that have a first `bar` child element starting with `'hell'`, one could use the following expression:

```
/descendant-or-self::foo[starts-with(child::bar, 'hell')]
```

This expression again identifies `foo1`.

On the same note, the following expression identifies all `foo` elements that have child `baz` elements containing the text `'orl'`:

```
/descendant-or-self::foo[contains(child::baz, 'orl')]
```

This expression identifies both `foo` elements.

The `string-length` function is useful for filtering nodes by string length. For instance, this expression finds all element nodes within the document that have child text nodes containing `string`s with exactly 5 characters:

```
/descendant-or-self::node()[string-length(child::text()) = 5]
```

This expression identifies both `baz` elements containing the text `'world'`.

XPath also provides a set of `boolean` functions for performing common `boolean` operations. These functions are listed in Table 3.7. The `boolean` function can be useful for testing `node-set`s, `string`s, or numeric values. For instance, the following expression returns the root element node's child element nodes that have one or more child elements themselves:

```
/child::*/child::*[boolean(child::*)]
```

Table 3.7   Boolean Functions

Function	Description
boolean	Converts the object to a `boolean` (non-empty `node-set`s, `string`s of non-zero length, and non-zero numbers evaluate to true)
not	Returns true if argument is false, returns false otherwise
true	Returns true
false	Returns false
lang	Returns true if the `xml:lang` attribute of the context node matches the argument

This expression identifies both `foo` elements when applied to the `foos` document shown earlier. The `not` function can be used to return the opposite of this expression: all of the child element nodes of the root element that *don't* have any children themselves.

```
/child::*/child::*[not(boolean(child::*))]
```

When this expression is applied to the document shown earlier, the result is a `null node-set` because there are no children of `foos` that don't also have children themselves.

The last `boolean` function worth mentioning is the `lang` function. `lang` is a convenience function for testing the context node for a given `xml:lang` attribute value. The `lang` function returns true if the `xml:lang` attribute of the context node is the same as the argument or a sublanguage of the argument indicated by a hyphen-separated language name. Consider the following document fragment:

```
<guitar id='guitar1' xml:lang='en-us'>
    <model id='model1'/>
</guitar>
```

For this document, either of the following expressions will select the `guitar` element node:

```
/child::guitar[lang('en')]
/child::guitar[lang('en-us')]
```

Furthermore, since `xml:lang` attributes are inherited by child elements, the following expression identifies both the `guitar1` and `model1` element nodes:

```
/descendant::*[lang('en')]
```

The last set of functions provided by XPath is for dealing with numeric values. These functions are listed in Table 3.8. The `number` function converts the

Table 3.8   Numeric Functions

Function	Description
number	Converts the argument to a number[8]
sum	Returns the sum of the numeric values of each node in the argument node-set
floor	Returns the largest number that is not greater than the argument and that is an integer
ceiling	Returns the smallest number that is not less than the argument and that is an integer
round	Returns the number closest to the argument and that is an integer

argument to a numeric value; how this is done depends on the type of object passed in. The sum function takes a node-set argument and calculates the sum of all the converted node values within the set. For example, assuming this document fragment

```
<Invoices>
   <Invoice id='inv1'>
      <Item>10</ItemItem>15</ItemItem>25</Item>
   </Invoice>
   <Invoice id='inv2'>
      <Item>0</ItemItem>5</ItemItem>10</Item>
   </Invoice>
</Invoices>
```

the sum function makes it trivial to find all Invoice element nodes that have an Item total greater than 20. For instance, the following expression does just this and identifies the first Invoice element node:

```
/descendant::Invoice[sum(child::Item) > 20]
```

The last three numeric functions—floor, ceiling, and round—are simple helper functions for dealing with floating point numbers.

---

[8]See section 4.4 of the XPath specification for conversion details.

ESSENTIAL XML: BEYOND MARKUP

As this section has illustrated, the four groups of XPath functions make it possible to build powerful location paths through more sophisticated predicate expressions. The breadth of functionality offered by the XPath function library adds significantly to XPath's flexibility and expressiveness.

XPath Abbreviations

The XPath language defines several abbreviations that can be used as shorthand for the more commonly used parts of the language. The abbreviated form of most location path expressions requires considerably fewer characters and are arguably more readable. Table 3.9 shows the complete list of expression abbreviations.

The most common abbreviation is omitting the `child` axis identifier. Because `child` is the most commonly used axis identifier, location steps that have the `child` axis can safely omit the `child::` prefix with no change in meaning. For instance, the following location path expressions are equivalent:

```
/child::guitars/child::guitar/child::model
/guitars/guitar/model
```

Whenever a location step doesn't contain an axis identifier, the `child` axis is implied.

Table 3.9: XPath Syntax Abbreviations

Verbose	Abbreviated
`child::`	`(omitted)`
`attribute::`	`@`
`self::node()`	`.`
`parent::node()`	`..`
`/descendant-or-self::node()/`	`//`
`[position() = number]`	`[number]`

Since attributes are also commonly used within expressions, `attribute::` can be abbreviated to `@`. The following location path expressions are equivalent:

```
/child::guitar/attribute::type
/guitar/@type
```

Another common task is to search the entire document tree from the root down, looking for nodes that match the specified criteria. The location path that identifies all nodes within the document tree, `/descendant-or-self::node()/`, can be abbreviated to `//`. This would have made several of the examples shown in this chapter much more compact. For example, the following location paths are identical:

```
/descendant-or-self::node()/child::model
//model
```

In many situations, it's necessary to refer to the current context node using the `self::node()` expression. This expression can be abbreviated to `.`, which is intuitive since it's the same syntax for referring to the current directory in most file systems. The following location paths, which find all `model` elements from the context node down, are identical:

```
./descendant-or-self::node()/child::model
.//model
```

Similarly, specifying the context node's parent requires the following somewhat cumbersome expression `parent::node()`. This can also be abbreviated to familiar `..` path notation. For instance, the following location paths are equivalent:

```
parent::node()/child::model
../model
```

It's also quite common to use the `position()` function within predicate expressions. For that reason, when a predicate expression contains only a number, it's considered shorthand for `[position() = number]`. Both of these location paths are the same.

```
/child::guitar/child::model[position() = 2]
/guitar/model[2]
```

Another not so obvious abbreviation has to do with text node values. When comparing an element node's child text node values, one typically uses the `text()` node test like this.

```
child::guitar[child::model/child::text() = 'Strat']
```

As long as the `model` element node only has a single child text node, the `/child::text` portion of the location path can be omitted and still produce the same results.

```
child::guitar[child::model = 'Strat']
```

Although using `text()` is more explicit, it's quite common to see it left out.

Navigation and URIs

The XPath language is useful for intradocument navigation. Despite its expressiveness, XPath stops short of supporting interdocument navigation. Rather, the Internet bias of XML relies heavily on the IETF Uniform Resource Identifier specification (RFC2396) for referencing XML documents from other XML documents. While both URNs and URLs are supported, the practical reality of today's Internet is that everything is referenced using URLs.

A URL can be absolute or relative. When an absolute URL appears in an XML document, there is no ambiguity as to how to dereference it. When a relative URL appears in an XML document, several factors come into play. By default, the URL is assumed to be relative to the entity in which it appears. Each entity information item has a `[base URI]` property that is based on where the entity was originally loaded. This property is replicated on the element and processing instruction information items as well, based on the entities in which they originally appeared.

The `[base URI]` property is used to resolve relative URLs into absolute URLs. For example, if an attribute information item had a value of "../foo.xml," this relative URL would be evaluated relative to the [base URI] property of the [owner element] of the attribute. This allows suites of external entities to safely use relative URLs without concern for where the collection of entities is located. At the time of this writing, the W3C was in the process of finalizing the XML Base (XBase) specification, which allows an element to override the [base URI] property using an explicit attribute named xml:base.

The most obvious application of URI in XML is the entity declaration. However, at the time of this writing, the W3C is working on the XML Inclusion (XInclude) specification. XInclude provides an alternative to external general entities that (1) uses normal XML syntax and (2) works at the Infoset level, not the serialized entity level. XInclude is the moral equivalent of the EntityReference node type from the DOM, as it exists solely as a placeholder for the content that it references. An XInclude-aware processor will silently replace the XInclude reference with the content that it references. This is similar to the way entity references are expanded, the difference being that XInclude does its magic after, not during, parsing.

The XInclude specification defines one element (include) with two attributes (href and parse). The href attribute contains a URI reference to the included content. The parse attribute controls the interpretation of the referenced data. When the attribute is absent or its value is 'xml', the referenced data is interpreted as well-formed XML; when the value is 'text' or 'cdata', the referenced data is interpreted as plain text and any embedded markup characters should be escaped using either entity references or CDATA sections respectively. Consider the following serialized document that uses a general parsed entity:

```
<?xml version='1.0' ?>
<!DOCTYPE foo [
  <!ENTITY bar SYSTEM "bar.xml">
]>
<foo>&bar;</foo>
```

The following XInclude-based document is functionally equivalent:

```
<?xml version='1.0' ?>
<foo xmlns:xinc='http://www.w3.org/1999/XML/xinclude'
><xinc:include href='bar.xml'/></foo>
```

ESSENTIAL XML: BEYOND MARKUP

Note that XInclude can be combined with XBase to control the interpretation of relative URI.

```
<?xml version='1.0' ?>
<foo  xml:base='http://www.develop.com/xml/'
      xmlns:xinc='http://www.w3.org/1999/XML/xinclude'
><xinc:include href='bar.xml'/></foo>
```

In this case the content found at `http://www.develop.com/xml/bar.xml` will be used no matter where the source document entity is located.

URI + XPath == XPointer

The examples so far have used URI for document entities. It is also possible to combine the URI of a document entity with an XPath expression to narrow the scope of the referent. This is the role of the XML Pointer Language (XPointer) language.

XPointer defines how XPath expressions can be used within URI fragment identifiers to identify subsets of particular XML documents. URI fragment identifiers are commonly used in Web documents to address a particular location within a document. For example, the following URI specifies that the User-Agent should navigate to the location within the document identified by the `gohere` ID:

```
http://www.guitars-r-us.com/guitarlist.htm#gohere
```

The URI fragment identifier is the part that comes after the document location and is delimited with a hash # symbol (in this case, `#gohere`). XPointer defines how to use XPath expressions within this type of URI fragment identifier with any Internet resource of type `text/xml` or `application/xml`.[9]

An XPointer expression consists of one or more *fragment parts.* Each fragment part consists of a *scheme* and a scheme-specific *expression,* as shown in Figure 3.9. The scheme identifies the syntax of the subsequent expression. The only

---

[9]A recent Internet Draft (`http://www.ietf.org/internet-drafts/draft-murata-xml-01.txt`) also suggests the use of a naming convention, `*/*-xml`, for specialized media types based on XML.

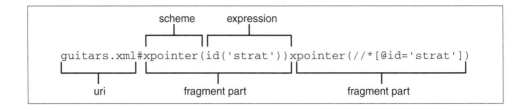

Figure 3.9   XPointer expression, fragment parts

scheme currently defined is `xpointer`, which identifies the use of XPath as the expression addressing language. Nevertheless, the scheme acts as an extensibility point of the language that future XML languages/specifications can leverage.

As with XPath expressions, the fragment parts of an XPointer expression are evaluated left to right in order. The difference, however, is that once a fragment part expression evaluates successfully, the evaluation process terminates. If a fragment part fails, the next fragment part is evaluated and so on. If the processor doesn't recognize the scheme, or if there is something about the expression that causes it to fail, the processor moves on to the next fragment part. For example, consider the following XPointer expression that consists of two fragment parts:

```
guitars.xml#xpointer(id('g1'))xpointer(//*[@type='g1'])
```

The first fragment part uses the XPath `id` function, which relies on the presence of metadata such as an XML Schema or DTD. If metadata is not present, the first fragment will fail and the next fragment part will be evaluated. That fragment doesn't rely on a DTD but instead compares the value of the `type` attribute.

There is an abbreviated XPointer expression form that allows developers to omit the `xpointer` scheme and the `id` function when used together. For instance, the following two XPointer expressions are equivalent:

```
guitars.xml#xpointer(id('g1'))
guitars.xml#g1
```

The context of an XPointer expression is always initialized to the root node of the XML resource identified by the URI. For that reason, the first XPath

ESSENTIAL XML: BEYOND MARKUP

location step with a given fragment part always operates on the resource's root node.

Because XPointer expressions exist within URIs, care must be taken with certain URI-unsafe characters. RFC 2396 outlines exactly what characters are unsafe along with the safe encoding mechanism. All unsafe characters must be replaced with a the %-prefixed hexadecimal value of the Unicode code point. Developers typically accomplish this by running the raw URI string through a standard URI-encoding library before using the resulting URI.

XPointer expressions can also be used within XML documents. Certain XPointer expressions that contain special XML 1.0 characters (e.g. <, >, etc.) can cause problems when used in document content. In these situations, character or entity references should always be used to avoid potential processor problems. For instance, the following XPointer expression uses the safe version of the less-than symbol within the document content:

```
<xinclude:include
    href ='foo.xml#xpointer(//f/g[position() &lt; 3])'/>
```

This example illustrates how XPointer expressions can be used with XInclude (and potentially XBase) to explicitly reference an external subset of a document.

XPointer is primarily about URI-enabling XPath expressions; so far this section hasn't introduced any new language constructs. The main extensions that XPointer does make to the XPath language have to do with *ranges* and *points*.

Ranges and Points

In XPath, every location path expression produces a `node-set`. XPointer, on the other hand, identifies portions of the document that are not considered typical XPath `node-sets`. Consider the task of describing a document portion that begins in the middle of one text node and spans to the middle of another text node in a sibling subtree. This is not possible today with standard XPath expressions. To satisfy this need, XPointer generalizes XPath's notion of node and `node-set` with *location* and *location-set*. In XPointer, every location is either a *point,* a *range,* or a standard XPath node. XPath expressions always produce node locations, whereas XPointer expressions can also produce point and range locations.

A *point location* identifies a standard node along with an *index* into its child data. If the node can have children (element nodes), the index refers to a position within the child nodes collection. If the node cannot have children (e.g., text nodes), the index refers to an offset within the node's character data.

A *range location* consists of two points: a start point and an end point. Everything within these two points (in document order) is part of the range location. XPointer introduces a new *range expression* for producing range location-sets. The following example illustrates how to build a simple range expression:

```
#xpointer(id('g2')/child::model[1] to
         id('g5')/child::model[last()])
```

This expression produces a location-set containing a range that begins with the first child `model` element of the `g2` element and ends with the last child `model` element of the `g5` element. Notice that this example is nothing more than two distinct XPath expressions separated by the XPointer-specific `"to"` keyword.

XPointer adds two new node tests to filter by range and point locations (`range()` and `point()`) along with a new set of supporting functions, including the following: `range`, `range-inside`, `start-point`, `end-point`, `here`, `origin`, `unique`, `string-range`. At the time of this writing, XPointer is a W3C Working Draft in last call. Nevertheless, the major concepts presented in this section will most likely not change drastically between now and when it becomes a W3C Recommendation.

Where Are We?

XPath offers a concrete syntax for identifying subsets of an XML document. An XPath location path expression consists of one or more location steps, each of which contains an axis identifier, a node test, and one or more predicate expressions. These simple XPath constructs make it possible to precisely identify document subsets of interest. While XPath is for intradocument addressing, XPointer makes it possible to perform interdocument addressing by placing XPath expressions within URI fragment identifiers. XPointer also extends the XPath data model by making it possible to address points and ranges within a document's Infoset. Finally, XBase and XInclude provide an XPointer and Infoset-based alternative to general external entities.

Chapter 4

XML Schemas

```
typedef struct tagPOINT {
  long x;
  long y;
}  POINT;
typedef struct tagRECT {
  POINT origin;
  POINT corner;
}  RECT;
```

Anonymous, 1981

XML documents that are exchanged between software agents rarely consist of arbitrary, unconstrained markup. Rather, these documents follow a common form or structure that is shared by many XML documents in a given problem domain. To allow both XML-aware software and humans to know what content is expected in a given scenario, these common structures need to be documented in a machine-readable and human-readable format. This is the primary motivation behind the XML Schema specification.

The XML Schema specification defines an XML vocabulary that can be used to describe XML documents. XML Schema subsumes the functionality of the ELEMENT and ATTLIST declarations from Document Type Definitions (DTDs), which are a holdover from XML's roots in document management systems. Unlike DTDs, an XML Schema-based definition is based primarily on types, not on tag names. This makes XML Schema much more adaptable to existing systems such as programming languages and databases. Unlike DTDs, XML Schema descriptions are namespace-aware and arguably namespace-centric. Also unlike DTDs, XML Schema descriptions are themselves XML documents that can be parsed and generated using the same technology used to parse and generate the XML documents they describe. The primary advantage of DTDs is that at the time of this writing, they are a full W3C recommendation (actually, they are just part of the XML 1.0 recommendation). At the time of this writing, the XML Schema specification was a work in progress and not yet a full W3C recommendation. That caveat in place, it is the authors' collective opinion that DTDs are a dead end and that the XML Schema definition language is the sanest way to describe XML documents even though the specification is still a moving target.[1]

The XML Schema specification introduces the term *schema-valid*. When processing an XML document, a schema-aware processor may enforce schema validity based on the constraints specified in the corresponding schema. Additionally, a schema-aware processor is expected to add schema-specific properties to the information set. In particular, a schema-aware processor adds the corresponding type definition to each element and attribute so that applications can interrogate the type information of each node in the document.

Schema Basics

The XML Schema specification assumes that at least two XML documents are in use: an *instance* document and at least one *schema* document. The instance document contains the actual information we care about. The schema documents describe the structure and type of the instance document. The distinction between instance and schema is similar to the distinction between object and class in object-oriented programming languages. A class describes an object much like a schema describes an instance document.[2]

---

[1] This chapter was written against the April 7, 2000 versions of the XML Schema public working drafts. These versions were in "last call" prior to being promoted to Candidate Recommendation status. Please check the supporting Web site for this book for a discussion of postpublication changes.

[2] In fact, class-to-schema compilers are one likely application for XML Schema.

The XML Schema specification relies on two fundamental namespace URIs. The schema URI (`http://www.w3.org/1999/XMLSchema`) is used to qualify all constructs that appear in *schema* documents. The instance URI (`http://www.w3.org/1999/XMLSchema-instance`) is used to qualify the XML Schema attributes that may appear in *instance* documents.[3] The conventional namespace prefix for the schema URI it is `xsd`, and for the instance URI it is `xsi`. Throughout this book, when these namespace prefixes appear in XML fragments, it is assumed that they have been aliased to these two namespace URI.

An XML Schema definition describes a target XML namespace. A schema definition is rooted by the `schema` element and primarily consists of named type definitions and element declarations.

```
<schema xmlns='http://www.w3.org/1999/XMLSchema'
        targetNamespace='urn:schemas-zoo-org:mammals'
        version='1.0' <!-- informational only -->
>
   <!-- named type definitions/elem declarations go here -->
</schema>
```

The schema definition above describes types, elements, and attributes in the `urn:schemas-zoo-org:mammals` namespace. A corresponding instance document would associate itself with this namespace using the standard XML technique.

```
<myzoo xmlns='urn:schemas-zoo-org:mammals' />
```

Since a given XML instance document can have elements and attributes from multiple namespaces, more than one schema definition may be required to describe the entire XML document.

Recall that an XML namespace URI should be treated as an opaque identifier. This means that given an XML namespace URI that appears in an instance document, one cannot necessarily find the corresponding schema definition

---

[3] A third namespace URI (`http://www.w3.org/1999/XMLSchema-datatypes`) is also defined as a distinct namespace for the built-in simple types. Its use in XML schema documents is discouraged.

simply by dereferencing the URI as if it were a URL that points to a schema definition. To support mapping each namespace URI to its corresponding schema definition, instance documents can use the `xsi:schemaLocation` attribute. The `xsi:schemaLocation` attribute contains a whitespace-delimited list of whitespace-delimited namespace-URI/location pairs of the form

```
nsuri1 schemaloc1 nsuri2 schemaloc2 . . .
```

The following instance document uses the `xsi:schemaLocation` attribute to indicate the locations of its corresponding schema definitions:

```
<myzoo xmlns='http://lazoo.org'
       xmlns:mml='urn:schemas-zoo-org:mammals'
       xmlns:xsi='http://www.w3.org/1999/XMLSchema-instance'
       xsi:schemaLocation='http://lazoo.org
                 http://lazoo.org/thezoo.xsd
                 urn:schemas-zoo-org:mammals
                 http://zoo.org/mammals.xsd'
/>
```

As shown in Figure 4.1, the `xsi:schemaLocation` attribute indicates that the schema definition for `http://lazoo.org` can be found at `http://lazoo.org/thezoo.xsd` and that the schema definition for `urn:schemas-zoo-org:mammals` can be found at `http://zoo.org/mammals.xsd`. In both cases, the corresponding `.xsd` files are assumed to be XML documents that contain a `schema` element as their root. Note that the `xsi:schemaLocation` attribute is optional, and when present, it simply acts as a hint to processing software (which is free to ignore the hint and use a schema definition that was discovered *a priori*). Also, the `xsi:schemaLocation` attribute can appear at any element, not just an element where the namespace is in direct use. Moreover, the effects of a given `xsi:schemaLocation` attribute remain in effect for the remainder of the XML document, not just for descendant elements.

The schema description of a target namespace can span multiple `schema` elements (potentially in multiple XML documents). To allow one `schema` document to use components from another `schema` document that also describes aspects in

ESSENTIAL XML: BEYOND MARKUP

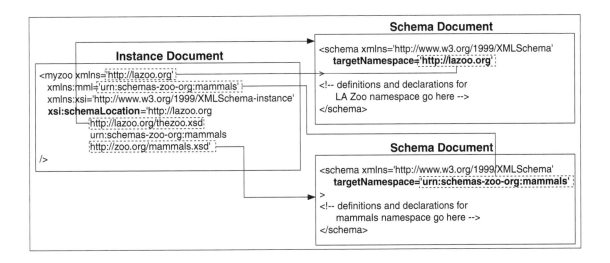

Figure 4.1   Relating schemas and instances

the same target namespace, the `include` mechanism is provided. The `include` element specifies the location of a `schema` document that describes additional aspects of the same target namespace. The `include` element must appear before any type definitions or element declarations, as shown here.

```
<schema xmlns='http://www.w3.org/1999/XMLSchema'
        targetNamespace='urn:schemas-zoo-org:mammals'
>
  <include schemaLocation='http://zoo.org/mam1.xsd' />
  <include schemaLocation='http://zoo.org/mam2.xsd' />
  <!-- named type definitions/elem declarations go here -->
</schema>
```

This schema definition assumes that the schema definitions contained in `http://zoo.org/mam1.xsd` and `http://zoo.org/mam2.xsd` describe portions of the `urn:schemas-zoo-org:mammals` namespace (if they do not, then it is an error). It is legal for the included schema documents to have no `targetNamespace` attribute, in which case the contained schema components will adopt the target namespace of the including schema. The XML Schema specification is worded in such a way as to allow multiple `include`s of the same schema document. It is an error, however, if a given named component has multiple definitions that are not 100 percent identical, even across multiple `included` schema definitions.

It is often the case that a given target namespace will rely on components from another namespace. Because `xsd:include` only works for intranamespace inclusion, some other mechanism is needed to signal the use of components from a foreign namespace. This is the purpose of the `xsd:import` directive. In addition to identifying the foreign namespace URI, the `xsd:import` directive can also specify the location of the foreign schema definition, but as with the `xsi:schemaLocation` attribute used in instance documents, this is optional. The following schema definition refers to two other namespace descriptions:

```
<schema xmlns='http://www.w3.org/1999/XMLSchema'
        targetNamespace='urn:schemas-zoo-org:mammals'
>
  <import namespace='http://lazoo.org'
          schemaLocation='http://lazoo.org/thezoo.xsd' />
  <import namespace='urn:schemas-zoo-org:reptiles' />
  <!-- named type definitions/elem declarations go here -->
</schema>
```

The `import` and `include` elements can appear in any order, but collectively they must precede all components of the schema definition.

Type Definitions

Arguably, the most useful component in a schema definition is a named type definition. XML Schemas supports two distinct categories of types: complex types and simple types (described in parts 1 and 2 of the XML Schemas specification respectively). Complex types describe the `[children]` and `[attributes]` of elements in an instance document. Simple types are the set of types that are represented purely as strings with no elements or attributes and are used to describe the `[children]` of attributes and text-only elements. Simple types are defined using the `simpleType` construct. Complex types are defined using the `complexType` construct described later in this chapter.

Part 2 of the XML Schema specification describes a set of "built-in" datatypes that map to either natural programmatic types (*e.g.,* `double`, `string`) or common XML productions (*e.g.,* `NMTOKEN`). These built-in types are directly useable in element or attribute declarations and can act as base types for user-defined type definitions. Roughly one-fourth of the built-in simple types are primitive or *ab initio* datatypes that are intrinsic to the XML Schema definition language. The remaining built-in types are derived using the standard `simpleType` construct. These derived types are always defined in terms of another built-in simple type, either via restriction or list generation. Figure 4.2 shows the built-in datatypes at the time of this writing.

The built-in simple types all belong to the `http://www.w3.org/1999/XMLSchema` namespace.[4] If a schema document uses that namespace URI in

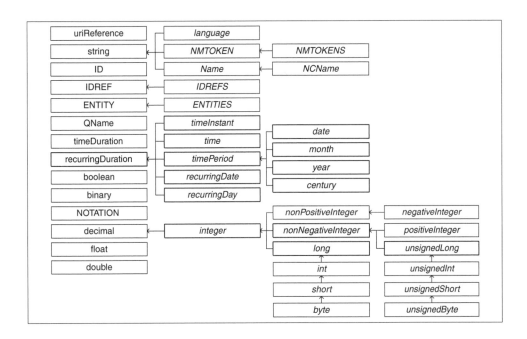

Figure 4.2   The built-in simple types

---

[4]A parallel set of names referring to the same types is available under the http://www.w3.org/1999/XMLSchema-datatypes namespace URI.

its default namespace declaration, then the built-in type names can be used without prefixes.

```
<schema xmlns='http://www.w3.org/1999/XMLSchema'
      targetNamespace='urn:schemas-zoo-org:mammals'
      xmlns:target='urn:schemas-zoo-org:mammals'
>
<!-- can now refer to string, NMTOKEN, long, etc -->
</schema>
```

If, however, a schema document does not have a default namespace declaration that is bound to the XML Schemas namespace URI, references to the built-in types must use prefixed QNames.

```
<xsd:schema xmlns='urn:schemas-zoo-org:mammals'
      xmlns:xsd='http://www.w3.org/1999/XMLSchema'
      targetNamespace='urn:schemas-zoo-org:mammals'
>
<!-- must refer to xsd:string, xsd:NMTOKEN, xsd:long, etc-->
</schema>
```

This chapter, like many schema documents, will use the former style of namespace management.

New simple types are defined in terms of an existing simple type by using the simpleType construct. The simpleType construct supports two forms of derivation: list generation and restriction. List generation is the simplest to understand. Consider the difference between the intrinsic XML productions NMTOKEN and NMTOKENS. NMTOKENS is simply a whitespace-delimited list of one or more NMTOKEN values. Derivation by list generation defines a new datatype as a whitespace-delimited list of another datatype. The following is a fragment from the normative schema for built-in datatypes:

```
<simpleType name='NMTOKENS'
          base='NMTOKEN'
          derivedBy='list'
/>
```

One can use this mechanism to define lists of arbitrary datatypes. For example, consider the following schema fragment:

```
<schema xmlns='http://www.w3.org/1999/XMLSchema'>
  <simpleType name='floats'
              base='float'
              derivedBy='list'
  />
</schema>
```

This schema definition states that instances of type floats consist of a whitespace-delimited list of floating-point numbers. This means that while the following is a schema-valid instance of type floats

```
34.1 25.1E5 -0.04E-6
```

the following is not

```
Hello, World
```

The ability to constrain character data based on user-defined types is one of many benefits that XML Schemas has over DTDs.

The more common form of derivation is by restriction, in which a new type is defined in terms of an existing simple type by placing one or more restrictions on the legal values of that type, in essence describing a subset of the valid values of the base type. These restrictions are defined in terms of a fixed number of pre-defined constraining facets that are listed in Table 4.1. Consider the following schema fragment:

```
<simpleType name='humanAges' base='double'
            derivedBy='restriction'
>
  <minInclusive value='0.0' />
  <maxExclusive value='150.0' />
</simpleType>
```

Table 4.1 — Simple Type Facets. The first four facet columns (ordered, bounded, finite, numeric) are grouped under "Fundamental"; the columns from length through duration are grouped under "Constraining".

Type	ordered	bounded	finite	numeric	length	minLength	maxLength	pattern	enumeration	maxInclusive	maxExclusive	minExclusive	minInclusive	precision	scale	encoding	period	duration	Base Type
string	y				y	y	y	y	y	y	y	y	y						
boolean		y						y											
float	y	y	y	y				y	y	y	y	y	y						
double	y	y	y	y				y	y	y	y	y	y						
decimal	y			y				y	y	y	y	y	y	y	y				
timeDuration	y							y	y	y	y	y	y						
recurringDuration								y	y	y	y	y	y				y	y	
binary					y	y	y	y	y							y			
uriReference					y	y	y	y	y										
ID	y				y	y	y	y	y	y	y	y	y						
IDREF	y				y	y	y	y	y	y	y	y	y						
ENTITY	y				y	y	y	y	y	y	y	y	y						
NOTATION	y				y	y	y	y	y	y	y	y	y						
QName	y				y	y	y	y	y	y	y	y	y						
language	y				y	y	y	y	y	y	y	y	y						string
IDREFS					y	y	y		y										IDREF
ENTITIES					y	y	y		y										ENTITY
NMTOKEN	y				y	y	y	y	y	y	y	y	y						string
NMTOKENS	y				y	y	y		y										NMTOKEN
Name	y				y	y	y	y	y	y	y	y	y						string
NCName	y				y	y	y	y	y	y	y	y	y						Name
integer	y			y					y	y	y	y	y	y	y				decimal
nonPositiveInteger	y			y					y	y	y	y	y	y	y				integer
negativeInteger	y			y					y	y	y	y	y	y	y				nonPositiveInteger
long	y	y	y	y					y	y	y	y	y	y	y				integer
int	y	y	y	y					y	y	y	y	y	y	y				long
short	y	y	y	y					y	y	y	y	y	y	y				int
byte	y	y	y	y					y	y	y	y	y	y	y				short
nonNegativeInteger	y			y					y	y	y	y	y	y	y				integer
unsignedLong	y	y	y	y					y	y	y	y	y	y	y				nonNegativeInteger
unsignedInt	y	y	y	y					y	y	y	y	y	y	y				unsignedLong
unsignedShort	y	y	y	y					y	y	y	y	y	y	y				unsignedInt
unsignedByte	y	y	y	y					y	y	y	y	y	y	y				unsignedShort
positiveInteger	y			y					y	y	y	y	y	y	y				nonNegativeInteger
timeInstant	y								y	y	y	y	y	y			y	y	recurringDuration
time	y								y	y	y	y	y	y			y	y	recurringDuration
timePeriod	y								y	y	y	y	y	y			y	y	recurringDuration
date	y								y	y	y	y	y	y			y	y	timePeriod
month	y								y	y	y	y	y	y			y	y	timePeriod
year	y								y	y	y	y	y	y			y	y	timePeriod
century	y								y	y	y	y	y	y			y	y	timePeriod
recurringDate	y								y	y	y	y	y	y			y	y	recurringDuration
recurringDay	y								y	y	y	y	y	y			y	y	recurringDuration

Table 4.1   Simple Type Facets

ESSENTIAL XML: BEYOND MARKUP

This definition states that all instances of the `humanAge` datatype must be a `double` that adheres to the following constraints:

```
0.0 <= value < 150.0
```

Instances with values outside of this range are considered schema-invalid.

One particularly interesting facet is the enumeration facet. When the enumeration facet is in use, the new simple type is defined in terms of a base type and a list of one or more literal values. All instances of the new type must match one of the enumerated values in order to be schema valid. The following is a simple enumeration type definition:

```
<simpleType name='yesno' base='NMTOKEN'>
  <enumeration value='yes' />
  <enumeration value='no' />
</simpleType>
```

Assuming that the element `answer` is of type `yesno`, the following are schema-valid instances:

```
<answer>yes</answer>
<answer>no</answer>
```

Note that since the enumerator lists only two literal values, no lexical values other than `yes` and `no` are legal content for an `answer` element.

Element Declarations

The conventional technique for associating types with elements is to use an element declaration. Element declarations come in two forms: global declarations and local declarations. Global element declarations must be named and must appear as [children] of the `schema` element. Local element declarations appear as part of a content model definition (typically inside a `complexType` definition) and are described later in this chapter. Local element declarations are typically more specific, and when both a global and local element declaration might be applicable, the local element declaration always takes precedence.

An element declaration binds a type to an element name in a context. For local element declarations, the context is the surrounding complex type. For global element declarations, the context is typically the "root" element of a document or an element matching a wildcard particle (more on this later). Consider the following simple type definition:

```
<schema xmlns='http://www.w3.org/1999/XMLSchema'
  targetNamespace='urn:schemas-zoo-org:mammals'
>
  <simpleType name='comment' base='string'>
    <maxLength value='1024'/>
  </simpleType>
</schema>
```

The following global element declaration binds the `about` element to the `comment` type.

```
<schema xmlns='http://www.w3.org/1999/XMLSchema'
        xmlns:mml='urn:schemas-zoo-org:mammals'
        targetNamespace='http://lazoo.org'
>
  <import namespace='urn:schemas-zoo-org:mammals' />
  <element name='about' type='mml:comment' />
</schema>
```

Note that this global element declaration binds the element name `about` (in the namespace) to the type named `comment` (in the `urn:schemas-zoo-org:mammals` namespace). In this example, the element declaration is global, which means that it applies to all namespace-qualified `about` elements in the instance document unless a local element declaration has masked its application. For example, in the following instance document, there are three instances of type `comment`:

```
<myzoo xmlns='http://lazoo.org'>
  <about>This is a comment</about>
  <monkey>
    <about>and so is this</about>
    <about>this is too</about>
```

ESSENTIAL XML: BEYOND MARKUP

```
    </monkey>
  </myzoo>
```

Because the `about` elements are in the `http://lazoo.org` namespace, the global element declaration applies and their type is implicitly `comment`.

XML Schemas maintains separate symbol spaces for each variety of schema component (*e.g.,* type definitions, element declarations, attribute declarations). That means that the following schema fragment

```
<schema xmlns='http://www.w3.org/1999/XMLSchema'
  targetNamespace='urn:schemas-zoo-org:mammals'
>
  <simpleType name='comment' base='string' />
  <simpleType name='comment' base='NMTOKENS' />
</schema>
```

is illegal because the name `comment` is multiply defined for a single component type (in this case, a simple type definition). However, the following fragment is schema-valid

```
<schema xmlns='http://www.w3.org/1999/XMLSchema'
  targetNamespace='urn:schemas-zoo-org:mammals'
      xmlns:tns='urn:schemas-zoo-org:mammals'
>
  <simpleType name='comment' base='string' >
    <maxLength value='1024' />
  </simpleType>
  <element name='comment' type='tns:comment' />
</schema>
```

because the name `comment` is only used once per schema component type.

In the previous schema definition, the named type definition can be eliminated if the type `comment` will only be used by elements named `comment`. If that is the case, then the `comment` element declaration can contain an anonymous type definition as shown here.

```
<schema xmlns='http://www.w3.org/1999/XMLSchema'
  targetNamespace='urn:schemas-zoo-org:mammals'
```

```
>
  <element name='comment' >
    <simpleType base='string' > <!-- anonymous type -->
      <maxLength value='1024' />
    </simpleType>
  </element>
</schema>
```

The net effect of this schema definition is functionally identical to the previous schema definition. The primary difference is that with the latter schema definition there is no type named comment that can be applied elsewhere in this or any other schema. Rather, the type of the comment element is an anonymous type that cannot be used anywhere except as the private description of the comment element. In the previous schema, comment was a named type that could be applied in multiple contexts.

In general, named type definitions should be used unless there is a compelling reason not to. The primary reason to choose anonymous type definitions over named type definitions is to make a type definition private by prohibiting its reuse in other contexts. Choosing an anonymous type definition not only disallows application of the type to other elements, it also disallows use of the type as a base for other type definitions. Ultimately, anonymous types in XML Schema definition fill the same shorthand role that anonymous structure definitions fill in the C programming language and should be used judiciously.

Complex Types

The discussion so far has focused on simple textual type definitions. While simple types are extremely useful, they are not nearly as expressive as complex type definitions. The XML Schema specification supports the definition of complex types that describe the content model and attribute inventory of a given class of element. A complex type definition fundamentally consists of a content model definition followed by a list of legal attributes. Like simple types, complex types can be named or anonymous and are associated with elements in the same manner, typically using an element declaration in the schema document. Unlike other schema components, complex types and simple types share a symbol space, which means it is illegal to have a complex type named bob and a simple type named bob in the same target namespace.

The content model of a complex type is defined in terms of *particles,* the most interesting of which is the local element declaration. Local element declarations override any global element declarations that may be in effect. Consider the following schema that contains a global element declaration:

```
<schema xmlns='http://www.w3.org/1999/XMLSchema'
        xmlns:mml='urn:schemas-zoo-org:mammals'
        targetNamespace='http://lazoo.org'
>
   <import namespace='urn:schemas-zoo-org:mammals' />
   <element name='about' type='mml:comment' />
</schema>
```

This schema states that all elements named about in the http://lazoo.org namespace must be of type comment irrespective of where they occur in an instance document. It is often preferable to associate named elements with types only when they are used in a specific context. For example, what if the about element needs to be of a different type when used as a subelement of monkey? This is where local element declarations and complex type definitions come into play.

A local element declaration must appear as a direct descendant to a complexType or model group element. Consider the following schema definition:

```
<schema xmlns='http://www.w3.org/1999/XMLSchema'
        xmlns:mml='urn:schemas-zoo-org:mammals'
        targetNamespace='http://lazoo.org'
            xmlns:tns='http://lazoo.org'
>
   <import namespace='urn:schemas-zoo-org:mammals' />
<!-- global element declaration -->
   <element name='about' type='mml:comment' />
   <complexType name='monkey' content='elementOnly'>
<!-- local element declaration -->
      <element name='about' type='mml:simianComment' />
```

```
        </complexType>
        <element name='monkey' type='tns:monkey' />
    </schema>
```

This schema states that elements named `about` in the `http://lazoo.org` namespace are always of type `comment`. However, when an unqualified `about` element appears as a child element of `monkey`, its type is `simianComment`. Consider the following instance document:

```
<lazoo:zoo xmlns:lazoo='http://lazoo.org' >
    <lazoo:about>This is my first comment</lazoo:about>
    <lazoo:monkey><about>Monkey stuff</about></lazoo:monkey>
</lazoo:zoo>
```

Note that there are two `about` elements. Because the first is in the `http://lazoo.org` namespace, the global element declaration applies to it and its type is `comment`. However, the second `about` element appears as a child element to `monkey` and must match the content model of type `monkey`. Because type `monkey` has a local element declaration named `about`, that declaration applies and the type of the `about` element is `simianComment`, not `comment`.

Note that in the previous instance document, the second `about` element belongs to no namespace. By default, that is how local element (and attribute) declarations are interpreted—that is, that they describe elements (and attributes) whose surrounding context controls their interpretation, not their namespace URI. This is a reasonable viewpoint and, though it makes the use of default namespace declarations cumbersome, captures the spirit of locally scoped declarations. That stated, there are a nontrivial number of XML vocabularies that expect each and every element name to be namespace-qualified, not just the name of the topmost element (the schema language itself is one such vocabulary). To support these types of vocabularies, local element (and attribute) declarations may have a `form` attribute indicating the namespace affiliation of that declaration. This attribute may have two values: `unqualified` or `qualified`. The former states that the name of the corresponding element or attribute is not affiliated with any namespace. The latter states that the corresponding element or attribute is affiliated with the namespace identified by the

ESSENTIAL XML: BEYOND MARKUP

surrounding complex type's `targetNamespace`. If no `form` attribute is provided, the values specified by the schema element's `elementFormDefault` or `attributeFormDefault` attributes are used. If there is no corresponding default provided at the schema level, then the declaration is processed as if the `form` attribute's value was `unqualified`.

To grasp how the `form` attribute affects namespace affiliation of local declarations, consider the following schema document:

```
<schema xmlns='http://www.w3.org/1999/XMLSchema'
        targetNamespace='urn:dogs:pugland'
         xmlns:target='urn:dogs:pugland'
        elementFormDefault='qualified' >
  <complexType name='Pug' content='elementOnly' >
    <element name='snout' form='qualified' />
    <element name='tail'  form='unqualified' />
    <element name='ears' />
  </complexType>
  <element name='pug' type='target:Pug' />
</schema>
```

Given this schema definition, the following document would be schema-valid:

```
<?xml version='1.0' ?>
<pl:pug xmlns:pl='urn:dogs:pugland' >
  <pl:snout/>
  <tail/> <!-- note that tail is unaffiliated -->
  <pl:ears/>
</pl:pug>
```

Had the schema's `elementFormDefault` attribute been absent or had the value `unqualified`, the following would be schema-valid instead:

```
<?xml version='1.0' ?>
<pl:pug xmlns:pl='urn:dogs:pugland' >
  <pl:snout/>
  <tail/> <!-- note that tail is unaffiliated -->
  <ears/> <!-- note that ears is unaffiliated -->
</pl:pug>
```

In general, one is expected to set the `elementFormDefault` and `attribute-FormDefault` at the schema level and only use the declaration-level `form` attribute for odd cases.

While `unqualified` is the default for both element and attribute local declarations, `unqualified` elements present a small inconvenience. Consider the following schema document that relies on `unqualified` local element declarations:

```
<schema xmlns='http://www.w3.org/1999/XMLSchema'
        targetNamespace='urn:dogs:pugland'
           xmlns:target='urn:dogs:pugland' >
  <complexType name='Pug' content='elementOnly' >
    <element name='snout' />
    <element name='tail' />
    <element name='ears' />
  </complexType>
  <element name='pug' type='target:Pug' />
</schema>
```

Given this schema definition, the following document would be schema-valid:

```
<?xml version='1.0' ?>
<pl:pug xmlns:pl='urn:dogs:pugland' >
  <snout/>
  <tail/>
  <ears/>
</pl:pug>
```

Note that no default namespace declaration is used. Had the `pug` element used a default namespace declaration, the child elements would each need to suppress that declaration as shown in this schema-valid instance document:

```
<?xml version='1.0' ?>
<pug xmlns='urn:dogs:pugland' >
  <snout xmlns=""/>
  <tail  xmlns=""/>
  <ears  xmlns=""/>
</pl:pug>
```

This naturally means that newer vocabularies based on local *unqualified* element declarations rarely use default namespace declarations.

It is possible for a complex type's content model to reference global element declarations, in essence allowing namespace-qualified child elements. An `element` element in a content model may use a `ref` attribute in lieu of `name` and `type` attributes to reference a global element declaration by its `QName`. When a reference to a global element declaration is used, the target namespace, element name, and type of the referenced element declaration will be used at validation-time. For example, the following schema definition

```
<schema xmlns='http://www.w3.org/1999/XMLSchema'
        targetNamespace='http://lazoo.org'
             xmlns:tns='http://lazoo.org'
>
   <simpleType name='bearComment' base='string'/>
   <element name='about' type='tns:bearComment' />
   <complexType name='bear' content='elementOnly'/>
      <element ref='tns:about' />
      <element ref='tns:about' />
   </complexType>
</schema>
```

is functionally equivalent to the following

```
<schema xmlns='http://www.w3.org/1999/XMLSchema'
        targetNamespace='http://lazoo.org'
             xmlns:tns='http://lazoo.org'
>
   <simpleType name='bearComment' base='string'/>
   <complexType name='bear' content='elementOnly'/>
      <element name='about' form='qualified'
              type='tns:bearComment' />
      <element name='about' form='qualified'
              type='tns:bearComment'/>
   </complexType>
</schema>
```

References to global element declarations always imply instance elements whose names are affiliated with the global element declaration's targetNamespace. This implies that the `form` attribute is prohibited on references to global element declarations. That stated, references to global element declarations are one way to get `[children]` elements whose namespace affiliation is different from that of the surrounding complex type.

In general, for new XML vocabularies, local element declarations are preferable to global element declarations. There are exceptions to that rule. If the element declaration is going to act as an exemplar for an equivalence class (more on this later), it must be a global element declaration. If a given namespace-qualified element name should be usable in unanticipated contexts, you must use a global element declaration. In the common case, however, local element declarations are a much more expressive mechanism and more closely model other type systems one is likely to encounter.

Content Models and Particles

Complex type definitions specify the constraints on the `[children]` and `[attributes]` for a given type of element information item. The content model of an element's `[children]` is composed of *particles*. A particle is a local element declaration or reference to a global element declaration (`element`), a compositor (`sequence`, `choice`, or `all`), a reference to a named content model group (`group`), or an element wildcard (`any`). With a few exceptions, anywhere one type of particle is allowed, the other five are allowed as well. A complex type definition contains a sequence of particles that indicate which elements can appear in instances of that type. All of the local element declarations shown in the previous section were particles of the containing type's content model.

The particles shown so far have all corresponded to mandatory elements. For example, all instances of type `bear` were required to have exactly two `about` elements—no more, no less. It is possible to indicate that a particle is optional—that is, that instances of the type can legally omit the corresponding element(s) and still be considered schema-valid. It is also possible to indicate that the instance elements corresponding to a given particle can appear multiple times. These characteristics are specified using the `minOccurs` and `maxOccurs` attributes, respectively. These two attributes can be applied in several contexts, but their basic meaning is the same. The minOccurs attribute indicates the minimum number of occurrences that are expected as a non-negative integer. The maxOccurs attribute indicates the maximum number of occurrences that are expected as a non-negative integer, with 'unbounded' indicating no limit on the number of occurrences. For content model particles (*e.g.*, local element declarations), the default value of the minOccurs attribute is always 1, and the default value for the maxOccurs attribute is either 1 or value of the minOccurs attribute, whichever is greater. In the following type definition

```
<complexType name='bear' content='elementOnly'>
  <element name='about' type='string' />
  <element name='about' type='string'
             minOccurs='1' maxOccurs='1'/>
</complexType>
```

the two local element declarations are identical, since the first element has neither a minOccurs or maxOccurs attribute. If a local element declaration has only a minOccurs attribute, the implied value of the maxOccurs attribute varies depending on the minOccurs value. Consider the following type definition:

```
<complexType name='cow' content='elementOnly'>
  <element name='head' type='head' minOccurs='1' />
  <element name='tail' type='tail' minOccurs='0' />
  <element name='leg' type='leg'  minOccurs='4' />
</complexType>
```

The maxOccurs attribute defaults to 1 for the 'head' and 'tail' element declarations and defaults to '4' for the 'leg' declaration. An alternative way to look at the minOccurs and maxOccurs attributes is to map them onto their regular expression counterparts. Table 4.2 shows the four common combinations of these attributes as well as their regular expression equivalents.

XML Schemas also supports providing default values for local element declarations whose content model only allows character data. Consider the following schema fragment:

```
<schema xmlns='http://www.w3.org/1999/XMLSchema'
        targetNamespace='someURI' xmlns:tns='someURI'>
  <complexType name='ABC' content='elementOnly' >
    <element name='a' type='string' minOccurs='0' />
    <element name='b' type='string' minOccurs='0'
                      default='bhere'/>
    <element name='c' type='string' minOccurs='0'
                      fixed='bhere'/>
  </complexType>
  <element name='am' type='tns:AnnotateMe' />
</schema>
```

If one were to present this instance to an XML Schema-aware processor

```
<ns:am xmlns:ns='someURI'/>
```

the a element would appear to be absent, but the b and c elements would appear to be present with the value 'bhere' just as if the instance document had looked like this:

```
<ns:am xmlns:ns='someURI'>
  <b>bhere</b>
  <c>bhere</c>
</ns:am>
```

Because the c element has a fixed value, no other value can appear as [children] of that element. That means that the following instance is schema-invalid

Table 4.2   minOccurs/maxOccurs

minOccurs	maxOccurs	Meaning	RegExp
0	1	Optional nonrepeatable	head?
1	1	Mandatory nonrepeatable	head
0	unbounded	Optional repeatable	head*
1	unbounded	Mandatory repeatable	head+

```
<ns:am xmlns:ns='someURI'>
  <c>This isn't legal due to the fixed attribute</c>
</ns:am>
```

since only the string `bhere` is allowed.

It is sometimes desirable to distinguish between an element that is absent and an element that is present but has no value. This is especially useful when mapping object references or nullable database columns to XML Schemas. For example, consider the following Java code fragment:

```
String a = "";
String b = null;
```

Note that a and b have distinct values. The `a` variable refers to the empty string `""`, whereas the `b` variable has the distinguished value `null`.

To support elements with a null value, XML Schemas define the `xsi:null` attribute that allows instance elements to indicate their "nullness." For this attribute to appear in an instance element, the corresponding element declaration must explicitly allow nulls using the boolean `nullable` attribute. Consider the following schema fragment:

```
<schema xmlns='http://www.w3.org/1999/XMLSchema'
        targetNamespace='someURI' xmlns:tns='someURI'>
  <complexType name='pair' content='elementOnly'>
    <element name='a' type='string' />
    <element name='b' type='string' nullable='1' />
  </complexType>
  <element name='pair' type='tns:pair />
</schema>
```

This type definition indicates that the `a` subelement of `pair` cannot be null, but the `b` sub-element can. The following is a schema-valid instance of type `pair`:

```
<t:pair xmlns:t='someURI'
    xmlns:xsi='http://www.w3.org/1999/XMLSchema-instance'>
  <a/>
  <b xsi:null='1' />
</t:pair>
```

Note that the values of a and b are different. The a element contains the empty string `""`, whereas the b element contains the distinguished value null. Elements that are marked `xsi:null='1'` must have an empty [children] property, but it is still legal to have namespace declarations and any attributes that would otherwise be allowed.

XML Schemas allows content models to be grouped together using compositors. There are three kinds of compositors that differ in how their contents are interpreted. The simplest compositor, sequence, interprets its subparticles as an ordered list that must correspond to a like-ordered collection of elements in the instance element's [children]. For example, consider the following schema fragment:

```
<schema xmlns='http://www.w3.org/1999/XMLSchema'
        targetNamespace='someURI' xmlns:tns='someURI'>
  <complexType name='TaxTable' content='elementOnly'>
    <sequence maxOccurs='unbounded'>
      <element name='state' type='string' />
      <element name='rate' type='double' />
    </sequence>
  </complexType>
  <element name='tt' type='tns:TaxTable' />
</schema>
```

This type definition states that a TaxTable instance contains one or more instances of the sequence state/rate.

```
<t:tt xmlns:t='someURI'>
  <state>CA</state><rate>8.25</rate>
  <state>OR</state><rate>0</rate>
  <state>WA</state><rate>7.5</rate>
</t:tt>
```

The choice compositor interprets its subparticles as an unordered list, only one of which will be selected and used in the actual instance. For example, consider the following schema fragment:

```
<schema xmlns='http://www.w3.org/1999/XMLSchema'
        targetNamespace='someURI' xmlns:tns='someURI'>
```

```
<complexType name='DogCat' content='elementOnly'>
  <element name='hair' type='string' />
  <choice>
    <element name='purr' type='double' />
    <element name='bark' type='double' />
  </choice>
</complexType>
<element name='fido' type='tns:DogCat' />
</schema>
```

This type definition states that a `'DogCat'` instance begins with a `hair` element and ends with either a `purr` element or `bark` element but not both. For example, the following is a schema-valid `DogCat`

```
<t:fido xmlns:t='someURI'>
  <hair>Brown</hair><bark>8.1</bark>
</t:fido>
```

but the following is not

```
<t:fido xmlns:t='someURI'>
  <hair>Red</hair><purr>1</purr><bark>8</bark>
</t:fido>
```

since the compositor in effect was `choice`, not `sequence`.

The `all` compositor interprets its subparticles as an unordered list, each of which must appear in the instance but may appear in any order. For example, consider the following schema fragment:

```
<schema xmlns='http://www.w3.org/1999/XMLSchema'
        targetNamespace='someURI' xmlns:tns='someURI'>
  <complexType name='Toupe' content='elementOnly'>
    <all>
      <element name='color' type='string' />
      <element name='length' type='string' />
    </all>
  </complexType>
  <element name='rug' type='tns:Toupe' />
</schema>
```

Instances of type `Toupe` must have one `color` and `length` element, but they can occur in any order. This means that the following is a schema-valid `Toupe`

```
<t:rug xmlns:t='someURI'>
  <color>red</color><length>2</length>
</t:rug>
```

as is

```
<t:rug xmlns:t='someURI'>
  <length>2</length><color>red</color>
</t:rug>
```

since the `all` compositor allows the declared elements to appear in any order as long as all of the declared elements actually appear. The `all` compositor has a variety of restrictions on its use. The `all` compositor may only appear as the immediate child of a complex type definition (it cannot appear as a subparticle to another particle). The `all` compositor may only contain element particles (not other compositors), and those particles' `maxOccurs` can only have the value 1 (the `minOccurs` attribute may be 0 however).

It is legal for `choice` and `sequence` compositors to contain other `choice` and `sequence` compositors in addition to element declarations. Consider the following schema fragment:

```
<schema xmlns='http://www.w3.org/1999/XMLSchema'
        targetNamespace='someURI' xmlns:tns='someURI'>
  <complexType name='Headpiece' content='elementOnly'>
    <choice>
      <element name='cap' type='string' />
      <sequence>
        <element name='color' type='string' />
        <element name='length' type='string' />
      </sequence>
    </choice>
  </complexType>
  <element name='hp' type='tns:Headpiece' />
</schema>
```

ESSENTIAL XML: BEYOND MARKUP

The type `Headpiece` contains a `choice` compositor indicating that instances must contain either a `cap` element or a `color` element followed by a `length` element. Additionally, `minOccurs` and `maxOccurs` can be applied to either compositor.

```
<schema xmlns='http://www.w3.org/1999/XMLSchema'
        targetNamespace='someURI' xmlns:tns='someURI'>
  <complexType name='Headpiece' content='elementOnly'>
    <choice minOccurs='0' >
      <element name='cap' type='string' />
      <sequence maxOccurs='unbounded' >
        <element name='color' type='string' />
        <element name='length' type='string' />
      </sequence>
    </choice>
  </complexType>
  <element name='hp' type='tns:Headpiece' />
</schema>
```

In this case, instances of type `Headpiece` can be empty, can contain exactly one `cap` element, or can contain one or more `color`/`length` element pairs.

XML Schemas allows content models to be grouped into named model groups using the `group` construct. The `group` construct makes a model group definition reusable in multiple contexts. A named `group` definition can appear at the root of a `schema` definition and be referenced as a particle in other content models. The following schema fragment uses named `groups` to replicate the previous `complexType` definition:

```
<schema xmlns='http://www.w3.org/1999/XMLSchema'
        targetNamespace''someURI' xmlns:tns='someURI'>
  <group name='cl' >
    <sequence>
      <element name='color' type='string' />
      <element name='length' type='string' />
    </sequence>
  </group>
  <group name='ccl' >
    <choice>
      <element name='cap' type='string' />
```

```
        <group ref='tns:cl' maxOccurs='unbounded' />
      </choice>
    </group>
    <complexType name='Headpiece' content='elementOnly'>
      <group ref='tns:ccl' minOccurs='0' />
    </complexType>
    <element name='hp' type='tns:Headpiece' />
  </complexType>
```

Note that references to named model groups are particles just like local element declarations and compositors.

The previous examples in this chapter have all used `elementOnly` content models. A complex type definition uses the `content` attribute to indicate the basic content model of the type. The `content` attribute can be applied to a `complexType` element and must be one of the following four values: `textOnly`, `empty`, `elementOnly`, or `mixed`. If a type's content model is `textOnly`, then the `[children]` of the corresponding instance element can only contain character data[5] and cannot contain elements. Assuming the element `about` is an instance of a `textOnly` type, the following would be schema-valid:

```
<someabouts>
  <about>Hello</about>
  <about/>
  <about><![CDATA[This is some text]]></about>
</someabouts>
```

If a complex type's content model is `empty`, the corresponding instance element's `[children]` cannot contain character data or elements. Assuming the element `about` is an instance of a `content='empty'` type, the following would be schema-valid:

```
<someabouts>
  <about/>
  <about></about>
</someabouts>
```

---

[5]Technically, entity references and CDATA start/end markers are still allowed.

ESSENTIAL XML: BEYOND MARKUP

Because instances of `content='textOnly'` or `content='empty'` types cannot contain child elements, the corresponding `complexType` definition cannot contain content model particles.

The `mixed` and `elementOnly` content models are virtually identical except for two minor differences. Instance elements whose content model is `mixed` may have character data interleaved between `[children]` elements. Instance elements whose content model is `elementOnly` cannot have any character data `[children]`. In both cases, the rules relating to particles discussed so far apply in full. The second minor difference is that if a complex type's content model does not consist of exactly one `all`, `sequence`, `choice`, or `group` particle, the content model is reinterpreted as if an additional particle containing the content model as subparticles were present. The type of particle that is introduced varies depending on whether the content model is `mixed` or `elementOnly`. Consider the following complex type definition:

```
<complexType name='AB' content='elementOnly' >
  <element name='a' type='string'/>
  <element name='b' type='string'/>
</complexType>
```

Because this is an `elementOnly` content model, a schema-aware processor will treat this type as if it were defined as follows:

```
<complexType name='AB' content='elementOnly' >
  <sequence minOccurs='1' maxOccurs='1' >
    <element name='a' type='string'/>
    <element name='b' type='string'/>
  </sequence>
</complexType>
```

The former is simply short-hand for the latter. Had the AB type definition been defined as `content='mixed'`, a schema-aware processor would have treated the type as if it were defined like this:

```
<complexType name='AB' content='mixed' >
  <choice minOccurs='0' maxOccurs='unbounded' >
    <element name='a' type='string'/>
```

```
      <element name='b' type='string'/>
    </sequence>
  </complexType>
```

Again, this is simply a more explicit form of the same type definition.[6]

Attributes

Element declarations bind a complex or simple type to an element name in a context. Attribute declarations bind a simple type to an attribute name in a context. Like element declarations, attribute declarations can be global or local, and the mechanisms and issues relating to this choice are the same, but there are even fewer reasons to use global attribute declarations than there are for using global element declarations.

In addition to describing the content model used for an element's [children], a complex type definition describes the members of the [attributes] property as well. A complex type's attribute inventory is described immediately after the content model particles. Attribute inventory is described using local attribute declarations, references to global attribute declarations, and references to named attribute groups. Of these three constructs, the first two may have a use and value attribute indicating the usage constraint for that attribute. The meaning of these two attributes is described in Table 4.3.

As the following XML Schema fragment shows, attribute declarations are strikingly similar to element declarations:

```
<schema xmlns='http://www.w3.org/1999/XMLSchema'
        targetNamespace='someURI' xmlns:tns='someURI'>
  <complexType name='CommentedText' content='mixed' >
    <element name='b' type='string' />
    <attribute name='comment' type='string'
               use='required'/>
    <attribute name='extra' type='boolean' />
    <attribute name='note' type='string'
               use='default' value='nothing said'/>
```

---

[6]Readers experienced in XML DTDs may recognize this as providing the expected behavior for legacy mixed content models.

Table 4.3: Attribute Declaration Attributes

use/value Attributes	Interpretation
`use='optional'`	Attribute is allowed but not mandatory and can have any value compatible with the associated simple type.
`use='required'`	Attribute is mandatory and can have any value compatible with the associated simple type.
`use='required' value='some-value'`	Attribute is mandatory and must have the value `'some-value'`.
`use='default' value='some-value'`	Attribute is allowed but not mandatory and can have any value compatible with the associated simple type. If the attribute does not appear, schema-aware processors will introduce the value `"some-value"` as if it had been explicitly provided.
`use='fixed' value='some-value'`	Attribute is allowed but not mandatory and, when present, must have the value `'some-value'`. If the attribute does not appear, schema-aware processors will introduce the value `"some-value"` as if it had been explicitly provided.
`use='prohibited'`	Attribute is never allowed.

```
  </complexType>
  <element name='ct' type='tns:CommentedText' />
</schema>
```

This type definition indicates that elements of type `CommentedText` must have a `comment` attribute and may have an `extra` and `note` attribute. No other attributes are allowed. If the `note` attribute is not provided in the instance element, a schema-aware processor will add the default value "nothing said" as if it had been explicitly provided in the original document.

Finally, it is possible to define reusable groups of local attribute declarations using named attribute groups. Named attribute groups must appear as [children] of the schema element and contain one or more attribute declarations.

```
<schema xmlns='http://www.w3.org/1999/XMLSchema'
        targetNamespace='someURI' xmlns:tns='someURI'>
  <attributeGroup name='annotations' >
    <attribute name='comment' type='string'
               use='required'/>
    <attribute name='extra' type='boolean' />
    <attribute name='note' type='string'
               use='default' value='nothing said'/>
  </attributeGroup>
</schema>
```

An attribute group reference can appear in a type definition alongside other local attribute declarations and attribute group references.

```
<schema xmlns='http://www.w3.org/1999/XMLSchema'
        targetNamespace='someURI' xmlns:tns='someURI'>
  <complexType name='CommentedText' content='mixed' >
    <element name='b' type='string' />
    <attributeGroup ref='tns:annotations' />
  </complexType>
</schema>
```

This type definition is equivalent to the earlier definition of the CommentedText type that used local attribute declarations.

Extensibility

Defining types in XML Schemas is no different from defining types in other languages or systems. Invariably, one defines a type in order to reuse it in multiple contexts. Assuming that the original type definition is perfect for the new context, the techniques for associating types with elements and attributes discussed so far are sufficient to achieve reuse. However, it is often the case that the new context really requires a somewhat modified version of an existing type. Fortunately, XML Schemas support several extensibility models that allow a type to be further refined or enhanced without modifying its original definition.

The simplest form of extensibility is the use of wildcards. Wildcard declarations allow unanticipated elements or attributes to appear in instances of the type in which they are declared. There are two types of wildcard declarations. The `any` declaration acts as a placeholder declaration for unanticipated elements. Exactly one `anyAttribute` declaration may appear after the complex type's attribute declarations and attribute group references and acts as a placeholder for unanticipated attributes. Both forms of wildcards allow the schema designer to enforce namespace-based constraints on wildcard replacements.

The `any` declaration is a content model particle and can appear anywhere a compositor particle can appear. Like all content model particles, it can have a `minOccurs` and `maxOccurs` attribute. Consider the following schema fragment:

```
<schema xmlns='http://www.w3.org/1999/XMLSchema'
    targetNamespace='someURI' xmlns:tns='someURI'
>
    <complexType name='entry' >
      <element name='name' type='string' />
      <any/>
    </complexType>
    <element name='entry' type='tns:entry />
</schema>
```

This type definition indicates that an `entry` starts with a `name` element followed by exactly one element whose name and type are not specified in the type definition. This means that the following is a schema-valid instance:

```
<t:entry xmlns:t='someURI'>
    <name>Don</name>
    <authorInfo>Write <b>less</b></authorInfo>
</t:entry>
```

In this instance, the `authorInfo` is used to satisfy the wildcard constraint. If an unlimited number of additional elements were to be allowed, the type definition would have used `minOccurs/maxOccurs` like this:

```
<complexType name='entry' >
    <element name='name' type='string' />
```

```
      <any minOccurs='0' maxOccurs='unbounded'/>
   </complexType>
```

For this version, all that is required is that all `entry` instances begin with a `name` subelement. They can be followed by any number of other elements whose names (and types) are provided in the instance document.

The `any` element wildcard can have a `processContent` attribute that controls what constraints (if any) are placed on the replacement elements. If the wildcard is marked `processContent='strict'` or has no `processContent` attribute, the replacement element must be schema-valid based on the schema definition derived from the namespace-qualified element name. If the wildcard is marked `processContent='skip'`, the replacement element must simply consist of well-formed XML and the consumer should not attempt to schema-validate the element. If the wildcard is marked `processContent='lax'`, the consumer should schema-validate recognized element types but is free to ignore unrecognized element types in terms of determining schema-validity.

Element and attribute wildcards can have a `namespace` attribute that is used to constrain what namespaces can or cannot be used. If no `namespace` attribute is provided, then the instance element or attribute can be from any namespace. If the `namespace` attribute is present, then it must have one of the values shown in Table 4.4. Consider the following type definition:

```
<schema xmlns='http://www.w3.org/1999/XMLSchema'
        targetNamespace='http://lazoo.org'
              xmlns:tns='http://lazoo.org'
>
   <complexType name='mostlyOpen' >
     <any namespace='##targetNamespace' />
     <any namespace='##other' />
     <anyAttribute namespace='urn:schemas-zoo-org:mammals' />
   </complexType>
   <element name='mo' type='tns:mostlyOpen' />
   <element name='monkey' type='string' />
</schema>
```

Instances of type `mostlyOpen` must have one element from the `http://lazoo.org` namespace followed by one element from any namespace other

ESSENTIAL XML: BEYOND MARKUP

Table 4.4: Wildcard Namespace Constraints

namespace attribute value	Meaning
##any	Any well-formed XML element or nonconflicting attribute
##local	Any well-formed XML element or nonconflicting attribute that belongs to no namespace
##targetNamespace	Any well-formed XML element or nonconflicting attribute from the targetNamespace of the containing schema
##other	Any well-formed XML element or nonconflicting attribute *not* from the targetNamespace of the containing schema
One or more URI references (space delimited)	Any well-formed XML element or nonconflicting attribute from the listed namespaces

than `http://lazoo.org`. Additionally, instances of type `mostlyOpen` can have zero or more attributes from the `urn:schemas-zoo-org:mammals` namespace. An instance of type `mostlyOpen` might look like this.

```
<laz:mo xmlns:laz='http://lazoo.org'
        xmlns:sdz='http://sdzoo.com'
        xmlns:mml='urn:schemas-zoo-org:mammals'
        mml:comment='Monkeys are mammals too'
>
    <laz:monkey>Eeek</laz:monkey>
    <sdz:ape>Oook</sdz:ape>
</laz:mo>
```

The use of wildcards allows a content model to be open to arbitrary extension. However, because no type-based constraints can be placed on the unspecified elements or attributes,[7] this style of extensibility is best suited to building generic container types or allowing arbitrary third-party annotations to be

---

[7]Wildcards are the moral equivalent of C++'s void * or Java's java.lang.Object.

applied to a set of otherwise fixed types. In general, it is preferable to use the type-based extensibility support offered by substitution.

XML Schemas supports a hierarchical type model much like the inheritance model in object-oriented programming languages. In XML Schemas, one type can derive from another type. As in most programming languages, derivation implies two side effects. The most obvious side effect of derivation is that the derived type inherits the definition of the base type and can provide additional properties or constraints. The less obvious side effect of derivation is that instances of the derived type are generally accepted wherever instances of the base type are expected. This principle is known as substitution.

XML Schemas supports two styles of complex type inheritance: extension and restriction. When a complex type derives from another type by extension, the derived type's declarations augment those of the base type by allowing additional elements and/or attributes not specified in the base type. When a type derives from another type by restriction, the derived type's declarations restrict those already present in the base type by placing additional constraints on the number of occurrences or types of elements or attributes beyond those imposed by the base type. The style of inheritance used is indicated using the `derivedBy` attribute in the derived type definition. In the absence of this attribute, the implied value is `restriction`.

A complex type definition can indicate its base type using the `base` attribute, which must contain the name of either a complex or simple type. If the `base` attribute refers to a simple type, then the derived type's content model is implicitly `textOnly`. If the `base` attribute refers to a complex type, then the derived type's content model is implicitly whatever the base type's content model is. For example, consider the following schema definition:

```
<schema xmlns='http://www.w3.org/1999/XMLSchema'
        targetNamespace='someURI' xmlns:tns='someURI'>
  <complexType name='sn' base='float'
               derivedBy='extension'>
    <attribute name='style' type='string' />
  </complexType>
  <complexType name='p' content='elementOnly'>
    <element name='b' type='string' />
  </complexType>
```

```
<complexType name='p2' base='tns:p' derivedBy='extension'>
  <element name='i' type='string' />
</complexType>
</schema>
```

Because type `sn` extends a simple data type, its content model is `textOnly`. Because type `p2` extends a complex type whose content model is `elementOnly`, p2's content model is also `elementOnly`.

Derivation by extension has the effect of prepending the derived type's element and attribute declarations with those from the base type. Consider the following schema fragment:

```
<schema xmlns='http://www.w3.org/1999/XMLSchema'
        targetNamespace='someURI' xmlns:tns='someURI'>
  <complexType name='vehicle' >
    <element name='topSpeed' type='float' />
    <element name='airborne' type='boolean' />
  </complexType>
  <complexType name='car' base='tns:vehicle'
               derivedBy='extension' >
    <element name='wheelsize' type='float' />
  </complexType>
  <element name='transportation' type='tns:vehicle' />
  <element name='carrera' type='tns:car' />
</schema>
```

This schema indicates that type `car` is an extension of type `vehicle` and that instances of type `car` will have a `wheelsize` element following the content model of the base type `vehicle` (which in this case is a `topSpeed` element followed by an `airborne` element). The following is a schema-valid instance of type `car`:

```
<t:carrera xmlns:t='someURI'>
<!-- vehicle content model -->
    <topSpeed>186</topSpeed>
    <airborne>0</airborne>
<!-- car content model -->
    <wheelsize>18</wheelsize>
</t:carrera>
```

It is also legal for an extended type to add attribute declarations. However, the order in which attributes appear in instance documents is always insignificant.

Note that in the previous schema fragment, the `transportation` element was bound to type `vehicle`. However, because type `car` derives from type `vehicle`, it is substitutable provided that the instance indicates which derived type is in use. This is accomplished using the `xsi:type` attribute. The value of the `xsi:type` attribute is the `QName` of the derived type that is being substituted. That means that the following is a schema-valid instance document

```
<t:transportation xmlns:t='someURI' xsi:type='t:car'
  xmlns:xsi='http://www.w3.org/1999/XMLSchema-instance' >
    <topSpeed>186</topSpeed>
    <airborne>0</airborne>
    <wheelsize>18</wheelsize>
</t:transportation>
```

but the following is not

```
<t:transportation xmlns:t='someURI'>
    <topSpeed>186</topSpeed>
    <airborne>0</airborne>
    <wheelsize>18</wheelsize>
</t:transportation>
```

since there is no explicit type substitution in the second instance document and the original type of `transportation` (type `vehicle`) does not allow a `wheelsize` subelement.

Derivation by extension looks and feels very much like object-oriented inheritance, as instances of the derived type always have additional information not found in the base type. XML Schemas also support derivation by restriction, which allows the derived complex type to apply additional constraints to the information already described in base type. A type that is derived by restriction can add no new content model particles or attribute declarations. Rather, it can only place additional constraints on particles and attributes from the base type, in essence identifying a subset of the base type. Because content model particles are typically order-sensitive, the derived type must redeclare the base type's particles in the order in which they originally appear. Consider the following schema fragment:

```
<schema xmlns='http://www.w3.org/1999/XMLSchema'
        targetNamespace='someURI' xmlns:tns='someURI'>
  xmlns='http://www.w3.org/1999/XMLSchema'>
  <complexType name='cola' >
    <element name='calories' type='float' minOccurs='0'/>
    <element name='taste' type='string'
            minOccurs='0' maxOccurs='unbounded'/>
  </complexType>
  <complexType name='dietcola' base='tns:cola'
                      derivedBy='restriction' >
    <element name='calories' type='float' minOccurs='1'/>
    <element name='taste' type='string' maxOccurs='0'   />
  </complexType>
  <element name='drink' type='tns:cola' />
</schema>
```

This schema indicates that an instance of type `dietcola` must have a `calories` subelement and that the `taste` subelement(s) are no longer allowed.

It may not be immediately obvious what the benefits of derivation were in this instance, since each of the base type's particles were duplicated in the derived type. The primary reason to use derivation by restriction is create a named subset of a given type. This subset has the benefit of being substitutable with the original type. The previous schema above states that an instance of type `dietcola` can be substituted anywhere an instance of type `cola` is allowed (such as a `drink` element as declared in the previous schema). For example, the following instance is schema-valid based on the previous schema

```
<d:drink xmlns:d='someURI' xsi:type='d:dietcola'
    xmlns:xsi='http://www.w3.org/1999/XMLSchema-instance'>
  <calories>1</calories>
</d:drink>
```

but the following is not

```
<d:drink xmlns:d='someURI' xsi:type='d:dietcola'
    xmlns:xsi='http://www.w3.org/1999/XMLSchema-instance'>
  <taste>Not as good as cola</taste>
  <taste>Not as good as cola</taste>
</d:drink>
```

Since instances of `dietcola` are required to have a `calories` subelement and are not allowed to have a `taste` subelement. Note, however, that had the substitution not taken place, both instances would be schema-valid, as both are valid instances of type `cola`.

In addition to tightening `minOccurs`/`maxOccurs` constraints, it is also legal to restrict the type of an element particle to a substitutable type. One can also provide a default value in the restricted type or constrain the value of an attribute or text-only element by specifying a fixed value.

Types Revisited

As with many object-oriented programming languages, it is possible to define a type as being abstract using XML Schemas. This is accomplished using the boolean `abstract` attribute on the type definition. Given the following schema

```
<schema xmlns='http://www.w3.org/1999/XMLSchema'
        targetNamespace='http://flowers.org'
        xmlns:tns='http://flowers.org' >
  <complexType name='flower' abstract='1' />
  <element name='bouquet' type='tns:flower' />
</schema>
```

the `bouquet` element declaration refers to an abstract type. This means that one must provide a derived type in order to use the `bouquet` element in an instance document. When an element declaration refers to an abstract type, all instances of that element must use the `xsi:type` attribute to indicate a concrete derived type. This means that the following instance is *not* schema-valid

```
<bouquet xmlns='http://flowers.org' />
```

but the following instance is

```
<bouquet xmlns='http://flowers.org' xsi:type='t:rose'
        xmlns:t='http://roses.org'
        xmlns:xsi='http://www.w3.org/1999/XMLSchema-instance'

/>
```

where `t:rose` is defined as follows

```
<schema xmlns='http://www.w3.org/1999/XMLSchema'
        targetNamespace='http://roses.org'
        xmlns:f='http://flowers.org'>
  <import namespace='http://flowers.org' />
  <complexType name='rose' base='f:flower'
        derivedBy='extension'/>
</schema>
```

Because the default value for the `abstract` attribute is false, type `rose` is concrete, not abstract, and therefore can legally appear in instance documents. Also, the XML Schema substitutability rules require all types used in instances of the `bouquet` element to derive from type `flower` either directly or indirectly.

Given the potential for substitution, the strength of a type definition or element declaration may seem somewhat weak, since any type can be successively restricted and extended to no longer resemble the original type in any significant way. This is why XML Schemas provides the `final` and `block` attributes. The `final` attribute can be applied to a complex type definition and controls which styles of derivation (if any) may be used with the current type as a `base` type. The `block` attribute can be applied to a complex type definition or an element declaration and controls which style of derivation (if any) may be used for substitution of the element's declared type. Both the `final` and `block` attributes can have a space-delimited list of prohibited derivation styles or the string "`#all`", which indicates that all styles of derivation are prohibited. Consider the following schema fragment:

```
<schema xmlns='http://www.w3.org/1999/XMLSchema'
        targetNamespace='someURI' xmlns:tns='someURI'>
  <complexType name='a' final='#all' />
  <complexType name='b' final='restriction' />
  <complexType name='c' final='extension' />
</schema>
```

This schema indicates that type `a` is never a valid base type, type `b` is only a valid base type for derivation by extension, and type `c` is only a valid base type for derivation by restriction. Note that the definition of type a could have also been written like this

```
<complexType name='a' final='restriction extension' />
```

but the original schema used the more convenient "#all" instead.

The final attribute explicitly prohibits derivation of new types that use the current type as a base. Often, all that is desired is to prohibit substitution without prohibiting derivation. For this, XML Schemas provides the block attribute. The block attribute can be applied to complex type definitions or to element declarations. The block attribute lists the derivation styles for which substitution is prohibited. Consider the following schema fragment:

```
<schema xmlns='http://www.w3.org/1999/XMLSchema'
        targetNamespace='someURI' xmlns:tns='someURI'>
 <complexType name='d' block='#all' />
 <complexType name='e' block='restriction' />
 <complexType name='f' block='extension' />
 <complexType name='d2e' base=' t:d'
              derivedBy='extension' />
 <complexType name='d2r' base='t:d'
              derivedBy='restriction' />
 <complexType name='e2e' base=' t:e'
              derivedBy='extension' />
 <complexType name='e2r' base=' t:e'
              derivedBy='restriction' />
 <complexType name='f2e' base='t:f'
              derivedBy='extension' />
 <complexType name='f2r' base='t:f'
              derivedBy='restriction' />
 <element name='delem' type='t:d' />
 <element name='eelem' type='t:e' />
 <element name='felem' type='t:f' />
</schema>
```

This schema states that the delem element must always be of type d and that no substitution is allowed. However, the eelem element may be of type e2e and the felem element may be of type f2r (provided that the xsi:type attribute is used to indicate the substitution). The block attribute in types e and f indicates that an `eelem` element cannot be of type `e2r` and an `felem` element cannot be of type `f2e`.

It is also legal to use the `block` attribute on an element declaration to restrict substitution independent of the `block` attribute of the referent type. Consider the following element declarations:

```
<schema xmlns='http://www.w3.org/1999/XMLSchema'
        targetNamespace='someURI' xmlns:tns='someURI'>
 <complexType name='d' />
 <complexType name='e' />
 <complexType name='f' />
 <complexType name='d2e' base=' t:d'
              derivedBy='extension' />
 <complexType name='d2r' base='t:d'
              derivedBy='restriction' />
 <complexType name='e2e' base='t:e'
              derivedBy='extension' />
 <complexType name='e2r' base='t:e'
              derivedBy='restriction' />
 <complexType name='f2e' base='t:f'
              derivedBy='extension' />
 <complexType name='f2r' base='t:f'
              derivedBy='restriction' />
 <element name='delem' type='t:d' block='#all' />
 <element name='eelem' type='t:e' block='restriction' />
 <element name='felem' type='t:f' block='extension' />
</schema>
```

This schema is effectively identical to the previous schema with respect to the `delem`, `eelem`, and `felem` elements. The difference in this case is that the types `d`, `e`, and `f` have no exactness restrictions when used in other contexts besides the three element declarations shown here.

Type-based substitution maps extremely well to a classic object-oriented view of inheritance. An element declaration acts as a variable declaration, and the type definition acts as a class definition. Consider the following simple schema:

```
<schema xmlns='http://www.w3.org/1999/XMLSchema'
        targetNamespace='someURI' xmlns:tns='someURI'>
  <complexType name='Person' abstract='1' />
```

```
<complexType name='Man' base='tns:Person'
                     derivedBy='extension' />
<complexType name='Woman' base='tns:Person'
                     derivedBy='extension' />
<complexType name='Marriage' >
  <element name='husband' type='tns:Person' />
  <element name='wife' type='tns:Person' />
</complexType>
<element name='wedding' type='tns:Marriage' />
</schema>
```

One could imagine a mapping to Java that looked like this.

```
abstract class Person {}
class Man extends Person {}
class Woman extends Person {}
class Marriage {
  Person husband;
  Person wife;
}
```

Because Java and XML Schemas support substitution in a similar fashion, the following would be a valid use of these Java classes:

```
Marriage wedding = new Marriage( );
wedding.husband = new Man( );
wedding.wife = new Woman( );
```

In general, type-based substitution is adequate for most new XML Schema-based designs. However, type-based substitution assumes that the element name will remain fixed. In more document-oriented schema, it is sometimes preferable to allow substitution based on elements instead of types. To support this type of substitution, XML Schemas supports element equivalence classes based on exemplars.

An element equivalence class is a set of global element declarations that declare their equivalence to a particular global element declaration that acts as the exemplar of the class. All element declarations in an equivalence class must bind to a type that is substitutable for the exemplar's type. Membership in an equivalence class is indicated using the `equivClass` attribute that must refer to the exemplar of the class. Consider the following schema fragment:

```
<schema xmlns='http://www.w3.org/1999/XMLSchema'
        targetNamespace='someURI' xmlns:tns='someURI'>
  <complexType name='Person' abstract='1' />
  <complexType name='Man' base='tns:Person'
                         derivedBy='extension' />
  <complexType name='Woman' base='tns:Person'
                         derivedBy='extension' />
<!-- spouse is the exemplar -->
  <element name='spouse' type='tns:Person' />
<!-- husband/wife are in the spouse equivalence class -->
  <element name='husband' type='Man'
           equivClass='tns:spouse' />
  <element name='wife' type='Woman'
           equivClass='tns:spouse' />
  <complexType name='Marriage'>
      <element ref='tns:spouse' />
      <element ref='tns:spouse' />
  </complexType>
  <element name='wedding' type='tns:Marriage' />
</schema>
```

This schema states that a `Marriage` consists of two elements that are in the equivalence class formed by the `spouse` element declaration. This means that the following is a schema-valid instance

```
<wedding><husband/><wife/></wedding>
```

as is this

```
<wedding><wife/><husband/></wedding>
```

and this

```
<wedding><wife/><wife/></wedding>
```

Note that the substitution is based on replacing the element name, not the type name. When substitution based on equivalence classes is used, the type of the substituted element is implicitly based on corresponding element declaration rather than explicitly specified via the `xsi:type` attribute.

The `abstract` attribute can be used to control substitution based on element equivalence classes. An exemplar element declaration can use the boolean `abstract` attribute to indicate that it can never appear in instance documents. Consider the previous schema fragment. Note that the `spouse` exemplar was not defined as abstract. However, the following is *not* a schema-valid instance

```
<wedding><spouse/><spouse/></wedding>
```

since the `Person` type is abstract. However, one could still use the `spouse` element by applying type-based substitution as shown in the following schema-valid instance:

```
<wedding>
  <spouse xsi:type='Man' />
  <spouse xsi:type='Woman' />
</wedding>
```

To prevent the `spouse` element from ever appearing and to force element substitution, the `spouse` exemplar itself should be declared as abstract as follows:

```
<element name='spouse' type='tns:Person' abstract='1' />
```

Had the `spouse` exemplar been declared this way, instances of type `Marriage` would always require element substitution for both sub-elements.

One can also use the `final` and `block` attributes to control element substitution. A global element declaration can use the `final` attribute to control membership in the equivalence class for which it acts as an exemplar for. If the `final` attribute value is `restriction`, then all elements in the equivalence class must be of types that derive from the exemplar's type by extension. If the `final` attribute value is `extension`, then all elements in the equivalence class must be of types that derive from the exemplar's type by restriction. If the final attribute value is #all, then no elements may elect this element as an exemplar.

An element reference inside a content model can use the block attribute to control element substitution based on equivalence classes. In addition to the restriction and extension values described earlier, one can also specify equivClass to prohibit element-based substitution as well as type-based substitution. Additionally, when an element reference is marked block='#all', no substitution of any kind is allowed.

As a convenience, the schema element can use the two attributes finalDefault and blockDefault, which apply to element declarations and type definitions that do not explicitly provide a final or block attributes. These defaults only apply to schema components that appear as descendant elements of the schema element, not to imported or included schema definitions.

One issue that has not been discussed so far is what is the implied base type when no base attribute is present? The XML Schemas specification describes an implicit type, ur-type, that is the implied base of all types that do not explicitly provide a base attribute. The implicit definition of type ur-type is as follows:

```
<complexType content='mixed' block=" final=" abstract='0'>
  <any />
  <anyAttribute />
</complexType>
```

The ur-type cannot be explicitly referenced from schema components, rather its use is implied by the absence of a base attribute on a complex type definition and by the absence of a type reference or definition on an element declaration. This means that the following element declaration

```
<element name='bob' />
```

is semantically identical to the following declaration

```
<element name='bob' type='ur-type' />
```

The difference is that the latter definition is illegal, since the type ur-type is never explicitly defined but rather is an implied type.

Reference and Uniqueness Constraints

The ID and IDREF datatypes from XML 1.0 provide a simple mechanism for uniquely identifying elements in a document and ensuring referential integrity for attributes (and elements if XML Schemas are in use) that refer to those elements. However, compared to the uniqueness and referential integrity constraints provided by most database technologies, ID and IDREF are extremely limited. The XML Schema specification outlines a mechanism for describing uniqueness and referential integrity constraints in terms of modified XPath expressions.

XML Schemas defines three constructs for specifying uniqueness and reference constraints. The unique construct is morally equivalent to a primary key constraint in a DBMS. The key and keyref constructs provide the moral equivalent to DBMS-style referential integrity. All three constructs consist of two or more XPath expressions: a selector followed by one or more fields. The selector describes a range of instance nodes over which the constraint applies. For example, the following selector describes all child elements named person that have a name attribute

```
<selector>person[@name]</selector>
```

and the following selector identifies person elements that are children of a child element named people

```
<selector>people/person</selector>
```

A selector can contain a list of |-delimited XPath expressions whose resultant node-sets are combined to describe the range over which the constraint applies. For example, the following selector describes all child elements named person or dog:

```
<selector>person|dog</selector>
```

Each field identifies a single instance node that is used as a constraint. The expression is interpreted as a relative XPath expression with respect to an element in the selector range. For example, the following refers to an attribute named ss-no

```
<field>@ss-no</field>
```

and the following refers to a child element named `address`

```
<field>address</field>
```

The `selector` and `field` elements shown here use a very minimal subset of XPath. The exact limitations on allowable XPath expressions were in flux at the time of this writing.

Uniqueness and reference constraints must appear at the end of an element declaration. The `selector` expressions are interpreted relative to the element currently being declared and can only constrain subelements relative to the element in which they are declared. The schema

```
<schema xmlns='http://www.w3.org/1999/XMLSchema'
        targetNamespace='someURI' xmlns:tns='someURI'>
  <element name='bag'>
    <unique>
      <selector>bag-item</selector>
      <field>@name</field>
    </unique>
  </element>
</schema>
```

applies only to the range of `bag-item` subelements from a particular instance of the `bag` element.

Uniqueness constraints are the easiest to understand, since they map naturally to both the `ID` datatype and DBMS-style primary keys. A uniqueness constraint indicates that the combination of one or more node values (each described by a `field` subelement) must be unique across a range of instances elements (described by the `selector` subelement). The following is the simplest possible uniqueness constraint:

```
<schema xmlns='http://www.w3.org/1999/XMLSchema'
        targetNamespace='someURI' xmlns:tns='someURI'>
  <complexType name='person_t' >
    <attribute name='ss-no' type='string' />
    <attribute name='name' type='string' />
    <attribute name='spouse' type='string' />
  </complexType>
```

```
<element name='person' type='tns:person_t' />
<element name='people' >
  <complexType>
    <element ref='person' maxOccurs='unbounded' />
  </complexType>
  <unique name='Person_PK' >
    <selector>person</selector>
    <field>@ss-no</field>
  </unique>
</element>
</schema>
```

This uniqueness constraint states that the ss-no attribute must contain unique
values across all instances of the person element that appear as [children]
of a particular people element. This means that the following instance is not
schema-valid

```
<people>
  <person ss-no='522-11-1111' name='Don' />
  <person ss-no='522-11-1111' name='Aaron' />
</people>
```

since two instances of the person element have identical ss-no attribute values.
     The keyref construct allows a referential integrity constraint to be
expressed in terms of either a unique or key constraint. The following schema
fragment ensures that the spouse attribute always refers to a valid person element by its ss-no attribute:

```
<schema xmlns='http://www.w3.org/1999/XMLSchema'
        targetNamespace='someURI' xmlns:tns='someURI'>
  <complexType name='person_t' >
    <attribute name='ss-no' type='string' />
    <attribute name='name' type='string' />
    <attribute name='spouse' type='string' />
  </complexType>
  <element name='person' type='tns:person_t' />
  <element name='people' >
    <complexType>
```

```
            <element ref='person' maxOccurs='unbounded' />
        </complexType>
        <unique name='Person_PK' >
          <selector>person</selector>
          <field>@ss-no</field>
        </unique>
        <keyref name='SpouseIsValid' refer='tns:Person_PK' >
          <selector>person</selector>
          <field>@spouse</field>
        </keyref>
      </element>
    </schema>
```

The `keyref` must refer to a valid `unique` or `key` element using the `refer` attribute. The constraint named by the `refer` attribute is called the *target* of the constraint. The `selector` of the `keyref` identifies an arbitrary range of instance nodes that is not necessarily the same range of nodes identified by the corresponding target range. Each `field` of the `keyref` is matched to the corresponding `field` in the target constraint. Each element in the range identified by the `keyref` must match an element is the target range field-for-field. Otherwise, the instance document is not schema-valid. Given the previous schema definition, this is a schema-valid instance

```
    <people xmlns='someURI' >
      <person ss-no='522-111-1111' name='Don'
              spouse='522-111-2222' />
      <person ss-no='522-111-2222' name='Barbara' />
    </people>
```

since the `spouse` attribute value appears as a `ss-no` attribute value in the target range of elements. However, this is not schema-valid

```
    <people xmlns='someURI' >
      <person ss-no='522-111-1111' name='Don'
              spouse='522-111-3333' />
      <person ss-no='522-111-2222' name='Barbara' />
    </people>
```

since the `spouse` attribute does not match an `ss-no` value anywhere in the scope of the referential integrity constraint.

The previous example used a `unique` constraint as the target for referential integrity. It is also possible to impose referential constraints based on nonunique values in the target range by using a `key` constraint in lieu of a `unique` constraint. Consider the following variation on the previous schema fragment:

```
<schema xmlns='http://www.w3.org/1999/XMLSchema'
        targetNamespace='someURI' xmlns:tns='someURI'>
  <element name='person'>
   </complexType>
    <attribute name='ss-no' type='string'/>
    <attribute name='name' type='string'/>
    <attribute name='spouse' type='string'/>
    </complexType>
  </element>
  <element name='people'>
    </complexType>
     <element ref='person' maxOccurs='unbounded'/>
    </complexType>
    <key name='Person_SS-NO'>
     <selector>person</selector>
      <field>@ss-no</field>
    </key>
    <keyref name='SpouseIsValid' refer='tns:Person_SS-NO' >
      <selector>person</selector>
      <field>@spouse</field>
     </unique>
  </element>
  </schema>
```

Because a key constraint is used, this schema has the same referential integrity constraints as the previous example; however, it has no uniqueness constraint on the ss-no attribute. This means that the following instance document

```
<people xmlns='someURI'>
  <person ss-no='522-111-1111' name='Don'
     spouse='522-111-2222'   />
  <person ss-no='522-1111-2222' name='Barbara'    />
```

```
   <person ss-no='522-1111-2222' name='Joan'    />
   <person ss-no='522-1111-2222' name='Sherry'   />
</people>
```

is now schema-valid, as duplicate ss-no attribute values are no longer prohibited.

It is possible to enforce uniqueness and referential constraints based on more than one node value simply by listing multiple fields per constraint. The following schema fragment allows duplicate ss-no attribute values provided that no two person elements share a combination of identical ss-no and name attribute values.

```
<schema xmlns='http://www.w3.org/1999/XMLSchema'
        targetNamespace='someURI' xmlns:tns='someURI'>
  <element name='person' >
    <complexType>
      <attribute name='ss-no' type='string' />
      <attribute name='name' type='string' />
      <attribute name='spouse' type='string' />
    </complexType>
  </element>
  <element name='people' >
    <complexType>
      <element ref='person' maxOccurs='unbounded' />
    </complexType>
    <unique name='Person_PK' >
      <selector>person</selector>
      <field>@ss-no</field>
      <field>@name</field>
    </unique>
  </element>
</schema>
```

This schema allows the following instance

```
<people xmlns='someURI' >
  <person ss-no='522-11-1111' name='Don' />
  <person ss-no='522-11-1111' name='Aaron' />
</people>
```

but not the following instance

```
<people xmlns='someURI' >
  <person ss-no='522-11-1111' name='Don' />
  <person ss-no='522-11-1111' name='Don' />
</people>
```

since the combination of the two constrained field values is not unique. When a
`keyref` targets a multifield constraint, the `keyref` must have the same number
of fields. Consider the following schema fragment:

```
<schema xmlns='http://www.w3.org/1999/XMLSchema'
        targetNamespace='someURI' xmlns:tns='someURI'>
  <element name='person' >
    <complexType>
      <element name='dear' type='string' minOccurs='0'/>
      <attribute name='ss-no' type='string' />
      <attribute name='name' type='string' />
      <attribute name='spouse' type='string' />
    </complexType>
  </element>
  <element name='people' >
    <complexType>
      <element ref='person' maxOccurs='unbounded' />
    </complexType>
    <unique name='Person_PK' >
      <selector>person</selector>
      <field>@ss-no</field>
      <field>@name</field>
    </unique>
    <keyref name='SpouseIsValid' refer='tns:Person_PK' >
      <selector>person</selector>
      <field>@spouse</field>
      <field>dear</field>
    </keyref>
  </element>
</schema>
```

This schema would allow the following instance

```
<people xmlns='someURI' >
  <person ss-no='522-11-1111' name='Don'
          spouse='522-11-2222' >
    <dear>Barbara</dear>
  </person>
  <person ss-no='522-11-2222' name='Barbara' />
</people>
```

but not this instance:

```
<people xmlns='someURI' >
  <person ss-no='522-11-1111' name='Don'
          spouse='522-11-2222' >
    <dear>Babs</dear>
  </person>
  <person ss-no='522-11-2222' name='Barbara' />
</people>
```

since there is no `person` element whose `ss-no` attribute is `'522-11-2222'`
and whose `name` attribute is `'Babs'`.

Where Are We?

This chapter has described the XML Schema definition language. XML Schemas
are a type-centric XML-based description language for describing XML documents. XML Schemas are likely to supplant DTDs as the dominant mechanism
for validating instance documents and documenting XML vocabularies. An XML
Schema definition is fundamentally a collection of type definitions and element
(and attribute) declarations that belong to a particular XML namespace. XML
Schemas are highly adaptable to domains beyond XML such as database and
object technologies.

Chapter 5

Transforms

```
<customer name='Bob'>
  <?age 31 ?>
  <address street='main'>
    <number value='123'/>
    <city name='Anytown'>
      <state>CA</state>
      <country value=US'/>
    </city>
    <zip><five>90277</five><four subcode='3255'/></zip>
  </address>
</customer>
```

Anonymous, 1999

The previous chapter presented the XML Schema definition language as a way to describe the type and structure of XML documents. XML Schemas provide the basic infrastructure for building interoperable systems based on XML, as there is now a common language for describing XML that is based on proven software engineering principles. That stated, the expressiveness of XML Schemas makes it is possible (if not likely) that multiple organizations modeling the same set of domain-specific abstractions will come up with different schema documents. Yes, this problem could be solved via industry consortia defining canonical schema for each domain, but until that happens, dealing with multiple schema definitions of the same basic information is a fact of life. Enter XSLT.

The *XSL Transformations (XSLT)* specification defines an XML-based language for expressing transformation rules from one class of XML document to another. The XSLT language can be thought of as a programming language, and indeed, there are at least two XSLT execution engines currently available that can directly execute an XSLT document as a program. That stated, XSLT documents are useful as a general-purpose language for expressing transformations from one schema type to another. In fact, one could imagine using an XSLT document as but one form of input to an arbitrary XML translation engine.

XSLT excels at mapping one XML-based representation onto another. Consider the following XML document:

```
<?xml version="1.0"?>
<product title="Essential XML" xmlns="http://awl.com">
  <writer name='Don Box' />
  <writer name='Aaron Skonnard'/>
  <writer name='John Lam'/>
</product>
```

Note that the element names belong to a namespace (and schema) defined by Addison-Wesley (the publisher of this book). Now consider this second representation of the same information:

```
<?xml version="1.0"?>
<content xmlns="http://www.develop.com/Schemas/book">
  <name>Essential XML</name>
  <contributors>
    <staff principal="true">Don Box</staff>
    <staff>Aaron Skonnard</staff>
    <staff>John Lam</staff>
  </contributors>
</content>
```

This time the element names belong to a namespace (and schema) defined by DevelopMentor (the home of the authors).

These two documents appear to contain roughly the same information. However, appearances can often be deceiving. Without human intervention, it is impossible to algorithmically determine whether there is any correlation whatsoever between the two underlying schema, even in the presence of similar or identical local element and attribute names. That stated, once a human capable of understanding the semantics of the two schema has determined that there is in fact some relationship, it would be useful to have a language for describing the transformations necessary to convert instances of one schema into instances of the other.

One way to describe these transformations is to simply write code in a traditional programming language. The following is an example of a DOM-based Java program that translates the first document into the second:

```java
import org.w3c.dom.*;
Document transform(Document source) throws Exception {
    String tns = "http://www.develop.com/Schemas/book";
    DOMImplementation dom = source.getImplementation();
    Document target = dom.createDocument(tns, "content",
                                         null);
    Element sourceRoot = source.getDocumentElement();
    String title = sourceRoot.getAttribute("title");
    Element e1 = target.createElementNS(tns, "name");
    e1.appendChild(target.createTextNode(title));
    target.getDocumentElement().appendChild(e1);
    e1 = target.createElementNS(tns,"contributors");
    boolean bFirst = false;
    for (Node author = sourceRoot.getFirstChild();
         author != null; author = author.getNextSibling()) {
      if (author.getNodeType() != Node.ELEMENT_NODE)
        continue;
      String name = ((Element)author).getAttribute("name");
      Element e2 = target.createElementNS(tns, "staff");
      e2.appendChild(target.createTextNode(name));
      if (!bFirst)
        e2.setAttributeNS("", "principal", "true");
      e1.appendChild(e2);
      bFirst = true;
    }
    target.getDocumentElement().appendChild(e1);
    return target;
}
```

While this program is functional, it is only readable by virtual machines and, assuming the source code is provided, humans that can read Java code. Moreover, this program is very brittle and would require a significant amount of modification to track the independent evolution of both the source and target schema.

In contrast, consider the following XSLT document that accomplishes the same task as the previous Java program:

```
<?xml version="1.0"?>
<content xmlns="http://www.develop.com/Schemas/book"
      xmlns:xsl="http://www.w3.org/1999/XSL/Transform"
      xsl:exclude-result-prefixes='src'
      xsl:version='1.0'
      xmlns:src="http://awl.com"
>
  <name><xsl:value-of select="/src:product/@title"/></name>
  <contributors>
    <xsl:for-each select='/src:product/src:writer'>
      <xsl:if test='position() = 1' >
        <staff principal='true'
        ><xsl:value-of select="@name"/></staff>
      </xsl:if>
      <xsl:if test='position() > 1'>
        <staff><xsl:value-of select="@name"/></staff>
      </xsl:if>
    </xsl:for-each>
  </contributors>
</content>
```

This XML document reflects both the source and target schemas and can be fed to an XSLT processor to translate instances of the source schema into instances of the target schema. As shown here, schema transformations are described by implementing an exemplar of the target schema in terms of its deltas from the source. More importantly, this document can be read using a standard XML parser and can act as input to a wide variety of processing software, not just XSLT transformation engines.

This example illustrates that simply using XML does not ensure interoperation. Yes, the world now agrees on where the angle brackets go. But being able to interpret anything beyond that is a much tougher problem to solve. XML Schemas give us the tool for representing type definitions, but in the absence of a common schema, human intervention is still needed to bridge between organizational boundaries. XSLT provides an XML-centric way to build that bridge.

XSLT Basics

XSLT is an XML-based language that describes transformations from XML documents into arbitrary text-based formats (which may or may not be XML). As shown in Figure 5.1, XSLT assumes that three documents are in use: the source document, the XSLT stylesheet document, and the result document. The source document is simply a well-formed XML document that provides the input for the transformation. The stylesheet document is an XML document that uses the XSLT vocabulary for expressing transformation rules. The result document is a text document that is produced by running the source document through the transformations found in the XSLT stylesheet.

The XSLT stylesheet is an XML document that contains one or more *XSLT templates*. A template is a collection of *literal result elements* and *XSLT instructions.* Literal result elements are elements that are copied more or less verbatim into the result document. XSLT instructions are well-known elements that alter the processing of the template. Table 5.1 contains the complete list of XSLT instructions. XSLT instructions (and other constructs) are always qualified by the XSLT namespace URI (`http://www.w3.org/1999/XSL/Transform`), which is typically mapped to the namespace prefix `xsl`.

An XSLT stylesheet can be written as either a single-template literal result element or as an explicit stylesheet. The former is simply an exemplar of the target schema that has been adorned with namespace-qualified XSLT instructions. The latter is an XSLT-specific document format whose root element is `xsl:stylesheet` and is described in the next section. Literal result element-based stylesheets support a simple subset of the more flexible and expressive `xsl:stylesheet` vocabulary. The following is the simplest possible XSLT stylesheet written as a literal result element:

```
<?xml version='1.0' ?>
<doc>Hello, World</doc>
```

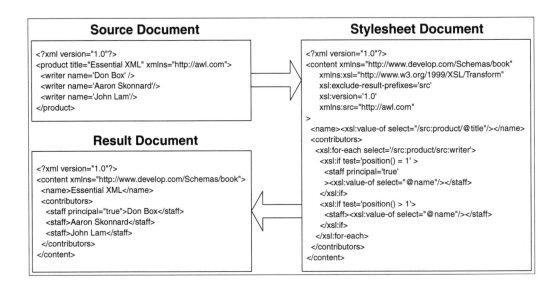

Figure 5.1   XSLT architecture

This stylesheet produces the same result document independent of the source document. Like the classic program from Kernighan and Richie, this version is extremely useless and produces the same output no matter what input is fed into it.

The easiest way to include content from the source document is via the `xsl:copy-of` instruction. The `xsl:copy-of` instruction works similarly to XInclude's `include` element; the primary difference is that `xsl:copy-of` is integrated into the context model of XSLT. Consider the following XSLT literal result element:

```
<?xml version='1.0' ?>
<doc xmlns:xsl='http://www.w3.org/1999/XSL/Transform'
     xsl:version='1.0'
><xsl:copy-of select='/book/author'/></doc>
```

Table 5.1: XSLT Instructions

Instruction	Syntax	Description
xsl:copy-of	`<xsl:copy-of` `select = expression />`	Emits the node-set corresponding to the select expression.

xsl:value-of	`<xsl:value-of`
	`select = string-expression`
	`disable-output-escaping = "yes" | "no" />`
		Emits the string corresponding to the select expression.

xsl:if	`<xsl:if`
	`test = boolean-expression>`
	`<!-- Content: template -->`
	`</xsl:if>`
		Evaluates the *template* if and only if the test expression evaluates to true.

xsl:choose	`<xsl:choose>`
	`<!-- Content: (xsl:when+, xsl:otherwise?)`
	`-->`
	`</xsl:choose>`
		Evaluates the template from the first xsl:when clause whose test expression evaluates to true. If none of the test expressions evaluate to true, then the *template* contained in the xsl:otherwise clause is evaluated.

xsl:for-each	`<xsl:for-each`
	`select = node-set-expression>`
	`<!-- Content: (xsl:sort*, template) -->`
	`</xsl:for-each>`
		Evaluates the *template* against each node in node-set returned by the select expression. The order of evaluation can be influenced using one or more xsl:sorts.

(Continued)

Table 5.1: XSLT Instructions (continued)

Instruction	Syntax	Description

xsl:call-template	`<xsl:call-template`
	`name`` = qname>`
	`<!-- Content: xsl:with-param* -->`
	`</xsl:call-template>`
		Invokes the template rule named by name.

xsl:variable	`<xsl:variable`
	`name`` = qname`
	`select = expression>`
	`<!-- Content: template -->`
	`</xsl:variable>`
		Declares a variable named name and initializes it using either the select expression or *template*.

xsl:text	`<xsl:text` `disable-output-escaping = "yes"	"no">` `<!-- Content: #PCDATA -->` `</xsl:text>`	Emits the text found in #PCDATA. Escaping of the five built-in entities is controlled using disable-output-escaping.
xsl:number	`<xsl:number` `level = "single"	"multiple"	"any"` `count = pattern` `from = pattern` `value = number-expression` `format = { string }` `lang = { nmtoken }` `letter-value = { "alphabetic"	"traditional" }` `grouping-separator = { char }` `grouping-size = { number } />`	Emits a number based on the XPath number expression found in value.

Instruction	Syntax	Description

xsl:copy	`<xsl:copy`
	`   use-attribute-sets = qnames>`
	`   <!-- Content: template  -->`
	`</xsl:copy>`
		Copies the current context node (and associated namespace nodes) to the result tree fragment.

xsl:apply-templates	`<xsl:apply-templates`
	`   select = node-set-expression`
	`   mode + qname>`
	`   <!-- Content: (xsl:sort | xsl:with-`
	`   param) * -->`
	`</xsl:apply-templates>`
		Invokes the best-match template rules against the node-set returned by the select expression.

xsl:apply-imports	`<xsl:apply-imports />`	Promote the current stylesheet in import precedence.
xsl:message	`<xsl:message` ` terminate = "yes"	"no">` ` <!-- Content: template -->` `</xsl:message>`	Emit a message in a processor-dependent manner.

xsl:fallback	`<xsl:fallback>`
	`   <!-- Content: template  -->`
	`</xsl:fallback>`
		Evaluate template when the parent instruction/directive is not supported by the current processor.

xsl:comment	`<xsl:comment>`
	`   <!-- Content:  template  -->`
	`</xsl:comment>`
		Emit an XML comment containing the template as its character data.

(Continued)

Table 5.1:   XSLT Instructions (*continued*)

Instruction	Syntax	Description
xsl:processing-instruction	```<xsl:processing-instruction
name = { ncname } >
<!-- Content: template -->
</xsl:processing-instruction>```	Emit an XML processing instruction whose [target] is name and whose [children] are based on *template*.
xsl:element	```<xsl:element
name = { qname }
namespace = { uri-reference }
use-attribute-sets = qnames>
<!-- Content: template -->
</xsl:element>```	Emit an XML element whose [local name] is name, and whose [namespace URI] is namespace, and whose [children] are based on *template*.
xsl:attribute	```<xsl:attribute
name = { qname }
namespace = { uri-reference }
<!-- Content: template -->
</xsl:attribute>```	Emit an XML attribute whose [local name] is name, and whose [name space URI] is namespace, and whose [children] are based on *template*.

The rules of XSLT indicate that the `xsl:copy-of` element will be replaced by the `node-set` produced by the `select` XPath expression. Assuming that the following source document

```
<?xml version="1.0"?>
<book title="Essential XML" >
   <author name='Don'   age='25' canadian='false'/>
   <author name='Aaron' age='19' canadian='false'/>
   <author name='John'  age='20' canadian='true'/>
</book>
```

is fed as input, the result document would look like this.

```
<?xml version='1.0' ?>
<doc>
   <author name='Don'   age='25' canadian='false/>
   <author name='Aaron' age='19' canadian='false'/>
   <author name='John'  age='20' canadian='true'/>
</doc>
```

The `xsl:copy-of` instruction is ideal for copying `node-set`s, but it is somewhat cumbersome for copying text from the source document. For this, XSLT provides two mechanisms: one for including source text as attribute [children], the other for including source text as element [children].

All attributes of literal result elements are interpreted as *attribute value templates.* Attribute value templates are simply strings that contain embedded XPath expressions that are evaluated to produce result text. XSLT treats the { and } characters specially when they appear as attribute [children]. When the { character is encountered, the subsequent characters (up to the closing }) are interpreted as a `string-value` XPath expression. For example, had the following attribute appeared in the literal result element

```
bookname='The book is {/book/@title} '
```

the corresponding attribute in the result document would look like this

```
bookname='The book is Essential XML'
```

To escape the { and } characters in attribute [children], one must use a redundant { or } to signal that no attribute value template is present. For example, the following attribute from a literal result element

```
curlies='{{}} '
```

would expand to this

```
curlies='{}'
```

in the result document. Attribute value templates are also allowed on a small subset of XSLT instructions.[1]

The { and } only receive special treatment when they appear as attribute [children]. To include source text as element [children], one must use the xsl:value-of instruction. The xsl:value-of instruction is similar to xsl:copy-of, the primary difference being that xsl:value-of's select expression is converted to a string prior to replacement. Consider the following literal result element:

```
<?xml version='1.0' ?>
<doc xmlns:xsl='http://www.w3.org/1999/XSL/Transform'
    xsl:version='1.0'
><xsl:value-of select='/book'/></doc>
```

This XSLT stylesheet indicates that the content of the doc element should consist of the text found by running the XPath expression /book against the source document. Since the select expression is a node-set, it is implicitly converted to a string prior to insertion using the XPath conversion rules described in Chapter 3. The following is the result document that corresponds to this XSLT stylesheet:

```
<?xml version='1.0' ?>
<doc/>
```

---

[1]One can tell immediately whether a given XSLT instruction attribute accepts attribute value templates by the presence of the surrounding { } in the syntax guide for that instruction and attribute in the XSLT specification or Table 5.1.

Note that because the source document contained no character data as element [children], the `select` expression (/book) yielded the empty string. Had the `select` expression been /book/author/@name, the result document would have looked like this

```
<?xml version='1.0' ?>
<doc>Don</doc>
```

since the `node-set` to string conversion rules state that the first node is converted to a `string-value`.

`xsl:copy-of` and friends are simple mechanisms for importing content from the source document. XSLT also provides a set of conditional evaluation instructions that should be familiar to developers coming from the procedural programming language world. The `xsl:if` instruction is equivalent to the `if` statement in C++ and Java. The `xsl:choose`, `xsl:when`, and `xsl:otherwise` instructions are the equivalent to C++ and Java's `switch`, `case`, and `default`, respectively. The simplest of these is, of course, the `xsl:if` instruction.

An element representing an `xsl:if` instruction must have a `test` attribute that contains a boolean XPath expression. If this expression evaluates to true, then the [children] of the `xsl:if` element (which is itself an XSLT template) will be processed. If the expression evaluates to false, then the [children] of the `xsl:if` element are ignored. Consider the following XSLT literal result element:

```
<?xml version='1.0' ?>
<doc xmlns:xsl='http://www.w3.org/1999/XSL/Transform'
     xsl:version='1.0'>
  <xsl:if test='count(//author) &gt; 4'>
    <cacophony/>
  </xsl:if>
</doc>
```

This XSLT stylesheet uses the `xsl:if` instruction to test the number of `author` elements. If the source document has more than four `author` elements, the result document will look like this.

```
<?xml version='1.0' ?>
<doc><cacophony/></doc>
```

If the source document has four or fewer `author` elements, the result document will look like this.

```
<?xml version='1.0' ?>
<doc/>
```

Note that the XPath expression used in the `test` attribute is a boolean expression similar to that found in an XPath predicate rather than a full-blown XPath location path.

The `xsl:choose` instruction provides the functionality of a Java or C++ `switch` statement. The `xsl:choose` instruction has one or more `xsl:when` clauses and an optional `xsl:otherwise` clause. The `xsl:when` and `xsl:otherwise` elements are represented as `[children]` of a containing `xsl:choose` element. Each `xsl:when` element can have a `test` attribute that contains a boolean XPath expression. Unlike a Java or C++ switch, multiple `xsl:when` clauses may have tests that evaluate to true. To resolve this potential nondeterminism, XSLT only allows the first `xsl:when` clause whose test is successful to be processed. Consider the following XSLT literal result element:

```
<?xml version='1.0' ?>
<doc xmlns:xsl='http://www.w3.org/1999/XSL/Transform'
     xsl:version='1.0'>
  <xsl:choose>
    <xsl:when test='count(//author) = 1'>
      <soloist/>
    </xsl:when>
    <xsl:when test='count(//author) &lt; 5'>
      <ensemble/>
    </xsl:when>
    <xsl:otherwise>
      <cacophony/>
    </xsl:otherwise>
  </xsl:choose>
</doc>
```

If the source document has exactly one `author` element, the result document will look like this.

```
<?xml version='1.0' ?>
<doc><soloist/></doc>
```

If instead the source document has between two and four `author` elements (or
no `author` elements at all), the result document will look like this.

```
<?xml version='1.0' ?>
<doc><ensemble/></doc>
```

Under any other circumstances, the result document will look like this.

```
<?xml version='1.0' ?>
<doc><cacophony/></doc>
```

Note that the `xsl:otherwise` has no `test` clause and fills the role of the
`default` clause from a Java or C++ `switch` statement. Also note that the
order of `xsl:when` clauses is important. Had the two `xsl:when` clauses
appeared in reverse order, the `<soloist/>` element would never be emitted, as
the expression

```
count(//author) = 1
```

would be masked by the expression ahead of it

```
count(//author) < 5
```

since 1 is less than 5.

In addition to conditional instructions, XSLT also provides instructions for rep-
etition and looping. The most basic of these instructions is `xsl:for-each`. The
`xsl:for-each` relies on an XPath expression to produce a `node-set` that controls the iteration of the loop. When an `xsl:for-each` element is encountered,
the XPath expression found in its `select` attribute is evaluated. Each node from
the resultant `node-set` is then fed into the `[children]` of the `xsl:for-each`
element for further processing. Consider the following XSLT literal result element:

```
<?xml version='1.0' ?>
<doc xmlns:xsl='http://www.w3.org/1999/XSL/Transform'
```

```
          xsl:version='1.0'
      >
        <xsl:for-each select='/book/author'>
          <by/>
        </xsl:for-each>
      </doc>
```

Assuming the source document used throughout this chapter, the following result document will be produced:

```
<?xml version='1.0' ?>
<doc><by/><by/></doc>
```

This `xsl:for-each` example is not all that interesting, as its content does not rely on the selected node from the node set. Accessing content from within an `xsl:for-each` instruction requires a bit more explanation.

XPath expressions that appear in XSLT stylesheets are evaluated relative to a context. This context consists of at least an XPath `node` and `node-set`. For absolute location paths, this context is largely immaterial. For relative location paths, however, this context means everything. For example, this XSLT instruction

```
<xsl:value-of select='position()' />
```

requires some notion of which `node` we are talking about and what `node-set` it belongs to. For the examples shown prior to the `xsl:for-each` instruction, the context `node` is the root node of the source document, and the context `node-set` is the set that contains only the root node. That stated, certain XSLT constructs can change the context used to evaluate XPath expressions. The `xsl:for-each` instruction is one such construct.

The `xsl:for-each` instruction alters the context of all XPath expressions found in its [children]. The context `node-set` is the `node-set` returned from the `select` expression. The context `node` changes for each iteration of the loop. For the *ith* iteration of the loop, the context `node` is the *ith* node of the context `node-set`. For example, consider the following XSLT literal result element:

```
<?xml version='1.0' ?>
<doc xmlns:xsl='http://www.w3.org/1999/XSL/Transform'
```

```
      xsl:version='1.0'
  >
    <xsl:for-each select='/book/author'>
      <by id='{position()} '>
        <xsl:value-of select='@name' />
      </by>
    </xsl:for-each>
  </doc>
```

The two XPath expressions that appear inside of the xsl:for-each instruction
(position() and @name) will be evaluated against the current node from the
node-set produced by the select expression. Given this XSLT stylesheet
and the source document shown previously, the result document would look
like this.

```
<?xml version='1.0' ?>
<doc><by id='1'>Don</by><by id='2'>Aaron</by><by id='3'
>John</by></doc>
```

Note that in this case the node-set produced by the xsl:for-each's
select expression contained each of the author elements from the source
document.

By default, the xsl:for-each instruction iterates over its node-set in
document order. This behavior can be changed using the xsl:sort instruction.
The xsl:sort elements must appear as the initial [children] of an
xsl:for-each element and must adhere to the following production:

```
<xsl:sort
  select = string-expression
  lang = { nmtoken }
  data-type = { "text" | "number" | qname-but-not-ncname }
  order = { "ascending" | "descending" }
  case-order = { "upper-first" | "lower-first" }  />
```

The most important attribute is the select attribute, which specifies an
XPath expression that is used as the sort key for the node-set. In the absence
of a select attribute, the XSLT processor assumes "." as the select

expression. To see `xsl:sort` in action, consider the following XSLT literal result element:

```
<?xml version='1.0' ?>
<doc xmlns:xsl='http://www.w3.org/1999/XSL/Transform'
     xsl:version='1.0'
>
  <xsl:for-each select='/book/author'>
    <xsl:sort select='@name' />
    <by><xsl:value-of select='@name' /></by>
  </xsl:for-each>
</doc>
```

When the source document used throughout this section is fed through this XSLT stylesheet, the following result document would be produced:

```
<?xml version='1.0' ?>
<doc><by>Aaron</by><by>Don</by><by>John</by></doc>
```

Note that the processing of the `node-set` produced by the XPath expression `/book/author` was processed in sorted order based on the `name` attribute. Had the following `xsl:sort` instruction been used instead

```
<xsl:sort select='@age' order='descending'
          data-type='number' />
```

the `node-set` would have been processed in descending order based on the `age` attribute, resulting in this document

```
<?xml version='1.0' ?>
<doc><by>Don</by><by>John</by><by>Aaron</by></doc>
```

The `data-type` attribute controls how the ordering of the value space is to be interpreted. There are two built-in constants (`text` and `number`), whose meaning is obvious. Additionally, the `QName` referring to an XML Schema datatype is supported in XSLT, but at the time of this writing no processors supported sorting based on schema types.

ESSENTIAL XML: BEYOND MARKUP

The `xsl:sort` instruction can also be used to specify more than one sort key for a `node-set`. The first `xsl:sort` instruction encountered within the content of an `xsl:for-each` instruction is considered the primary sort key. Subsequent `xsl:sort` instructions are interpreted as secondary sort keys. For example, consider the following XSLT literal result element:

```
<?xml version='1.0' ?>
<doc xmlns:xsl='http://www.w3.org/1999/XSL/Transform'
    xsl:version='1.0'
>
  <xsl:for-each select='/book/author'>
    <xsl:sort select='@canadian' order='descending'/>
    <xsl:sort select='@name' />
    <by><xsl:value-of select='@name' /></by>
  </xsl:for-each>
</doc>
```

Due to the multiply-sorted `xsl:for-each` instruction, this XSLT document would yield the following result:

```
<?xml version='1.0' ?>
<doc><by>John</by><by>Aaron</by><by>Don</by></doc>
```

Because the `canadian` attribute is used by the first `xsl:sort` instruction, it dominates the sort order.

Template-based Programming

The discussion so far has used a literal result element as the stylesheet. This is effective for simple transformations, but due to its linear structure, it is impossible to modularize into smaller chunks of reusable XSLT. For that reason, most nontrivial XSLT stylesheets don't use literal result elements as stylesheets in favor of the explicit `xsl:stylesheet` format.

An `xsl:stylesheet` is primarily a collection of one or more template rules. Template rules play the role of functions in XSLT and always appear as top-level [children] of the `xsl:stylesheet` element. A template rule binds a QName and/or pattern to a template. As stated early in this chapter, template is a collection of literal result elements and XSLT instructions. The QName is simply a symbolic name that is associated with a template. The following is a named XSLT template rule:

```
<xsl:template name='emitSignature' >
  <sig><xsl:value-of select='/book/@title'/></sig>
</xsl:template>
```

This template rule can be "called" from other templates using the xsl:call-template instruction.

```
<xsl:template name='enchilada' >
  <doc>
    <xsl:call-template name='emitSignature' />
  </doc>
</xsl:template>
```

Assuming the source document from the previous section, the enchilada template rule would yield the following result:

```
<>doc><sig>Essential XML</sig></doc>
```

Of course, to invoke the enchilada template rule, one would simply use an xsl:call-template instruction somewhere else in the stylesheet.

Like functions, template rules can be invoked with parameters. To support parameters, the template rule's [children] may begin with one or more xsl:param instructions that declare a named parameter and set its default value. All template parameters are added to the context of the template and are available to XPath expressions by prefixing the parameter name with a $ (e.g., $arg1). The syntax for the xsl:param instruction is defined as follows:

```
<xsl:param
  name = qname
  select = expression>
  <!-- Content: template -->
</xsl:param>
```

A parameter declaration can use either an XPath expression or a template as its [children] to set the default value of the parameter.

ESSENTIAL XML: BEYOND MARKUP

The following named template rule declares and uses two template parameters:

```
<xsl:template name='emitTop' >
  <xsl:param name='arg1' select='/book/author[2]/@name' />
  <xsl:param name='arg2' >true</xsl:param>
  <top>
    <xsl:if test='$arg2' >
      <sometimes/>
    </xsl:if>
    <one><xsl:value-of select='$arg1' /></one>
  </top>
</xsl:template>
```

If this template rule were to be invoked with no parameters, the default values would be derived based on either the `select` attribute or `[children]` of each `xsl:param` instruction. Given the source document used throughout this chapter, that would yield the following result tree fragment:

```
<top>
  <sometimes/>
  <one>Aaron</one>
</top>
```

To invoke a template rule using parameters, one simply provides one or more `xsl:with-param` instructions as `[children]` to the `xsl:call-template` instruction.

```
<xsl:call-template name='emitTop' >
  <xsl:with-param name='arg1' >Hello</xsl:with-param>
  <xsl:with-param name='arg2' select='false()' />
</xsl:call-template>
```

Other than the element name, the syntax of the `xsl:with-param` instruction is identical to that of the `xsl:param` instruction. Given this invocation of `emitTop`, the following result tree fragment would be produced:

```
<top>
  <one>Hello</one>
</top>
```

Note that because `arg2` evaluated to the boolean value `false`, the `[children]` of the `xsl:if` instruction are never evaluated.

The `xsl:param` element typically appears as `[children]` of a template rule. XSLT also allows the stylesheet itself to accept parameters. These stylesheet-level parameter declarations must appear as `[children]` of the `xsl:stylesheet` element. Exactly how an XSLT processor initializes the values of these parameters is processor specific. Appendix C shows how at least one XSLT processor deals with stylesheet-level parameters.

In addition to named parameters, XSLT also supports named variables via the `xsl:variable` instruction. The syntax of the `xsl:variable` instruction is identical to that of `xsl:param` except for the element name. The difference between `xsl:param` and `xsl:variable` is that parameters, unlike variables, can have their initial values overridden at template invocation time using `xsl:with-param`. Additionally, `xsl:param` instructions must appear at the top of the template in which they appear; `xsl:variable` instructions can appear anywhere an instruction is allowed. In either case, a given variable or parameter name can only be defined once per template. Variables and parameters defined as `[children]` of an `xsl:stylesheet` element are global in scope and are visible across all templates. However, a template can hide the global definition by defining a variable or parameter with the same name. That means that the following is a legal XSLT stylesheet

```
<xsl:stylesheet version='1.0'
   xmlns:xsl='http://www.w3.org/1999/XSL/Transform'>
  <xsl:param name='bob' select='2' />
  <xsl:template name='steve'>
    <xsl:variable name='bob' select='4'/>
  </xsl:template>
</xsl:stylesheet>
```

but the following is not

```
<xsl:stylesheet version='1.0'
   xmlns:xsl='http://www.w3.org/1999/XSL/Transform'>
  <xsl:template name='steve'>
    <xsl:param name='bob' select='2' />
```

```
    <xsl:variable name='bob' select='4'/>
  </xsl:template>
</xsl:stylesheet>
```

since the name `bob` is multiply defined in the same template.

It is important to note that there is no way to modify the value of a variable or parameter once it has been defined. This is because XSLT is a functional programming language, not an imperative language like C++ or Java. Unlike C++ or Java functions, XSLT templates cannot have side effects. Rather, they can only produce results that act as output of the overall stylesheet or as input to other templates. Part of the reason for this is to simplify the processing model of XSLT. Another reason is to support the parallel or out-of-order execution of template rules, as the execution of one rule is guaranteed not to interfere with the execution of another.

Namespaces and XSLT

The example source and stylesheet documents used throughout this chapter have made no use of namespaces other than the required affiliation of XSLT instructions and constructs with the XSLT namespace. This was intentional in order to make the literal result elements and XPath expressions more compact and readable. In general, this is unrealistic, as most interesting XML documents rely on namespaces quite heavily.

Recall that nonprefixed QNames that appear in XPath expression are assumed to be unaffiliated with respect to namespaces. This is true irrespective of any default namespace declaration that may be in effect. Prefixed QNames that appear in XPath expressions are always expanded prior to being used in a Node-Test or other QName-aware construct. Whenever an XPath expression appears as an attribute value of an XSLT element, XSLT adds the declarations found in the [in-scope namespace declarations] property (without any default namespace declaration that may be in-scope) to the XPath evaluation context.

When processing a literal result element, all namespace declarations that map to http://www.w3.org/1999/XSL/Transform are stripped out of the result.[2]

---

[2]In the same vein, all XSLT-specific attributes that are used when a literal result element acts as a stylesheet (e.g., xsl:version) disappear during the translation as well.

However, all other namespace declarations that appear in literal result elements are considered significant and will appear in the result document. This behavior can be suppressed using the `xsl:exclude-result-prefixes` attribute. This attribute can appear at the root element of the stylesheet document and contains a space-delimited list of namespace prefixes. Namespace declarations whose prefix appears in this list will *not* appear in the result document. For example, consider the following XSLT literal result element that makes use of namespaces:

```
<?xml version='1.0' ?>
<dm:out xmlns='http://example.com'
        xmlns:xsl='http://www.w3.org/1999/XSL/Transform'
        xmlns:dm=' http://www.develop.com/Schemas/doc'
        xmlns:awl='http://awl.com'
        xsl:version='1.0'
><xsl:value-of select='/awl:product/@title'/></dm:out>
```

As it sits, this stylesheet would produce the following output when evaluated against the first document of this chapter:

```
<?xml version='1.0' ?>
<dm:out xmlns='http://example.com'
        xmlns:dm='http://www.develop.com/Schemas/doc'
        xmlns:awl='http://awl.com'
>Essential XML</dm:out>
```

Because the `awl` namespace declaration existed only as context for the XPath expression in the template, it is superfluous in the result document. To suppress this unnecessary namespace declaration, one could have written the literal result element as follows:

```
<?xml version='1.0' ?>
<dm:out xmlns='http://example.com'
        xmlns:xsl='http://www.w3.org/1999/XSL/Transform'
        xmlns:dm=' http://www.develop.com/Schemas/doc'
        xmlns:awl='http://awl.com'
        xsl:exclude-result-prefixes='awl'
        xsl:version='1.0'
><xsl:value-of select='/awl:book/@title'/></dm:out>
```

This stylesheet would have yielded a result document with no `awl` namespace declaration:

```
<?xml version='1.0' ?>
<dm:out xmlns='http://example.com
        xmlns:dm='http://www.develop.com/Schemas/doc'
>Essential XML</dm:out>
```

To exclude the default namespace declaration as well, one can include the pseudo-prefix `#default` in the list of excluded prefixes. Had the `exclude-result-prefixes` attribute from the previous example looked like this

```
xsl:exclude-result-prefixes='awl #default'
```

the result document would have looked like this

```
<?xml version='1.0' ?>
<dm:out xmlns:dm='http://www.develop.com/Schemas/doc'
>Essential XML</dm:out>
```

Note that when an explicit `xsl:stylesheet` element is used, the `exclude-result-prefixes` (like the `version` attribute) attribute must not be prefixed.

The fact that all namespace declarations mapping to the XSLT namespace URI are suppressed introduces an interesting puzzle: How does one write a stylesheet that generates stylesheets as its result document. For example, consider the following stylesheet document:

```
<xsl:stylesheet version='1.0'
    xmlns:xsl='http://www.w3.org/1999/XSL/Transform'>
  <xsl:template name='emitStylesheet' >
    <xsl:stylesheet version='1.0'>
      <xsl:template name='{//@procName} ' />
    </xsl:stylesheet>
  </xsl:template>
</xsl:stylesheet>
```

The intent of this stylesheet is to emit the following result document:

```
<xsl:stylesheet version='1.0'
    xmlns:xsl='http://www.w3.org/1999/XSL/Transform'>
```

```
      <xsl:template name='func2' />
  </xsl:stylesheet>
```

However, there are two problems. Problem one is that the `xsl:stylesheet` element may not legally appear as [children] of an `xsl:template`. The second problem is that any namespace declarations binding the XSLT namespace URI will be suppressed in the result document. Both of these problems are addressed by the `xsl:namespace-alias` instruction.

The `xsl:namespace-alias` instruction alters the namespace URI of one namespace declaration by associating it with a second namespace declaration that provides the actual namespace URI to be used in the result document. The syntax of the `xsl:namespace-alias` is as follows:

```
<xsl:namespace-alias
    stylesheet-prefix = prefix | "#default"
    result-prefix = prefix | "#default"
/>
```

The `result-prefix` indicates which namespace declaration contains the actual namespace URI that will appear in the result document. The `stylesheet-prefix` indicates which namespace declaration should be "redeclared" prior to emitting the result document. Consider the following stylesheet document:

```
<xslt:stylesheet version='1.0'
    xmlns:xslt='http://www.w3.org/1999/XSL/Transform'
    xmlns:xsl='urn:fake:uri'>
  <xslt:namespace-alias stylesheet-prefix='xsl'
                        result-prefix='xslt' />
  <xslt:template name='emitStylesheet' >
    <xsl:stylesheet version='1.0'>
      <xsl:template name='{//@procName} ' />
    </xsl:stylesheet>
  </xslt:template>
</xslt:stylesheet>
```

Because the [children] of the `emitStylesheet` template are no longer affiliated with the XSLT namespace, they are treated as literal result elements.

However, any namespace declarations for the `urn:fake:uri` namespace URI will be morphed into declarations for the `http://www.w3.org/1999/XSL/Transform` namespace URI. That means that the `emitStylesheet` template would produce the following result document:

```
<xsl:stylesheet version='1.0'
    xmlns:xsl='http://www.w3.org/1999/XSL/Transform'>
  <xsl:template name='func2' />
</xsl:stylesheet>
```

Had the `xsl:namespace-alias` instruction not appeared in the stylesheet, the result document would have instead looked like this.

```
<xsl:stylesheet version='1.0'
    xmlns:xsl='urn:fake:uri'>
  <xsl:template name='func2' />
</xsl:stylesheet>
```

While it is possible to use namespace aliases with other namespaces, the XSLT namespace URI is the most obvious use of this feature.

Generated Output

There is a class of transformations that are not achievable using literal result elements. For example, if the local name or namespace URI of an element or attribute needs to be calculated based on XSLT processing, a literal result element cannot be used. Conditional emission of attributes is also complicated when using literal result elements. Additionally, any processing instructions or comments that appear in templates are stripped away during processing.

XSLT defines four instructions that can be used to algorithmically generate specific output nodes: `xsl:comment`, `xsl:processing-instruction`, `xsl:element`, and `xsl:attribute`. These instructions can be used in place of literal result elements, and because they make extensive use of attribute value templates, they are highly suited to dynamic output formats. Of the four, `xsl:comment` and `xsl:processing-instruction` are the easiest to understand. The productions for these two instructions are as follows:

```
<xsl:comment>
  <!-- Content: template -->
</xsl:comment>

<xsl:processing-instruction
  name= { ncname }
>
  <!-- Content: template -->
</xsl:processing-instruction>
```

Note that the `name` attribute of `xsl:processing-instruction` is an attribute value template, which allows the `[target]` of the processing instruction to be dynamically generated. To see these instructions in action, consider the following named template:

```
<xsl:template name='annotated' >
  <!-- comment number one -->
  <?Magnum PI?>
  <xsl:comment>comment number two</xsl:comment>
  <xsl:processing-instruction name='A'
    >PI</xsl:processing-instruction>
</xsl:template>
```

When executed, this named template would emit the following:

```
<!--comment number two--><?A PI?>
```

As mentioned earlier, literal comments and processing instructions that appear in templates are not emitted into the result document.

The `xsl:attribute` instruction adds an attribute to the `[attributes]` property of the "current" result element. The production for the `xsl:attribute` instruction is as follows:

```
<xsl:attribute
  name={qname}
  namespace={uri-reference} >
  <!-- Content: template -->
</xsl:attribute>
```

The `xsl:attribute` element's [children] are interpreted as text to produce the [children] of the resultant attribute. The `xsl:attribute` instruction may not be used after [children] have been added to the current result element. Consider the following named template:

```
<xsl:template name='simple' >
  <bob><xsl:attribute name='id'>32</xsl:attribute><x/></bob>
</xsl:template>
```

Because the `xsl:attribute` instruction appears as [children] of the `bob` element, the attribute will be associated with that element in the result document. This named template produces the following result:

```
<bob id='32'><x/></bob>
```

Note that the [children] of the `id` attribute were generated by evaluating the [children] of the `xsl:attribute` instruction as a template.

The power of the `xsl:attribute` instruction is its dynamism. Consider the following named template that uses `xsl:if` and attribute value templates:

```
<xsl:template name='fancy' >
  <xsl:param name='sAttName' select='bob' />
  <xsl:param name='bUseAttribute' select='true()' />
  <xsl:param name='sAttValue' />
  <bob>
    <xsl:if test='$bUseAttribute' >
      <xsl:attribute name='{$sAttName} '>
        <xsl:value-of select='$sAttValue' />
      </xsl:attribute>
    </xsl:if><x/>
  </bob>
</xsl:template>
```

When this named template is invoked as follows

```
<xsl:call-template name='fancy' >
  <xsl:with-param name='sAttName' >myAttr</xsl:with-param>
  <xsl:with-param name='bUseAttribute' select='true()' />
```

```
    <xsl:with-param name='sAttValue'>Hi, XSLT</xsl:with-param>
  </xsl:call-template>
```

this would be the result

```
    <bob myAttr='Hi, XSLT'><x/></bob>
```

As shown here, xsl:attribute provides a great deal of flexibility.

By default, the xsl:attribute emits an attribute that is not affiliated with any namespace. This behavior can be altered in one of two ways. The simplest way to affiliate an xsl:attribute instruction with a namespace is to use the namespace attribute

```
    <xsl:template name='ns1' >
      <bob>
        <xsl:attribute namespace='http://b.com'
         name='id' >32</xsl:attribute>
      </bob>
    </xsl:template>
```

This template will produce the following result:

```
    <bob xmlns:auto-ns1='http://b.com' auto-ns1:id='32/>
```

Note that because only the [local name] property was provided, the XSLT processor needed to manufacture a namespace declaration (and prefix). Which prefix is used can be controlled by specifying a QName instead of an NCName

```
    <xsl:template name='ns1' >
      <bob>
        <xsl:attribute namespace='http://b.com'
         name='b:id' >32</xsl:attribute>
      </bob>
    </xsl:template>
```

which produces the following result

```
    <bob xmlns:b='http://b.com' b:id='32/>
```

An alternative way to affiliate an `xsl:attribute` instruction with a namespace is to simply use a `QName` with no corresponding `namespace` attribute. This causes the XSLT processor to look at the `[in-scope namespace declarations]` property to derive the namespace URI. Consider the following named template:

```
<xsl:template name='ns1' xmlns:b='http://b.com'>
  <bob>
    <xsl:attribute name='b:id' >32</xsl:attribute>
  </bob>
</xsl:template>
```

This template produces an identical result to the previous example.

The fourth instruction in this family is `xsl:element`. The `xsl:element` instruction is an alternative to the literal result element. Both the `xsl:element` instruction and the literal result element cause an element to be emitted in the result document. Only the `xsl:element` instruction can generate the element name dynamically using XPath expressions. The production for the `xsl:element` instruction is as follows:

```
<xsl:element
  name={qname}
  namespace={uri-reference}
  use-attribute-sets=qnames
>
  <!-- Content: template -->
</xsl:element>
```

The basic usage model of `xsl:element` is the same as for a literal result element. For example, the following named template that uses a literal result element

```
<xsl:template name='elems' >
  <bob xmlns='http://example.com'><steve/></bob>
</xsl:template>
```

could be rewritten as follows

```
<xsl:template name='elems' >
 <xsl:element name='bob' namespace='http://example.com'>
  <xsl:element name='steve' namespace='http://example.com'/>
 </xsl:element>
</xsl:template>
```

or using this hybrid style

```
<xsl:template name='elems' >
  <xsl:element name='bob' namespace='http://example.com'>
    <steve xmlns='http://example.com'/>
  </xsl:element>
</xsl:template>
```

The namespace prefixes used by xsl:element are controlled the same way as for xsl:attribute.

As shown earlier, there are multiple ways to add to the [attributes] property of the result element. The most obvious way is to use the xsl:attribute instruction. The less obvious way is to use attribute sets. Attribute sets are named collections of xsl:attribute instructions that appear as [children] of the xsl:stylesheet element. Attribute sets are named by a QName and are referenced by the use-attribute-sets attribute of the xsl:element instruction or a literal result element. Consider the following stylesheet:

```
<xsl:stylesheet version='1.0'
     xmlns:xsl='http://www.w3.org/1999/XSL/Transform' >
  <xsl:attribute-set name='myAttrs' >
    <xsl:attribute name='a'>a-val</xsl:attribute>
    <xsl:attribute name='b'>b-val</xsl:attribute>
  </xsl:attribute-set>
  <xsl:attribute-set name='yourAttrs' >
    <xsl:attribute name='c'>c-val</xsl:attribute>
  </xsl:attribute-set>
  <xsl:template name='elems2' >
    <xsl:element name='bob'
         use-attribute-sets='myAttrs yourAttrs' >
      <steve xsl:use-attribute-sets='yourAttrs' />
    </xsl:element>
```

ESSENTIAL XML: BEYOND MARKUP

```
    </xsl:template>
  </xsl:stylesheet>
```

Given this stylesheet, the `elems2` template would produce the following result:

```
<bob a='a-val' b='b-val' c='c-val' ><steve c='c-val'/></bob>
```

It is also legal for one attribute set to include other attribute sets using the `use-attribute-sets` attribute in its definition.

Multiple Stylesheets

XSLT provides two mechanisms for breaking an `xsl:stylesheet` into multiple documents. The simplest mechanism is the `xsl:include` directive. The `xsl:include` directive references an external `xsl:stylesheet` by its URI. When an `xsl:include` directive appears as a child of an `xsl:stylesheet`, the XSLT directives found in the referenced document will be inserted into the current document just as if they were defined inline. For example, consider the following two XSLT stylesheets:

```
<?xml version='1.0' ?>
<!-- stylesheeta.xsl -->
<xsl:stylesheet version='1.0'
          xmlns:xsl='http://www.w3.org/1999/XSL/Transform'>
  <xsl:template name='func-a' ><a/></xsl:template>
</xsl:stylesheet>

<?xml version='1.0' ?>
<!-- stylesheetb.xsl -->
<xsl:stylesheet version='1.0'
          xmlns:xsl='http://www.w3.org/1999/XSL/Transform'>
  <xsl:include href='stylesheeta.xsl' />
  <xsl:template name='func-b' >
    <xsl:call-template name='func-a' />
  </xsl:template>
</xsl:stylesheet>
```

The second stylesheet uses the `xsl:include` directive to include the directives from the first. The resultant stylesheet is equivalent to the following:

```
<?xml version='1.0' ?>
<!-- stylesheetb.xsl -->
<xsl:stylesheet version='1.0'
          xmlns:xsl='http://www.w3.org/1999/XSL/Transform'>
  <xsl:template name='func-a' ><a/></xsl:template>
  <xsl:template name='func-b' >
    <xsl:call-template name='func-a' />
  </xsl:template>
</xsl:stylesheet>
```

Because it is an error to define the same template name more than once, it is dangerous at best to xsl:include a document multiple times.

In addition to wholesale inclusion, XSLT supports a collision-aware import mechanism using its xsl:import directive. Like xsl:include, xsl:import causes the contents of an external stylesheet to be merged with the importing stylesheet. The distinction between xsl:import and xsl:include is only evident when there are name collisions. When using xsl:include, it is an error if the external stylesheet defines a named construct (e.g., a template rule) with an identical identifier as the including stylesheet. When using xsl:import, it is expected that the external stylesheet may define a named construct (e.g., a template rule) with an identical identifier as the including stylesheet. In the case of such a collision, the construct in the importing stylesheet takes precedence. In fact, there is a hierarchy for determining precedence for colliding definitions.

1. If an xsl:import directive results in a collision with a construct defined in the importing stylesheet, the construct in the imported stylesheet is hidden by the construct in the importing stylesheet.

2. If two xsl:import directives in the same stylesheet result in a collision, the construct in the first imported stylesheet is hidden by the construct in the second imported stylesheet.

To maintain sanity, all xsl:import directives must appear as the initial [children] of an xsl:stylesheet element. It is illegal for an xsl:import element to appear after an xsl:include, xsl:template, or any other top-level stylesheet element.

ESSENTIAL XML: BEYOND MARKUP

Consider the following collection of stylesheets that use `xsl:import` to form an aggregate stylesheet:

```
<?xml version='1.0' ?>
<!-- root.xsl -->
<xsl:stylesheet version='1.0'
            xmlns:xsl='http://www.w3.org/1999/XSL/Transform'>
  <xsl:import href='first.xsl' />
  <xsl:import href='second.xsl' />
  <xsl:template name='func-b' >
    <xsl:call-template name='func-a' />
  </xsl:template>
</xsl:stylesheet>

<?xml version='1.0' ?>
<!-- first.xsl -->
<xsl:stylesheet version='1.0'
        xmlns:xsl='http://www.w3.org/1999/XSL/Transform'>
  <xsl:template name='func-a' ><first/></xsl:template>
</xsl:stylesheet>

<?xml version='1.0' ?>
<!-- second.xsl -->
<xsl:stylesheet version='1.0'
            xmlns:xsl='http://www.w3.org/1999/XSL/Transform'>
  <xsl:import href='third.xsl' />
  <xsl:template name='func-a' ><second/></xsl:template>
</xsl:stylesheet>

<?xml version='1.0' ?>
<!-- third.xsl -->
<xsl:stylesheet version='1.0'
            xmlns:xsl='http://www.w3.org/1999/XSL/Transform'>
  <xsl:template name='func-a' ><third/></xsl:template>
</xsl:stylesheet>
```

Assuming that the `root.xsl` stylesheet is the initial stylesheet, the result of calling the `func-b` template would be this:

```
<second/>
```

The definition of `func-a` in `first.xsl` is hidden by the definition in `second.xsl`. Even though `second.xsl` imports `third.xsl`, because `second.xsl` is considered the importing stylesheet, its definition of `func-a` hides the definition in `third.xsl`.

Pattern-based Templates

The template rules shown so far in this chapter have been named and invoked based on a symbolic name. XSLT also supports invoking template rules based on pattern-matching. An XSLT pattern is a stylized XPath expression that identifies subsets of the source document. An XSLT pattern contains one or more location paths separated by a `|`. Location paths contained in XSLT patterns can only use the `child` and `attribute` axes. That stated, a location path in an XSLT pattern can use also the `//` operator (but not the equivalent `descendant-or-self` axis).

Patterns are associated with a template rule using the `match` attribute instead of the `name` attribute.

```
<xsl:template match='author|illustrator' >
  <contributor />
</xsl:template>
```

This template rule matches elements whose name is either `author` or `illustrator`. Template rules can also use predicates and multiple location steps.

```
<xsl:template match='book//author[@name != "Don"]' >
  <contributor />
</xsl:template>
```

This template matches `author` elements that have a `book` element as an ancestor but do not have a `name` attribute whose `[children]` is the string "Don".

It is common for multiple template rules to match a given node. In those scenarios, the template rule that is actually used is determined by the following rules.

ESSENTIAL XML: BEYOND MARKUP

1. Only template rules whose `match` pattern matches the current node may be chosen.

2. Among matching template rules, template rules with higher import precedence are always chosen over template rules with lower import precedence.

3 Among matching template rules with the same import precedence, template rules with higher priority are always chosen over template rules with lower priority. The priority is calculated as follows.

    a. If the `xsl:template` has a `priority` attribute, the `decimal` number found there is used independent of rules c–f.

    b. Templates whose patterns use | to separate multiple alternatives are treated as distinct template rules, one per alternative.

    c. Templates whose patterns are of the form `child::QName`, `attribute::QName`, or `child::processing-instruction(literal)` (or their abbreviated equivalents) are assigned a default priority of 0.

    d. Templates whose patterns are of the form `child::NCName:*` or `attribute:: NCName:*` (or their abbreviated equivalents) are assigned a default priority of –0.25.

    e. Templates whose patterns are of the form `child::<node-test>` or `attribute:: <node-test>` (or their abbreviated equivalents) are assigned a default priority of –0.5.

    f. Templates whose patterns are not of the forms described in rules c–e and that do not have an explicit `priority` attribute are assigned a default priority of 0.5.

4. It is an error for more than one matching template rule with the same priority and import precedence. In the case of such an error, an XSLT processor may signal the error or recover by breaking the tie by choosing the template rule that occurs last in the enclosing stylesheet.

These rules appear in more detail in section 5.5 of the XSLT specification.

In general, the pattern-matching rules prefer the most specific match from the stylesheet whose import priority is highest. Consider the following stylesheet fragment:

```
<xsl:transform version='1.0' xmlns:a='http://awl.com'
        xmlns:xsl='http://www.w3.org/1999/XSL/Transform'>
  <xsl:template
            match='/a:product/a:writer'><a/></xsl:template>
  <xsl:template match='a:writer'        ><b/></xsl:template>
  <xsl:template match='a:*'             ><c/></xsl:template>
  <xsl:template match='*'               ><d/></xsl:template>
</xsl:transform>
```

Assuming the first XML document of this chapter, an element node corresponding to an `author` element would match any of these template rules. Because there is more than one match, the priorities must be taken into account. According to the rules just described, the default priorities for these template rules are (in order) 0.5, 0, –0.25, and –0.5. Since there is a uniquely highest-priority template rule (the first rule), that rule would be selected for execution. In contrast, the `book` element would only match the third and fourth template rules, and since the third rule has a higher priority, that rule would be selected. Note that these calculations assume that all template rules appear in the same stylesheet and that no importing stylesheet has matching template rules (note that in the matching rules, import precedence is the most important factor in choosing a template rule). Also note that explicit `priority` attributes would affect the prioritization considerably.

Pattern-based template rules are not invoked using the `xsl:call-template` instruction. Rather, they are invoked using the `xsl:apply-templates` instruction.

```
<xsl:apply-templates
  select=node-set-expresssion : node()
  mode=qname
>
  <!— Content: (xsl:sort | xsl:with-param)* —>
</xsl:apply-templates>
```

The `xsl:apply-templates` instruction is remarkably similar to the `xsl:for-each` instruction. Both instructions take a `node-set` and iteratively apply a template to each node in some order. For an `xsl:for-each` instruction, the template that is applied is simply the `[children]` of the `xsl:for-each` instruction. For an `xsl:apply-templates` instruction, the template is selected based on pattern-matching against all known template rules. Also, like the `xsl:for-each` instruction, invoking a template rule via `xsl:apply-templates` alters the context of the template being evaluated based on the `node-set` returned by the `select` expression and the current node in the iteration sequence.

Consider the following XSLT stylesheet that uses pattern-matching and `xsl:apply-templates` to invoke template rules:

```
<xsl:stylesheet version='1.0'
    xmlns:xsl='http://www.w3.org/1999/XSL/Transform'>
  <xsl:template match='author' >
    <by><xsl:value-of select='@name' /></by>
  </xsl:template>
  <xsl:template match='book' >
    <doc><xsl:apply-templates /></doc>
  </xsl:template>
  <xsl:template match='/' >
    <xsl:apply-templates/>
  </xsl:template>
</xsl:stylesheet>
```

Assuming the `book` source document used throughout this chapter, this stylesheet will emit the following result document:

```
<?xml version='1.0' ?>
<doc><by>Don</byby>Aaron</byby>John</by></doc>
```

It is illustrative to walk through the processing of this stylesheet.

XSLT processing always starts by executing the template rule that best matches the root node of the source document. This node is matched by the XSLT pattern `/`, which is always used to find the initial template rule. If no explicit template rule exists, there is a built-in template rule whose contents exactly matches the third template rule in this stylesheet (more on built-in template rules later in this section). In the case of this stylesheet, the third template rule will be selected as the initial template rule. That template rule simply invokes the `xsl:apply-templates` instruction with no `select` attribute, which, via defaults, is equivalent to

```
<xsl:apply-templates select='node()' />
```

Given the source document, this `select` expression will return a `node-set` containing one element node (`book`). Since there is only one template rule that matches the element node named `book` (the second rule), that rule is then invoked using the `book` element node as the "current" context node.

Upon evaluating the second template rule, the literal result element `doc` will be emitted. Inside of that element, however, there is another `xsl:apply-templates` instruction. The implicit `select` expression for that instruction will return a `node-set` containing the three `author` element nodes. The `xsl:apply-templates` instruction will find only one matching template rule (the first rule). Upon evaluating the final template rule, the literal result element `by` is encountered with an `xsl:value-of` as its `[children]`. Because `xsl:apply-templates` alters the context upon invocation of a template rule, the relative XPath expression used in the `xsl:value-of` instruction will be evaluated relative to the current `author` node.

XSLT defines a set of seven built-in template rules (one per node-type) that are implicitly considered during template rule matching. These built-in rules are given the lowest possible import precedence, which means they will only be selected when there is absolutely no viable template rule explicitly defined in any of the available stylesheets. The built-in rule for element and root nodes recursively applies the best-match template to all child nodes.

```
<xsl:template match='*|/' >
  <xsl:apply-templates select='node()' />
</xsl:template>
```

The built-in template rule for text and attribute nodes simply copies the text values through

ESSENTIAL XML: BEYOND MARKUP

```
<xsl:template match='text()|@*' >
  <xsl:value-of select='.' />
</xsl:template>
```

The built-in template rule for comments and processing instruction nodes discards the nodes from further processing:

```
<xsl:template match='processing-instruction()|comment()' />
```

The built-in template rule for namespace nodes also discards the nodes from further processing, but since XSLT patterns do not support matching namespace nodes, this built-in template rule cannot be overridden.

It is hard to discuss the built-in template rules and not discuss the `xsl:copy` instruction. Despite their similar names, the `xsl:copy` and `xsl:copy-of` instructions are quite different. The `xsl:copy` instruction emits a copy of the current context node independent of its type. If the node type is an element node, the associated namespace nodes are copied as well, but the [attributes] and [children] of the element are not copied. To copy these nodes as well, one must include an `xsl:apply-templates` instruction to recursively copy the subordinate nodes. The following is the identity transformation stylesheet:

```
<xsl:transform version='1.0'
    xmlns:xsl='http://www.w3.org/1999/XSL/Transform'>
  <xsl:template match='@*|node()' >
    <xsl:copy>
      <xsl:apply-templates select='@*|node()'/>
    </xsl:copy>
  </xsl:template>
</xsl:transform>
```

Note that this lone template rule matches all attribute nodes and all child nodes (including comment, processing instruction and text nodes). The template itself simply uses the `xsl:copy` instruction to pass the current node through. The subtemplate inside the `xsl:copy` instruction then recursively invokes the template rule against all of the child and attribute nodes.

Controlling Output

By default, an XSLT stylesheet produces an XML document. This can be changed using the `xsl:output` directive. The `xsl:output` directive must appear as a child element of the `xsl:stylesheet` element and must adhere to the following production:

```
<xsl:output
  method = "xml" | "html" | "text" | qname-but-not-ncname
  version = nmtoken
  encoding = string
  omit-xml-declaration = "yes" | "no"
  standalone = "yes" | "no"
  doctype-public = string
  doctype-system = string
  cdata-section-elements = qnames
  indent = "yes" | "no"
  media-type = string
/>
```

The most important of these attributes is the `method` attribute. The `method` attribute sets the output method of the XSLT stylesheet. If not provided, the default is typically XML.[3] XSLT provides two other output methods: text and html. The former assumes that the result document is simply a text file with no implicit structure. The latter assumes that the result document is a Web document whose version is controlled by the `version` attribute. Consider the following XSLT stylesheet:

```
<xsl:stylesheet version='1.0'
        xmlns:xsl='http://www.w3.org/1999/XSL/Transform' >
  <xsl:template match='/' >
    Hello, World
  </xsl:template>
</xsl:stylesheet>
```

---

[3]In the absence of an xsl:output element, a set of heuristics is used to detect Web documents as result documents. Consult the XSLT specification for the details of these heuristics.

As it stands, this XSLT stylesheet is illegal, as the result document is not well-formed XML. To make this stylesheet legal, an `xsl:output` directive is needed.

```
<xsl:stylesheet version='1.0'
        xmlns:xsl='http://www.w3.org/1999/XSL/Transform' >
  <xsl:output method='text' />
  <xsl:template match='/' >
    Hello, World
  </xsl:template>
</xsl:stylesheet>
```

Given this stylesheet, the following result document would be produced:

```
Hello, World
```

Because this is not an XML document, there is no XML declaration nor is there any expectation of well-formedness.

The output method also controls the handling of the five built-in entities (`lt`, `gt`, `amp`, `apos`, `quot`). In `method='text'` mode, all references to the five built-in entities are converted to their literal values prior to emission into the result document. In all other modes, the default behavior is to always emit entity references for the five *verboten* characters. This behavior can be disabled using the `disable-output-escaping` attribute. This attribute appears on both the `xsl:value-of` and `xsl:text` instructions. The `xsl:text` instruction is used to emit character data based on the character data [children] of the `xsl:text` instruction. Consider the following named template:

```
<xsl:template name='emitme' >
  Hel&lt;lo, <xsl:text>Wo&gt;rld</xsl:text>
</xsl:template>
```

In `method='text'` mode, the result of this template would look like this.

```
Hel<lo, wo>rld
```

In `method='xml'` mode, the result of this template would look like this:

```
Hel&lt;lo, wo&gt;rld
```

It is possible to suppress the appearance of the second entity reference using the `disable-output-escaping` attribute. Consider this slight variation on the previous named template:

```
<xsl:template name='emitme' >
  Hel&lt;lo, <xsl:text disable-output-escaping='yes'
             >Wo&gt;rld</xsl:text>
</xsl:template>
```

In `method='xml'` mode, the result of this template would look like this:

```
Hel&lt;lo, wo>rld
```

Note that in element content, a raw > is perfectly legal.

It is also possible to force the use of a `<![CDATA[` section in the result document. The `xsl:output` directive's `cdata-section-elements` attribute can contain a list of `QName`-based element names. When a text node is encountered, if its parent element's expanded name is in the list of `cdata-section-elements`, the text node will be emitted inside of a `<![CDATA[` section. Consider the following stylesheet:

```
<xsl:stylesheet version='1.0'
          xmlns:xsl='http://www.w3.org/1999/XSL/Transform' >
  <xsl:output method='xml' cdata-section-elements='bob'/>
  <xsl:template match='/' >
    <steve>
      <bob>&lt;Hello&gt;</bob>
      <george>&lt;Hello&gt;</george>
    </steve>
  </xsl:template>
</xsl:stylesheet>
```

This stylesheet would emit the following result document:

```
<steve>
  <bob><![CDATA[<hello>]]></bob>
  <george>&lt;Hello&gt;</george>
</steve>
```

Note that when a `<![CDATA[` section is emitted, all built-in entity references are expanded.

The discussion so far has managed to avoid the nasty issue of whitespace handling. XSLT provides a well-defined set of rules and mechanisms for controlling whitespace in result documents. In general, XSLT acknowledges the fact that mixed content is the exceptional case and strips all whitespace-only text nodes from the source document tree and from the stylesheet. This stripping can be suppressed by the presence of any `xml:space='preserve'` attributes that may be in effect. Additionally, the stylesheet can contain one or more `xsl:strip-space` or `xsl:preserve-space` directives that list the element names that require overriding behavior. Consider the following source document:

```
<?xml version='1.0' ?>
<root>
  <a>
    <e/>
  </a>
  <b xml:space='preserve'>
    <e/>
  </b>
  <c xml:space='default'>
    <e/>
  </c>
  <d>
    <e/>
  </d>
</root>
```

If no `xsl:strip-space` or `xsl:preserve-space` directives are in effect, this source document is identical to the following stripped source document:

```
<?xml version='1.0' ?>
<root><a><e/></a><b xml:space='preserve'>
    <e/>
  </b><c xml:space='default'><e//c><d><e//d></root>
```

Note that only the b element's whitespace was preserved. Assuming the following two directives were to appear in the stylesheet document

```
<xsl:strip-space elements='b' />
<xsl:preserve-space elements='a root'/>
```

the source document would be prestripped to be identical to the following

```
<?xml version='1.0' ?>
<root>
  <a>
    <e/>
  </a>
  <b xml:space='preserve'><e//b>
  <c xml:space='default'><e//c>
  <d><e//d>
</root>
```

Note that the xsl:strip-space directive can override the value of the xml:
space attribute. The stripping behavior just described applies to stylesheets as
well as source documents. The primary distinction is that the xsl:text element is automatically in the whitespace preserving list and does not need to be
explicitly listed in the xsl:preserve-space directive.

Where Are We?

XSLT is an XML-based language for expressing new documents in terms of old
ones. XSLT allows a stylesheet document to contain templates that act as exemplars of the target schema. Templates contain literal result elements and XSLT
instructions, both of which make extensive use of XPath expressions to incorpo-
rate information from the source document as part of the result document. The
XSLT language has many of the constructs found in traditional programming languages, including variables, functions, conditional statements, and iteration
statements.

ESSENTIAL XML: BEYOND MARKUP

Chapter 6

Beyond Interface-based Programming

```
typedef string LocType;
typedef short TempType;
interface Thermostat {
  LocType  get_location();
  TempType get_temperature();
  TempType get_nominal_temp();
  void     set_nominal_temp(in TempType t);
}
```

Michi Henning and Steve Vinoski, 1999

This book began by painting XML as the heir apparent to the component technologies of the late twentieth century. However, the intervening chapters have described a variety of XML technologies largely as independent entities with little attention paid to the application of XML as a replacement for the component technologies currently in use. This chapter begins by looking at the state of component software as we now know it and concludes by examining how XML may (or may not) change the way we write component software in the future.

Where Are We?

The dominant concept in component software is the interface, hence the term *interface-based programming.* Interfaces are abstract types that define a contract between two agents: the implementation (often referred to as the component) and the consumer (often referred to as the client). As shown in Figure 6.1, the implementation exposes its functionality via one or more interfaces. The consumer utilizes this functionality via the interfaces exposed by the implementation. In the purest application of the interface-based programming model, the consumer knows nothing about the implementation other than the interfaces it supports.

The interface-based programming model enforces encapsulation. Implementors are free to change the implementation details of their components provided they continue to adhere to the semantics (and syntax) of their supported interfaces. This degree of encapsulation is especially important when parts of an overall system need to be replaced one component at a time. Though some would argue that interface-based programming is overkill when incremental redeployment of a system is not required, the benefits of modularity and looser coupling that results from interface-based designs have been well documented in the literature.[1]

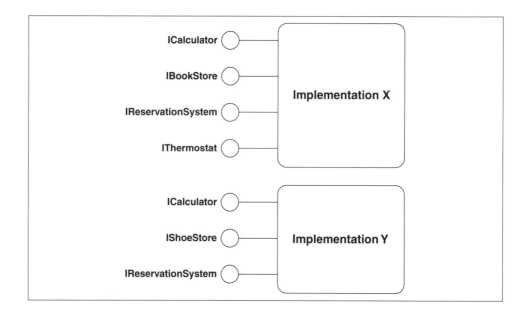

Figure 6.1   Components and interfaces

---

[1]*Large-Scale C++ Software Design* by John Lakos and *Component Software: Beyond Object-Oriented Programming* by Clemens Szyperski both come to mind.

Interfaces are often referred to as protocols or contracts. This is because interfaces make explicit the set of expectations that the two sides of the equation must live up to. It is difficult to decide exactly how precise this contract should be. If the contract is too vague, consumers (and implementations) can make almost no assumptions about the semantics (or perhaps even the syntax) of a given interface. If the contract is too specific, implementations may have virtually no freedom to innovate or evolve and still adhere to the constraints of the contract. A well-designed interface errs toward precision yet leaves room for "controlled uncertainty" in order to support evolution and polymorphism. Polymorphism is *the* enabling concept behind field-replaceable, interchangeable components and is the Holy Grail of software reuse.

Interfaces are not just warm and fuzzy ideas that technologists like to throw around to sound intelligent. Interfaces are real first-class concepts that are explicitly supported in many programming languages and runtime environments. While there are minor variations from system to system, the basic notion of what constitutes an interface is universal: An interface is a typed collection of operations a consumer can invoke on an implementation of that interface. Interfaces define the syntax and semantics of each individual operation as well as the semantics of the collection of operations as a whole.

An interface definition assigns a unique identifier to the interface itself as well as locally unique identifiers to each individual operation.[2] While the exact format of these identifiers varies across component systems, each system provides a mechanism to dynamically interrogate an implementation for support of a given interface. Because interfaces are themselves types, this mechanism is often integrated into the runtime-type system of the programming language in use. C++'s dynamic_cast operator, COM's QueryInterface method, and the Java virtual machine's checkcast and instanceof opcodes are all examples of such mechanisms.

Interfaces are generally considered indivisible types. That is, if an implementation supports an interface, it supports that interface as a whole, not just selected operations that make sense for that implementation. Doing otherwise weakens the strength and precision of the interface's contract. Properly factoring

---

[2]In the presence of overloading, the type signature acts as part of the overall local identifier.

an interface to avoid partial support requires foresight on behalf of the interface designer, as one must balance the desire to support unanticipated use-cases against the design and implementation downsides of having hundreds of single-operation interfaces. That stated, well-designed interface suites typically tend toward a collection of smaller, atomic types rather than a single, larger, "everything including the kitchen sink"-style interface.

Most of the interesting interfaces in nature have one or more operations. Each operation has an identifier, a type signature, and represents one aspect of the overall semantic contract of the containing interface. The identifier of the operation is scoped by the surrounding interface and is generally meaningless outside that scope.[3] The type signature of an operation is a list of formal argument names and types that are passed as parameters to the operation. Special keywords or attributes are often used to indicate which direction the values of these arguments flow. Arguments whose values flow from consumer to implementation are called *in-parameters.* Arguments whose values flow from the implementation to the consumer are called *out-parameters*. Arguments whose values flow in both directions are called *inout-parameters.* Most systems allow operations to return a single unnamed result in addition to any out- or inout-parameters that may be specified, however, this is just syntactic shorthand for expressing another out-parameter.

To make this discussion concrete, consider the following interface definition written in the Object Management Group's (OMG) Interface Definition Language (IDL):

```
module com {
  module develop {
    interface ICalculator {
      double add(     in double m,
                      in double n,
                      out boolean overflow);
      double multiply(in double m,
                      in double n,
```

---

[3]For example, the Java virtual machine's `invokeinterface` instruction requires both an interface identifier and a method identifier. This is in contrast with the `invokevirtual` instruction, which only requires the method identifier.

```
                        out boolean overflow);
        }
      }
   }
```

This interface definition states that implementations of `com.develop.ICalculator` support two operations: `add` and `multiply`. Both operations coincidentally share a type signature and accept two 64-bit floating point numbers as in-parameters and return a boolean and a 64-bit floating point number as out-parameters. Consumers that are handed a variable of type `com.develop.ICalculator` are expected to invoke these operations according to the type signatures just described. The results of doing otherwise are undefined.

The interface just described is an example of a typed contract. That is, the contract between the consumer and the implementation is expressed in terms of types. In the case of `com.develop.ICalculator.add` and `com.develop.ICalculator.multiply`, the types are fairly simple. That does not diminish the importance of type to the contract as a whole. For example, consider the following variation on the `com.develop.ICalculator` interface:

```
module com {
  module develop {
    interface ICalculator2 {
      any add(     in any m,
                   in any n,
                   out any overflow);
      any multiply( in any m,
                    in any n,
                    out any overflow);
    }
  }
}
```

The only difference between this interface and `com.develop.ICalculator` is that the argument types are now any, which is the OMG IDL mechanism for indicating that the argument is untyped.[4] This contract is considerably weaker than

---

[4]An OMG IDL any is similar to C++'s void *, COM's VARIANT, or Java's java.lang.Object.

the previous interfaces, since now either party is free to pass whatever type they like for each of the arguments. While that may sound liberating, the downside is that the receiver of the parameter value now must be able to handle literally any type supported by the system. If all types in the world were numeric, this wouldn't be that much of a problem. However, what if the consumer passes a string, date, or widget as the first parameter to `com.develop.` `ICalculator2.multiply`? What does it mean to multiply two widgets? If the implementation knew ahead of time what a widget was, it might be able to encode the semantics of widget multiplication into its code-base. However, because consumers can always define new types (with new semantics) and pass them as parameters to the `com.develop.ICalculator2.multiply` operation, there is no way for the type system to keep implementations from choking on unanticipated input.

One could carry the loosely typed approach used by the previous interface to the extreme. Consider the following interface definition:

```
module com {
  module develop {
    interface Interface {
      void operation(in any id,       // what should I do?
                     in any input,    // use this as input..
                     out any output); // here's what I got!
    }
  }
}
```

This interface completely abandons the type system and provides a single generic invocation operation. It expects the consumer to know what to pass for the id parameter to indicate which functionality is desired. It also expects both the consumer and implementation to know what types are expected for input and output for each possible id value. While this interface offers the ultimate in flexibility, it also offers no guarantees whatsoever about what the type `com.develop.Interface` really means, making it virtually useless as a typed contract. Yes, entire systems could be built using this interface and this interface alone, but in building such a system, one would likely wind up reimplementing an ad hoc type system in a proprietary, noninteroperable manner.

The seductive lure of untyped contracts is that they appear to require no forethought and offer the ultimate in extensibility. However, in order to be usable, one inevitably needs to define a set of conventions that constrain the set of formats and values that may be conveyed as parameters. When using a typed contract, these constraints are expressed in terms of value types that can be enforced by type-aware programming languages and plumbing.[5] When using an untyped contract, it is up to the consumer and implementation to get it right based on documentation, guesswork, or word of mouth, with no enforcement except the inevitable runtime error that occurs when one party gets it wrong. True, many modern component systems support runtime-type discovery, reflection, or introspection, but unless the *semantics* of these types can be discovered at runtime, there is little chance one can properly cope with arbitrary, unforeseen types.

Leaving Home

It is interesting to note that support for multiple parameters is largely a syntactic convenience. Consider the following variation on the `com.develop.ICalculator` interface:

```
module com {
  module develop {
    interface ICalculator3 {
      struct addRequest {
        double m, n;
      } ;
      struct addResponse {
        boolean overflow; double result;
      } ;
      addResponse add(in addRequest request);

      struct multiplyRequest {
        double m, n;
      } ;
```

---

[5]In fact, the presence of precise-type information enables tools and infrastructure to assist the development effort via code generation, smart-editors, and other type-driven convenience features.

```
        struct multiplyResponse {
          boolean overflow; double result;
        } ;
        multiplyResponse multiply(in muliplyRequest request);
      }
    }
  }
```

This interface passes exactly the same information to/from the add and multiply operations as the `com.develop.ICalculator` interface. The difference between the two interfaces is syntactic, not functional. Which interface is better is largely a matter of stylistic preference, but for systems that do not support out-parameters (*e.g.,* Java), the latter style of interface is quite common.

For any given interface, one could refactor it to use the struct in/struct out format of `com.develop.ICalculator3` with no loss of functionality. That is exactly the idea that permeates the remote procedure call (RPC) systems made popular in the late 1980s and 1990s. At their core, RPC systems transparently decompose an operation into two type definitions—one that represents the operation request and one that represents the operation response. To support transparent remote invocation, RPC systems transmit a serialized instance of the request type to the context of the implementation code. Once there, the request instance is deserialized and the operation is invoked. The resultant response instance is then serialized and sent back to the original context where it is deserialized prior to returning control to the consumer. RPC systems were the prehistoric ancestors to the component technologies currently in vogue.

Transparent remote invocation is extremely seductive. The notion that by simply reconfiguring a set of components to use remote invocation, an application will transparently receive the benefits of distributed computing is overwhelmingly attractive. Unfortunately, the concerns of integrating components into a single operating system process or virtual machine are not the same as the concerns of integrating independent processes across a potentially wide-area communications network. Interfaces designed to work well between component libraries in the same address space rarely make good communication protocols. Beyond the obvious efficiency concerns, issues such as concurrency management, partial failure, load balancing, availability, and scalability need to be addressed for a communication protocol to be viable.

This does not mean that interfaces in and of themselves are unsuitable as communication protocols. Quite the contrary; the notion of typed contracts is just as important in the distributed case as it is in the same-process case—and for the same reasons. That stated, one needs to reexamine what an interface truly represents when used as a communications protocol. In that context, an interface is a collection of message types that have request/response semantics. For each operation, there are two message types—one for the request and one for the response. The syntax and semantics of these types may be inferred from the syntax and semantics of the corresponding operation.

Transparent remoting is a special case of message-oriented communications. The consumer (a.k.a. the client) sends a request message to the implementation (a.k.a. the server) and blocks until the response is received. The implementation receives the request message, invokes the appropriate code, and sends back a response message. The fact that RPC systems hide this behind a transparent marshaling/dispatching layer does not change the fact that a message exchange has taken place. It would be just as valid a programming model if the client were to send the message and continue processing while the server was processing the operation in parallel. Assuming the operation yielded significant results, the client could arrange to be alerted to the arrival of the response message via any number of mechanisms. This asynchronous invocation style (which is supported by both DCOM and CORBA) blurs the notion of transparent remoting by promoting the message to first class status. This promotion in no way diminishes the importance of the interface; rather, the style of invocation is simply an implementation detail of the consumer that is largely immaterial to the implied contract of the interface.[6]

The request/response communications model of transparent remoting is but one form of message-oriented communications. Other models such as one-way,

---

[6]Careful readers may have noticed the weasel-word *largely.* Assuming the client does not invoke multiple operations against the same implementation in parallel, the weasel-word would not have been necessary. However, counsel has advised the authors that issuing parallel operations may or may not violate the constraints of a given contract, and that *largely* was sufficiently vague to cover our assets.

broadcast, multicast, queued, workflow, and transactional are also useful and often necessary to achieve efficient and/or correct operation. This does not diminish the importance of typed contracts; rather, it simply suggests that additional mechanisms for modeling the interactions between agents are in order. These interactions will invariably be based on the exchange of typed messages to avoid the randomness and chaos that results from untyped contracts. The CORBA messaging specification is one example of an attempt to adapt the typed contracts implied by interfaces to more general message-oriented communications.

XML as a Better Component Model

The last 30+ years of software engineering and distributed systems research and development has left a fairly extensive paper (and product) trail of ideas, concepts, and techniques that natural selection has weeded down to the ideas summarized in the previous several pages of prose. As a reader, you may be wondering, "What does all of this have to do with XML?" In a word: everything. XML was originally developed to solve a completely different class of problems than the ones just described. However, as the software industry looks to XML as a solution to all problems short of world hunger, there is a tendency to reinvent the entire automobile and highway system in the process of reinventing the wheel. In particular, applications that exchange XML documents between software agents inevitably wind up reinventing the paradigms and protocols popularized in the pre-XML era. As these new XML-based applications are developed, it is easy to ignore the 30 years of history in the field in favor of the "brave new world" that XML presents to the ambitious developer.

It is unlikely that XML will replace the component runtime systems and models that are currently in use. XML is so far removed from issues such as execution environments, concurrency management, and code management that component execution systems such as Java and COM have little to fear from XML. However, for cross-execution environment integration, XML shows a great deal of promise. Unlike its predecessors, such as CORBA, Java RMI, and DCOM, XML has already achieved universal support across platforms, programming languages, and vendors. Due to its relative simplicity and text-based orientation, adapting XML to a new platform or programming language is extremely straightforward, especially given the amount of freely available open-source software.[7]

Despite the hype surrounding XML at the time of this writing, simply adopting XML as an integration technology is fairly meaningless, as just being able to parse past the angle brackets is of limited utility. Rather, unless a set of conventions is agreed upon for exchanging application-level datatypes, there is little benefit to using XML. The XML schema specification makes explicit how to encode the so-called "primitive types" of most programming and runtime environments (*e.g.,* `double, boolean`). The XML schema specification also provides mechanisms for aggregating instances of these primitive types into constructed types, but the specification stops short of mandating exactly which of its many mechanisms should be used for this purpose. In the absence of such a mandate, it becomes difficult at best to build automated bridges between existing type systems and the type system of XML and XML Schemas. Enter SOAP.

The Simple Object Access Protocol (SOAP) is a specification that was submitted to the W3C by Ariba, Commerce One, DevelopMentor, Hewlett Packard, IBM, Iona, Microsoft, SAP, and UserLand. At the time of this writing, SOAP was not even a W3C working draft, but its submission was intended to act as the seed for a W3C activity leading toward (hopefully) a full recommendation. Whether that happens remains to be seen, but it is obvious (to the authors of this book and that specification at least) that something *like* SOAP is needed. Acknowledging that SOAP may change radically or be completely superseded by something else by the time you read this, the remainder of this chapter will focus on the core ideas of SOAP rather than the grueling details.

The SOAP specification can be summarized in two sentences: "read the XML Schema specification" and "just use elements." The former sentence refers to the fact that SOAP relies heavily on the XML Schema type system. The latter sentence refers to the fact that SOAP only uses attributes for SOAP-specific structural metadata, not for user/application information. As shown in Figure 6.2, the core value of SOAP is its type system and encoding rules, which are detailed in section 5 of the SOAP specification.

---

[7] James Clark's EXPAT is an excellent example of a portable open-source parser that is extremely adaptable to a broad spectrum of environments, both due to its small size and the fact that it is written in Standard C.

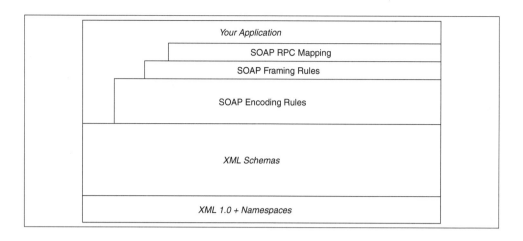

| Your Application |
| SOAP RPC Mapping |
| SOAP Framing Rules |
| SOAP Encoding Rules |
| XML Schemas |
| XML 1.0 + Namespaces |

Figure 6.2   The role of SOAP

As stated before, the XML Schema specification provides constructs for aggregating instances of primitive types into constructed types but stops short of mandating exactly which of its many constructs should be used for this purpose. SOAP's primary value is that it makes explicit which constructs should be used in order to ensure interoperability with non-XML-based type systems such as CORBA, Java, C++, and COM. SOAP defines two forms of constructed type: one whose subcomponents are accessed by a locally unique name and one whose subcomponents are accessed by position. The former corresponds to a C/C++ structure, Perl hash, database row, or Java/C++ class; the latter corresponds to a C/C++/Java array, CORBA sequence, or database table. In both cases, named `elementOnly` complex type definitions are used to represent the type. In both cases, the subcomponents are represented by local element declarations. Consider the following Java class definitions:

```
public class Person {
  public String firstName;
  public String lastName;
  public int    age;
}
public class Author extends Person {
  public boolean meetsDeadlines;
}
```

ESSENTIAL XML: BEYOND MARKUP

The SOAP representation of these classes would be the following XML Schema types:[8]

```
<complexType name='Person' content='elementOnly' >
  <sequence minOccurs='0' maxOccurs='1'>
    <element name='firstName' type='string' />
    <element name='lastName'  type='string' />
    <element name='age'       type='string' />
  </sequence>
  <attribute name='id' type='ID' />
  <attribute name='href' type='uriReference' />
  <anyAttribute
    namespace='http://schemas.xmlsoap.org/soap/encoding/"/>
  <anyAttribute
    namespace='http://schemas.xmlsoap.org/soap/envelope/"/>
</complexType>
<element name='Person' type='target:Person' />

<complexType name='Author' base='Person'
            derivedBy='extension' >
  <sequence minOccurs='0' maxOccurs='1'>
    <element name='meetsDeadlines' type='boolean' />
  </sequence>
</complexType>
<element name='Author' type='target:Author' />
```

These type definitions are fairly obvious, but two aspects require further explanation. For one, note that the attribute wildcard allows any attribute from two namespaces. The first namespace URI corresponds to SOAP's encoding rules. The second namespace URI corresponds to SOAP's framing rules. These wildcards allow the various structural attributes that SOAP may need to add to be added without violating schema-validity. The more interesting aspect of this type definition is the id and href attributes.

Most runtime environments support references in some form. If two references inside a graph of instances refer to the same instance, this fact needs to be retained in the serialized representation of the graph. Otherwise, there is loss

---

[8]At the time of this writing, SOAP stops short of mandating XML schemas, but the complex type definition shown here completely adheres to the SOAP encoding rules.

of information at best and stack overflow at worst. To support serializing instances that are referenced from more than one accessor, SOAP uses the id/href attributes to serialize multireference instances. Consider this Java class definition

```
public class Marriage {
  public Person husband;
  public Person wife;
}
```

and the corresponding complex type definition

```
<complexType name='Marriage' content='elementOnly' >
  <sequence minOccurs='0' maxOccurs='1'>
    <element name='husband' type='target:Person' />
    <element name='wife'    type='target:Person' />
  </sequence>
  <attribute name='id' type='ID' />
  <attribute name='href' type='uriReference' />
  <anyAttribute
    namespace='http://schemas.xmlsoap.org/soap/encoding/"/>
  <anyAttribute
    namespace='http://schemas.xmlsoap.org/soap/envelope/"/>
</complexType>
<element name='Marriage' type='target:Marriage' />
```

Assuming the rules of marriage that are prevalent in North America, an instance of Marriage would be serialized as follows

```
<package:Marriage xmlns:package='[URI-for-package]' >
  <husband>
    <firstName>John</firstName><lastName>Smith</lastName>
    <age>22</age>
  </husband>
  <wife>
    <firstName>Jane</firstName><lastName>Jones</lastName>
    <age>35</age>
  </wife>
</package:Marriage>
```

This is a fairly uninteresting example. For example, consider the case where a husband is allowed to be in more than one marriage at a time. The following intuitive encoding

```
<package:Marriage xmlns:package='[URI-for-package]' >
  <husband>
    <firstName>John</firstName><lastName>Smith</lastName>
    <age>22</age>
  </husband>
  <wife>
    <firstName>Jane</firstName><lastName>Jones</lastName>
    <age>35</age>
  </wife>
</package:Marriage>

<package:Marriage xmlns:package='[URI-for-package]' >
  <husband>
    <firstName>John</firstName><lastName>Smith</lastName>
    <age>22</age>
  </husband>
  <wife>
    <firstName>Sheila</firstName><lastName>Brown</lastName>
    <age>19</age>
  </wife>
</package:Marriage>
```

winds up serializing John Smith twice. Though this is wasteful in terms of resources, the more significant problem is that the identity of John Smith is now broken. There is no way for a deserializer to know that the same instance was serialized twice. If the underlying application was relying on this identity relationship, this style of serialization will not work—hence, the id/href attributes.

Instances that potentially can be referenced multiple times are never serialized as [children] of the element that references them. Rather, these multireference instances must be serialized as sibling elements to the root(s) of the serialization graph. When serialized in this manner, the element must carry a unique id attribute. All elements that reference that instance must use an href attribute containing a fragment identifier that refers to the instance. The following is the correct serialization of our bigamist graph:

```
<package:Marriage xmlns:package='[URI-for-package]' >
  <husband href='#xyz'/>
  <wife>
    <firstName>Jane</firstName><lastName>Jones</lastName>
    <age>35</age>
  </wife>
</package:Marriage>

<package:Marriage xmlns:package='[URI-for-package]' >
  <husband href='#xyz' />
  <wife>
    <firstName>Sheila</firstName><lastName>Brown</lastName>
    <age>19</age>
  </wife>
</package:Marriage>

<package:Person id='xyz' xmlns:package='[URI-for-package]'>
    <firstName>John</firstName><lastName>Smith</lastName>
    <age>22</age>
</package:Person>
```

SOAP does not require any particular values for the id and href attributes other than that all id attribute values must be unique (they are of type ID) and that all href attributes refer to an instance of the appropriate type.

SOAP relies on the XML Schema mechanisms for type-based substitution, null references, and primitive data types. SOAP does add a construct for handling arrays that is similar to the constructs just examined. The primary difference is that the [children] of an array are accessed by position, not by name, and that there is a well-known attribute (SOAP-ENC:arrayType) that describes the shape and element type of the array. For example, consider the following variation on the Marriage class:

```
class Marriage2 {
  public Person wife;
  public Person[] husband;
}
```

The corresponding schema type would look like this.

```
<complexType name='Marriage2' content='elementOnly' >
  <element name='wife' type='target:Person' />
  <element name='husband' type='SOAP-ENC:Array'
                          SOAP-ENC:auxType='Person[]'[9] />
<!-- attribute declarations elided for clarity -->
</complexType>
```

The type SOAP-ENC:Array is defined in the normative schema for SOAP and allows any element as its `[children]`. The rules of SOAP are much stricter than this. Instead, arrays must contain one element per item in the array. The name of the element is typically the same as the complex type name. Assuming wives and husbands could only belong to one marriage, an instance of Marriage2 would look like this:

```
<package:Marriage2 xmlns:package='[URI-for-package]' >
  <wife>
    <firstName>Iman</firstName><lastName/><age>41</age>
  </wife>
  <husband SOAP-ENC:arrayType='package:Person[2]'>
    <package:Person>
      <firstName>Fabio</firstName><lastName/><age>38</age>
    </package:Person>
    <package:Person>
      <firstName>Roy</firstName><lastName/><age>52</age>
    </package:Person>
  </husband>
</package:Marriage>
```

When arrays are encoded in SOAP, the `SOAP-ENC:arrayType` attribute is mandatory, as it provides the deserializer with the dimension information needed to properly allocate the array.

Given the primitives just described, it is fairly straightforward to map the type systems of existing programming environments onto XML Schema types. The SOAP serialization rules are not the only way to perform this mapping, but

---

[9]Note that this extension to schemas has not been endorsed by anyone, but something like it is inevitable.

their existence provides a common framework for interoperation that a more ad hoc encoding style would not provide.

Documents as Messages

To integrate software agents using XML, it is necessary but not necessarily sufficient to agree on how instances of application-specific types will be represented in XML. In order for these representations to be useful, some context is needed for defining when and where these representations will reside, how they will be transmitted, and the action that should be taken upon the receipt of a serialized instance. One way to provide this context is to model the serialized instance as a message that is transmitted from a sender to a receiver. By viewing an XML document as a transient message as opposed to a persistent well-known resource, one can easily adapt existing messaging/RPC communication models to use XML as their message format.

Ultimately, XML is a data representation format. XML is not a full-fledged communication protocol, as XML does not address transmission endpoints, protocol-style state machines, error correction/detection, flow control, and other protocol-esque features. This makes it difficult to build XML messaging applications using XML alone. Rather, some underlying transport protocol is needed. For RPC applications, TCP can be used either in the raw or using a layered protocol such as HTTP.[10] The advantages of HTTP include tons of existing infrastructure plus the intrinsic RPC-style semantics of HTTP's POST method. Equally important is HTTP's use of logical endpoints based on URI that are independent of physical TCP port numbers. The HTTP endpoint URI provides a flexible scheme for managing server-side resources that have persistent or transient identity. For more general messaging applications that are not request/response-based, other transports such as IBM's MQSeries or Microsoft's MSMQ can be used. No matter which underlying transport is used, the concepts of XML-based messaging and RPC remain constant.

To grasp XML as a message format, consider the OMG IDL interface definition of `com.develop.ICalculator` from earlier in this chapter. As was

---

[10]In fact, section 7 of the SOAP specification details exactly how this particular mapping must look.

demonstrated by the `com.develop.ICalculator3` interface, this interface could be refactored as a set of structure pairs, with two structures per method. Assuming that each of these structures were then mapped to XML schemas according to the SOAP encoding rules, one could invoke the add method by transmitting the following XML document to an implementation:

```
<?xml version='1.0' ?>
<itf:add xmlns:itf='[URI-for-ICalculator]'>
  <m>34.2</m>
  <n>87.3</n>
</itf:add>
```

Upon receiving this document, the implementation would then produce the following result document:

```
<?xml version='1.0' ?>
<itf:addResponse xmlns:itf='[URI-for-ICalculator]'>
  <overflow>0</overflow>
  <result>111.5</result>
</itf:addResponse>
```

Mapping these two XML documents to instances of programmatic types (and ultimately to stack frames) is an extremely straightforward process.[11] While the SOAP specification currently does not specify how to associate complex type definitions and element declarations with an interface definition, several approaches are currently being proposed. One set of proposals believes that minor extensions to the XML Schemas specification are the best approach. Another set of proposals seeks to replicate CORBA IDL in XML. It remains to be seen which approach will be endorsed by the W3C.

In most messaging applications, both the sender and receiver can be thought of as execution contexts.[12] When a message is sent from an execution context, that message invariably winds up being received and processed by an execution context other than the one that sent the message. History has shown

---

[11]Though one could just as easily write an XSLT that transformed the request message into the response message, turning XML messaging into "XSLT with a longer wire."

[12]An operating system process is one example of such an execution context.

that it is often desirable to transmit aspects of the sender's execution context in tandem with the interface-specific information that acts as the primary content of the message. Such context-related aspects include locale information, security identifiers and signatures, and information related to synchronization and transactions. More often than not, these context-related information items are completely orthogonal to the semantics and syntax of the operation being invoked. To allow execution contexts to convey this extended information, an XML messaging format must have a flexible mechanism for extensibility.

SOAP provides a framework for layering extensions into a message format. All messages in the SOAP protocol are contained in an Envelope element that contains two [children]: the Header element, which contains all extension information, and the Body element, which contains the primary information of the message. The Body element is mandatory; the Header element is optional. The following is a SOAP message for invoking the com.develop.ICalculator.add method:

```
<?xml version='1.0' ?>
<frame:Envelope
   xmlns:frame='http://schemas.xmlsoap.org/soap/envelope/' >
  <frame:Body>
    <itf:add xmlns:itf='[URI-for-ICalculator]'>
   <m>34.2</m>
   <n>87.3</n>
  </itf:add>
  </frame:Body>
</frame:Envelope>
```

This particular message contains no extensions. Any extensions must appear as [children] of the Header element, as shown here.

```
<?xml version='1.0' ?>
<frame:Envelope
   xmlns:frame='http://schemas.xmlsoap.org/soap/envelope/' >
  <frame:Header>
    <tip:Transaction xmlns:tip='[URI-for-TIP]' >
    <tid>tip:209.110.197.4?transid-78</tid>
    </tip:Transaction>
    <lcid:LocaleExtension xmlns:lcid='[URI-for-LCID]' >
```

ESSENTIAL XML: BEYOND MARKUP

```
          <country>us</country>
          <lang>en</lang>
        </lcid:LocaleExtension>
      </frame:Header>
      <frame:Body>
        <itf:add xmlns:itf='[URI-for-ICalculator]'>
        <m>34.2</m>
        <n>87.3</n>
        </itf:add>
      </frame:Body>
    </frame:Envelope>
```

This message contains a Transaction Internet Protocol (TIP) transaction ID that the receiver can use to compose the work of the add method with the sender's transaction. It also contains an extension that describes the locale of the sender.

SOAP, like XML Schemas, assumes that the corresponding element declaration binds the underlying type to a given context/usage. Along these lines, the namespace-qualified element name of the extension is sufficient to identify "who" the extension is meant for. That stated, SOAP adds an additional identifier (which is expressed via the `frame:Actor` attribute) that allows the recipient of the extension to be identified independently from the element name. If an extension's element name or `frame:Actor` is not recognized by the receiver, the receiver is free to ignore the extension *provided* that the extension has not been marked as a mandatory extension. Mandatory extensions have a namespace-qualified `frame:mustUnderstand` attribute with a value of '1'. For example, consider this variation on the previous message:

```
    <?xml version='1.0' ?>
    <frame:Envelope
       xmlns:frame='http://schemas.xmlsoap.org/soap/envelope/' >
      <frame:Header>
        <tip:Transaction xmlns:tip='[URI-for-TIP]'
                         frame:mustUnderstand='1'
        >
          <tid>tip:209.110.197.4?transid-78</tid>
        </tip:Transaction>
        <lcid:LocaleExtension xmlns:lcid='[URI-for-LCID]' >
          <country>us</country>
```

```
        <lang>en</lang>
      </lcid:LocaleExtension>
    </frame:Header>
    <frame:Body>
      <itf:add xmlns:itf='[URI-for-ICalculator]'>
      <m>34.2</m>
      <n>87.3</n>
      </itf:add>
    </frame:Body>
  </frame:Envelope>
```

In this message, the `lcid:LocaleExtension` is optional and can safely be
ignored. The `tip:Transaction` is mandatory and must be understood in
order to properly process the message. Receivers that cannot understand a
mandatory extension are required to reject the message as a whole and, in RPC
scenarios, signal the rejection using a well-known fault message.

Where Are We Going?

It is difficult to discuss RPC, messaging, and components without discussing
objects. The distributed object technologies made popular in the 1990s applied
the concepts of object orientation to network protocols. While the request/
response nature of RPC is very amenable to transparent method remoting, the
traditional notions of object identity made little sense when translating between
an object-oriented programming language such as C++ or Java, and a network
protocol, such as CORBA's GIOP/IIOP or DCOM. In particular, the lifecycles of
communication endpoints and language-level objects are rarely the same, yet
both CORBA and DCOM went to great lengths to try to make one look like the
other. Despite these efforts, at the end of the twentieth century the state-of-the-
practice in both of these technologies was to reject transparent remote access to
persistent application entities in favor of session-oriented communications models. This style of design was first popularized by Microsoft Transaction Server
and later formalized by Enterprise Java Beans. Both of these technologies owe a
great deal to HTTP, which validated the session-oriented communications model
by providing the substrate to the Internet as we now know it. HTTP supports
both persistent and transient endpoint identifiers through the use of URI and
cookies, respectively. Whether a server maps either or both of these identifiers to

"objects" is completely opaque to the HTTP client. The more sophisticated the server, the less likely it is to tie language-level objects to cookies or URI.

If HTTP diminishes the importance of objects as communication endpoints, XML messaging turns traditional object-oriented thinking on its head. The type model of XML messaging fundamentally changes the flavor of encapsulation and polymorphism, largely due to its reliance on XML schemas. Unlike traditional object-orientation, which attempts to hide representations, XML schemas are focused on documenting representations for all to see. Unlike traditional object-orientation, which uses polymorphism and inheritance to dynamically dispatch code to derived types, XML schemas use inheritance only for substitutability and extending representations.

The exhibitionist nature of XML schemas forces one to reevaluate exactly what an object is and whether the term is even meaningful in the context of XML messaging. XML messaging supports typed communication endpoints and typed serialized instances that are contained in messages, which are themselves typed. Attaching the term "object" to any of these abstractions (endpoint, instance, message) may help one sleep at night but ultimately obfuscates the core issues at hand. Instead, it is the authors' hope that XML messaging will give the software development community at large an opportunity to reexamine the atoms of distributed system development and build on these atoms using the growing body of XML, TCP, and HTTP-based tools and software.

Appendix A

The XML Information Set (Infoset)

This appendix contains the most recent *public* draft of the Infoset specification. During the production of this book, the W3C XML Core Working Group had produced several internal *private* drafts in preparation for entering the Candidate Recommendation phase. Despite the vast improvements in both accuracy and readability, W3C policy prevents us from reprinting that draft until it is released to the public. Be aware that the draft reprinted here is hopelessly out of date, however, the prose of the previous six chapters was informed by the more recent drafts that should be closer to where the final recommendation converges. You can view the most recent public version of the Infoset by pointing your browser at `http://www.w3.org/TR/xml-infoset`.

W3C Working Draft 20 December–1999

This version:

    http://www.w3.org/TR/1999/WD-xml-infoset-19991220

Latest version:

    http://www.w3.org/TR/xml-infoset

Previous versions:

    http://www.w3.org/TR/1999/WD-xml-infoset-19990517

Editors:

    John Cowan

    David Megginson

Abstract

This specification describes an abstract data set containing the information available from an XML document.

Status of this Document

The *XML Core Working Group,* with this 1999 December 20 Infoset *Last Call* working draft, invites comment on this specification. The Last Call period begins 20 December 1999 and ends 31 January 2000.

The W3C Membership and other interested parties are invited to review the specification and report implementation experience. Please send comments to *www-xml-infoset-comments@w3.org* (*archive*).

For background on this work, please see the *XML Activity Statement.* While we welcome implementation experience reports, the *XML Core Working Group* will not allow early implementation to constrain its ability to make changes to this specification prior to final release.

See *XML Information Set Requirements* for the specific requirements that informed development of this specification.

A list of current W3C Recommendations and other technical documents can be found at *http://www.w3.org/TR.*

Contents

1. Introduction

This document specifies an abstract data set called the **XML information set** (**Infoset**), a description of the information available in a well-formed XML document [*XML*].

Although technically well-formed XML 1.0, documents that do not conform to [*Namespaces*] are not considered to have meaningful information sets. This essentially bars documents that have element or attribute names containing colons that are used in other ways than as prescribed by [Namespaces]. There is no requirement for a XML document to be valid in order to have an information set.

An XML document's information set consists of two or more **information items** (the information set for any well-formed XML document will contain at least the *document information item* and one *element information item*). An information item is an abstract representation of some component of an XML document: each information item has a set of associated properties, some of which are core, and some of which are peripheral.

In earlier drafts, the term "required" was used rather than "core", and the term "optional" rather than "peripheral". The editor has made this change because "required" and "optional" suggest the behavior of an application rather than the status of part of a data structure.

For any given XML document, there are a number of corresponding information sets: a unique minimal information set consisting of the core properties of the core items and nothing else, a unique maximal information set consisting of all the core and all the peripheral items with all the peripheral properties, and one for every combination of present/absent peripheral items and properties in between. The in-between information sets must be fully consistent with the maximal information set.

All information sets are understood to describe the XML document with all entity references already expanded; that is, represented by the information items corresponding to their replacement text. In the case that an entity reference cannot be expanded, because an XML processor has not read its declaration or its value, explicit provision is made for representing such a reference in the information set.

The XML information set does not require or favor a specific interface or class of interfaces. This specification presents the information set as a tree for the sake of clarity and simplicity, but there is no requirement that the XML information set be made available through a tree structure; other types of interfaces, including (but not limited to) event-based and query-based interfaces are also capable of providing information conforming to the information set. As long as the information in the information set is made available to XML applications in one way or another, the requirements of this document are satisfied.

> **Note:** In this document, the words "must", "should", and "may" assume the meanings specified in RFC 2119 [RFC2119], except that the words do not appear in upper case.

> **Note:** To the best of the editors' knowledge and belief, the information set scheme described in this document satisfies the requirements of the XPointer-Information Set Liaison Statement [XPointer-Liaison].

> **Note:** To the best of the editors' knowledge and belief, the interface specified by the Document Object Model, Level 1 Core Recommendation [DOM] conforms to the XML Information Set as currently specified.

2. Information Items

The XML information set can contain fifteen different types of information items:

1. *a document information item* (core)
2. *element information items* (core)
3. *attribute information items* (core)
4. *processing instruction information items* (core)
5. *reference to skipped entity information items* (core)
6. *character information items* (core)
7. *comment information items* (peripheral)
8. *a document type declaration information item* (peripheral)
9. *entity information items* (core for unparsed entities, peripheral for others)
10. *notation information items* (core)
11. *entity start marker information items* (peripheral)

12. *entity end marker information items* (peripheral)

13. *CDATA start marker information items* (peripheral)

14. *CDATA end marker information items* (peripheral)

15. *namespace declaration information items* (core)

Every information item has properties, some of which are core and some of which are peripheral. Note that peripheral information items can, and do, have core properties. For ease of reference, each property is given a name, indicated **[thus]**.

2.1. The Document Information Item

XML Definition: document *(Section 2, Documents)*

XML Syntax: [1] Document *(Section 2.1, Well-Formed XML Documents)*

There is always one **document information item** in the information set, and all other information items are related to the document information item, either directly or indirectly.

2.1.1. Document: Core Properties

The document information item must have the following properties available in some form:

1. **[children]** An ordered list of references to child information items, in the original document order. The list must contain exactly one reference to an *element* information item, together with a reference to one *processing instruction information item* for each processing instruction preceding the document element (either in the document entity or in a lower-level entity) or following the document element. The list may contain references to other information items as well (see below).

2. **[notations]** An unordered set of references to *notation* information items, one for each notation declaration in the DTD.

3. **[entities]** An unordered set of references to *entity* information items, one for each unparsed entity declaration in the DTD.

2.1.2. Document: Peripheral Properties

The document information item may also have the following properties available in some form:

4. **[base URI]** The absolute URI of the document entity, as computed by the method of RFC 2396 [*RFC2396*], if that is known.

5. **[children—comments]** One reference to a *comment* information item for each comment outside the document element, added to the ordered list of child information items. The relative position of each comment information item in the list must reflect its position in the original document.

6. **[children—doctype]** A reference to exactly one *document type declaration* information item, added to the ordered list of child information items. The relative position of the document type declaration information item in the list must reflect its position in the original document.

7. **[entities—other]** One reference to an *entity* information item for each parsed general entity declaration in the DTD, added to the unordered set of entities. There can also be an entity information item for the document entity and for the external DTD subset.

2.2. Element Information Items

> ***XML Definition:*** element *(Section 3, Logical Structures)*
>
> ***XML Syntax:*** [39] Element *(Section 3, Logical Structures)*

There is one **element information item** for each element appearing in the XML document. Exactly one of the element information items corresponds to the document element (the root of the element tree), and all other element information items are contained within the document element, either directly or indirectly.

2.2.1. Elements: Core Properties

An element information item must have the following properties available in some form:

ESSENTIAL XML: BEYOND MARKUP

1. **[namespace URI]** The URI part, if any, of the element's name.

2. **[local name]** The local part of the element's name. This does not include any namespace prefix or following colon.

3. **[children]** An ordered list of references to *element, processing instruction, reference to skipped entity* and *character* information items, one for each element, processing instruction, reference to an unprocessed external entity, and character appearing immediately within the current element, in the original document order. If the element is empty, this list will have no members.

4. **[attributes]** An unordered set of references to *attribute* information items, one for each of the attributes (specified or defaulted) for this element. Namespace declarations are not represented as attribute information items. If there are no non-#IMPLIED attributes specified or defaulted for the element, this set will be empty.

5. **[declared namespaces]** An unordered set of references to *namespace declaration* information items, one for each of the namespaces declared in this element. If there are no non-#IMPLIED namespace declarations specified or defaulted for the element, this set will be empty.

2.2.2. Elements: Peripheral Properties

An element information item may also have the following properties available in some form:

4. **[children—comments]** A reference to a *comment* information item for each comment appearing immediately within the current element, added to the ordered list of children of the current element. The relative position of each comment information item in the list must reflect its position in the original document.

5. **[children—entity markers]** An ordered set of pairs of references to *entity start marker* information items and their corresponding *entity end marker* information items, one pair for each entity reference in the content of the element, added to the ordered list of children of the current element. The relative position of each marker information item in

the list must reflect its position in the original document. If an entity start marker is present, the corresponding entity end marker must also be present, and vice versa.

6. **[children—CDATA markers]** An ordered set of pairs of references to *CDATA start marker* information items and their corresponding *CDATA end marker* information items, one pair for each CDATA section in the content of the element, added to the ordered list of children of the current element. The relative position of each marker information item in the list must reflect its position in the original document. If a CDATA start marker is present, the corresponding CDATA end marker must also be present, and vice versa.

7. **[base URI]** The absolute URI of the *external* entity in which this element appears, as computed by the method of RFC 2396 [*RFC2396*]. If the element appears directly in the document entity, the URI is the absolute URI of the document entity, if that is known.

8. **[in-scope namespaces]** An unordered set, distinct from that previously mentioned, of references to *namespace declaration* information items, one for each of the namespaces in effect for this element. If there are no namespaces in effect for the element, this set will be empty. This set will include all of the members of the preceding set, except for any information item representing a declaration in the form `xmlns=""`, which does not declare a namespace but rather undeclares the default namespace.

2.3. Attribute Information Items

XML Definition: attribute *(Section 3.1, Start-Tags, End-Tags, and Empty-Element Tags)*

XML Syntax: [41] Attribute *(Section 3.1, Start-Tags, End-Tags, and Empty-Element Tags)*

There is one **attribute information item** for each attribute (specified or defaulted) for each element in the document instance. Namespace declarations are represented using namespace declaration information items, not attribute information items.

Attributes declared in the DTD with a default value of #IMPLIED and not specified in the element's start tag are not represented by attribute information items.

2.3.1. Attributes: Core Properties

An attribute information item must have the following properties available in some form:

1. **[namespace URI]** The URI part, if any, of the attribute's name.

2. **[local name]** The local part of the attribute's name. This does not include any namespace prefix or following colon.

3. **[children]** An ordered list of references to *character* information items, one for each character appearing in the normalized attribute value.

2.3.2. Attributes: Peripheral Properties

In addition, for each attribute information item, the following property may be available in some form:

4. **[specified]** A flag indicating whether this attribute was actually specified in the document instance, or was defaulted from the DTD.

5. **[default]** An ordered list of references to *character* information items, one for each character appearing in the default value specified for this attribute in the DTD, if any. A #FIXED value is considered a default value.

6. **[attribute type]** An indication of the type declared for this attribute in the DTD. Legitimate values are ID, IDREF, IDREFS, ENTITY, ENTITIES, NMTOKEN, NMTOKENS, NOTATION, CDATA, and ENUMERATED.

7. **[children—entity markers]** One reference to an *entity start marker* and a reference to its corresponding *entity end marker* information item for each entity reference in the attribute, added to the ordered list of children of the current attribute. The relative position of each marker information item in the list must reflect the beginning and ending of the entity in the original document. If an entity start marker is present, the corresponding entity end marker must also be present, and vice versa.

2.4. Processing Instruction Information Items

> *XML Definition:* processing instruction *(Section 2.6, Processing Instructions)*
>
> *XML Syntax:* [16] PI *(Section 2.6, Processing Instructions)*

There is one **processing instruction information item** for every processing instruction in the document. The XML declaration and text declarations for external parsed entities are not considered processing instructions.

2.4.1. Processing Instructions: Core Properties

A processing instruction information item must have the following properties available in some form:

1. **[target]** The target part of the processing instruction's content (an XML name).

2. **[content]** A string representing the content of the processing instruction, excluding the target and any whitespace immediately following it. The content may be the empty string.

2.4.2. Processing Instructions: Peripheral Properties

A processing instruction information item may also have the following properties available in some form:

3. **[base URI]** The absolute URI of the *external* entity in which this PI appears, as computed by the method of RFC 2396 [*RFC2396*]. If the PI appears directly in the document entity, the URI is the absolute URI of the document entity, if that is known.

2.5. Reference to Skipped Entity Information Items

> *XML Definition:* Section 4.4.3, Included If Validating

There is one **reference to skipped entity information item** for each reference to an entity not included by a non-validating XML processor because the XML processor does not include external parsed entities.

A validating XML processor will never generate reference to skipped entity information items for a valid XML document.

2.5.1. *Reference to Skipped Entity: Core Properties*

A reference to skipped entity information item must have the following information available in some form:

1. **[name]** The name of the entity referenced.

2.5.2. *Reference to Skipped Entity: Peripheral Properties*

A reference to skipped entity information item may also have the following properties available in some form:

2. **[referent]** A reference to the *entity* information item for the skipped entity (if the XML processor has read the declaration).

2.6. Character Information Items

> **XML Definition:** characters *(Section 2.2, Characters)*

> **XML Syntax:** [2] Char *(Section 2.2, Characters)*

There is one **character information item** for each non-markup character that appears within the document element, either literally, as a character reference, or within a CDATA section. There is also one character information item for each character that appears in a normalized attribute value.

Note, however, that a CR (#xD) character that is followed by a LF (#xA) character is not represented by any information item. Furthermore, a CR character that is *not* followed by a LF character is treated as a LF character. These rules do not apply to CR characters created by character references such as  or .

Each character is a logically-separate information item, but XML applications are free to chunk characters into larger groups as necessary or desirable.

2.6.1. *Characters: Core Properties*

A character information item must have the following properties available in some form:

1. **[character code]** The ISO 10646 character code (in the range 0 to #x10FFFF, but not every value in this range is a legal XML character code) of the character.

2.6.2. Characters: Peripheral Properties

A character information item may also have the following properties available in some form:

2. **[element content whitespace]** A flag indicating whether the character is whitespace appearing within element content (see [*XML*], 2.10 "White Space Handling"). Note that validating XML processors are *required by* XML 1.0 to provide this information.

3. **[predefined entity]** A flag indicating whether the character was included through one of the predefined XML entities.

2.7. Comment Information Items

> ***XML Definition:*** comment *(Section 2.5, Comments)*
>
> ***XML Syntax:*** [15] Comment *(Section 2.5, Comments)*

The peripheral **comment information item** corresponds to a single XML comment in the original document.

2.7.1. Comments: Core Properties

If a comment information item is included, the following properties must be available:

1. **[content]** A string representing the content of the comment.

2.8. The Document Type Declaration Information Item

> ***XML Definition:*** document type declaration *(section 2.8, Prolog and Document Type Declaration)*
>
> ***XML Syntax:*** [28] doctypedecl *(section 2.8, Prolog and Document Type Declaration)*

ESSENTIAL XML: BEYOND MARKUP

If the XML document has a document type declaration, then the information set may contain a single **document type declaration information item**. Note that although entities and notations are logically part of the document type declaration, they are provided as properties of the document information item, because XML processors must provide information on them.

2.8.1. Document Type Declaration: Peripheral Properties

A document type declaration information item may have the following properties available in some form:

1. **[external DTD]** A reference to the *entity* information item for the external DTD subset, if such an information item exists. The public and system identifiers for the external DTD subset are available through this information item.

2. **[children]** An ordered list of references to *comment information items* and *processing instruction information items* representing comments and processing instructions appearing in the DTD, in the original document order. Items from the internal DTD subset appear before those in the external subset.

2.9. Entity Information Items

XML Definition: entity *(section 4, Physical Structures)*

XML Syntax: [70] EntityDecl *(section 4.2, Entity Declarations)*

Entity information items are peripheral, except for information items representing unparsed external entities, which are core information items.

There is at most one entity information item for each general entity, internal or external, declared in the DTD: when the same entity is declared more than once, only the first declaration is used. Parameter entities are not represented by entity information items. There is also at most one entity information item for the document entity, and at most one for the DTD external subset (if there is one). It is perfectly all right for an XML processor to report some entities and not others.

2.9.1. Entities: Core Properties

The entity information item, if included, must have the following information available in some form:

1. **[entity type]** An indication of the type of the entity (internal general entity, external general entity, unparsed entity, document entity, or external DTD subset).

2. **[name]** The name of the entity. If the information item represents the document entity or the external DTD subset, the name is null.

3. **[system identifier]** The system identifier of the entity. If the information item represents an internal entity, the value of this property is always null, and if it represents the document entity, the value *may* be null; otherwise, it must have a non-null value.

4. **[public identifier]** The public identifier of the entity, if one is available. For internal entities, the value is always null.

5. **[base URI]** The absolute URI corresponding to the entity. If the information item represents an internal entity, the value of this property is always null, and if it represents the document entity, the value *may* be null; otherwise, it must have a non-null value.

6. **[notation]** A reference to the *notation* information item associated with the entity, if the entity is an unparsed (NDATA) entity. For entities other than unparsed entities, the value must be null.

2.9.2. Entities: Peripheral Properties

An entity information item may also have the following information available in some form:

6. **[content]** The replacement text of the entity, if it is an internal entity.

7. **[charset]** The name of the character encoding in which the entity is expressed. This property is derived from the XML or text declaration optionally present at the beginning of the document entity or an external entity respectively.

8. **[standalone]** An indication of the standalone status of the entity (which must be the document entity in this case), either "yes", "no", or "not present". This property is derived from the XML declaration optionally present at the beginning of the document entity.

2.10. Notation Information Items

XML Definition: notation *(section 4.7, Notation Declarations)*

XML Syntax: [82] NotationDecl *(section 4.7, Notation Declarations)*

There is one **notation information item** for each notation declared in the DTD.

2.10.1. Notations: Core Properties

A notation information item must have the following properties available:

1. **[name]** The name of the notation.
2. **[system identifier]** The system identifier of the notation, if one was specified.
3. **[public identifier]** The public identifier of the notation, if one was specified.
4. **[base URI]** The absolute URI corresponding to the notation.

2.11. Entity Start Marker Information Items

XML Definition: entity reference *(section 4.1, Character and Entity References)*

XML Syntax: [68] EntityRef *(section 4.1, Character and EntityReferences)*

Entity start marker information items are an peripheral part of the information set. They are inserted to mark the place where text included from an general entity (as a consequence of an entity reference) begins. They appear as children of an element or attribute information item.

Entity start marker information items are not used in connection with parameter entity references in the DTD.

2.11.1. Entity Start Markers: Core Properties

An entity start marker information item, if present, must have the following properties available in some form:

1. **[entity]** A reference to the entity information item referred to by the entity reference which triggered the insertion of this information item.

2.12. Entity End Marker Information Items

> **XML Definition:** entity reference *(section 4.1, Character and Entity References)*
>
> **XML Syntax:** [68] EntityRef *(section 4.1, Character and Entity References)*

Entity end marker information items are an peripheral part of the information set. They are inserted to mark the place where text included from an general entity (as a consequence of an entity reference) concludes. They appear as children of an element or attribute information item.

Entity end marker information items are not used in connection with parameter entity references in the DTD.

2.12.1. Entity End Markers: Core Properties

An entity end marker information item, if present, must have the following properties available in some form:

1. **[entity]** A reference to the entity information item referred to by the entity reference which triggered the insertion of this information item.

2.13. CDATA Start Marker Information Items

> **XML Definition:** CDATA sections *(section 2.7, CDATA sections)*
>
> **XML Syntax:** [18] CDSect *(section 2.7, CDATA Sections)*

CDATA start marker information items are an peripheral part of the information set. They are inserted to mark the place where text embedded in a CDATA section begins. They appear as children of an element information item.

CDATA start marker information items have no properties.

2.14. CDATA End Marker Information Items

XML Definition: CDATA sections *(section 2.7, CDATA sections)*

XML Syntax: [18] CDSect *(section 2.7, CDATA Sections)*

CDATA end marker information items are an peripheral part of the information set. They are inserted to mark the place where text embedded in a CDATA section concludes. They appear as children of an element information item.

CDATA end marker information items have no properties.

2.15. Namespace Declaration Information Items

XML Definition: attribute *(Section 3.1, Start-Tags, End-Tags, and Empty-Element Tags)*

XML Syntax: [41] Attribute *(Section 3.1, Start-Tags, End-Tags, and Empty-Element Tags)*

There is one **namespace declaration information item** for each namespace declaration (specified or defaulted) for each element in the document instance. Namespace declarations are syntactically like attribute declarations of attributes whose names begin with the string `xmlns`.

Namespace declarations declared in the DTD with a default value of `#IMPLIED` and not specified in the element's start tag are not represented by information items.

Note that the last two properties present the same underlying information in overlapping ways. XML processors may report either one or both, but must report at least one.

2.15.1. Namespace Declarations: Core Properties

A namespace declaration information item must have the following properties available in some form:

1. **[prefix]** The prefix being declared. Syntactically, this is the part of the attribute name following the `xmlns:` prefix. If the attribute name is simply `xmlns`, this property is a null string.

2. **[namespace URI]** The absolute URI (plus optional fragment identifier) of the namespace being declared. It may be a null string. *This property is considered a core property if and only if the following property is not present.*

3. **[children]** An ordered list of references to *character* information items, one for each character appearing in the normalized attribute value. There may also be a reference to an *entity start marker* and a reference to its corresponding *entity end marker* information item for each entity reference in the attribute. The relative position of each marker information item in the list must reflect its position in the original document. If an entity start marker is present, the corresponding entity end marker must also be present, and vice versa. This property is considered a core property if and only if the preceding property is not present.

3. Example

Consider the following example XML document:

```
<?xml version="1.0"?>

<msg:message dc:date="19990421"
             xmlns:dc="http://purl.org/metadata/dublin_core#"
             xmlns:msg="http://www.message.net/"
>Phone home!</msg:message>
```

The Information Set for this XML document will contain at least the following items in some form:

- A *Document* information item.

- An *Element* information item with the URI part `"http://www.message.net/"` and the local part "`message `".

- An *Attribute* information item with the URI part `"http://purl.org/metadata/dublin_core#"` and the local part "` date`".

- Eleven *Character* information items for the character data, and an additional 8 *Character* information items for the attribute value.

4. Conformance

An XML processor conforms to the XML Information Set if it provides all the core information items and all their core properties corresponding to that part of the document that the processor has actually read. For instance, attributes are core information items; therefore, an XML processor that does not report the existence of attributes, as well as their names and values (which are core properties of attributes), does not conform to the XML Information Set.

Some information items are peripheral, and some core information items have peripheral information associated with them. If an XML processor reports an information item, then it must supply at least the core properties defined by the XML Information Set in order to conform. For instance, if an XML processor chooses to supply entity information items, which are peripheral, then it is also required to supply names for the entities, since the XML Information Set specifies that the name of an entity information item is a core property. However, since entity information items are peripheral, an XML processor which does not supply them at all also conforms to the XML Information Set.

The XML 1.0 Recommendation *[XML]* explicitly allows non-validating XML processors to omit parsing the external DTD subset and external entities (both parsed general entities and parameter entities). As a result, it is possible that a non-validating XML processor will omit reading attribute and entity declarations or actual markup that will affect the quantity and quality of information included in the information set. Validating XML processors must report all core information; non-validating XML processors may omit core information that appears outside of the top-level document entity (either in the external DTD subset or in an external text entity) if they do not read the other entities.

XML Processors may optionally provide additional information not found in the XML Information Set; for instance, the XML Information Set excludes whitespace that occurs between attributes from the information set, but an XML Processor that provides this information will still conform to the Information Set as long as it provides the information that is required for conformance to the XML Information Set.

5. What is not in the Information Set

The following information is not represented in the current version of the XML Information Set:

1. The XML version number.

2. The content models of elements, from ELEMENT declarations in the DTD.

3. The grouping and ordering of attribute declarations in ATTLIST declarations.

4. Whitespace outside the document element.

5. The difference between the two forms of an empty element: `<foo/>` and `<foo></foo>`.

6. Whitespace within start-tags (other than significant whitespace in attribute values) and end-tags.

7. The difference between CR, CR-LF, and LF line termination.

8. The unnormalized form of attribute values (see *3.3.3 Attribute-Value Normalization [XML]*).

9. The order of attributes within a start-tag.

10. The order of declarations within the DTD.

11. The boundaries of conditional sections in the DTD.

12. Any ignored declarations, including those within an IGNORE conditional section, as well as entity and attribute declarations ignored because previous entity declarations override them.

Furthermore, the XML Infoset does not provide any method of assigning a single series of numbers to all child nodes of an element or of the document that is guaranteed to be reliable regardless of the underlying XML processor. Although such a method would be desirable, it is considered unachievable for XML, due to the difficulties produced by references to skipped entities, non-validating processors, and peripheral information items.

In other words, there is no reliable way to specify something like "the second child of this element" without restricting both the type of XML processor and the types of children being counted.

ESSENTIAL XML: BEYOND MARKUP

6. References

DOM

Document Object Model (DOM) Level 1 Specification, eds. Vidur Apparao, Steve Byrne, Mike Champion, et alii. 1 October 1998. Available at `http://www.w3.org/TR/REC-DOM-Level-1/` .

Namespaces

Namespaces in XML, eds. Tim Bray, Dave Hollander, and Andrew Layman. 14 January 1999. Available at `http://www.w3.org/TR/REC-xml-names`.

RFC2119

Key words for use in RFCs to Indicate Requirement Levels, ed. S. Bradner. March 1997. Available at `http://www.isi.edu/in-notes/rfc2119.txt`.

RFC2396

Uniform Resource Identifiers (URI): Generic Syntax, T. Berners-Lee, R. Fielding, L. Masinter. August 1998. Available at `http://www.isi.edu/in-notes/rfc2396.txt`.

XML

Extensible Markup Language (XML) 1.0, eds. Tim Bray, Jean Paoli, and Michael Sperberg-McQueen. 10 February 1998. Available at `http://www.w3.org/TR/REC-xml`.

XPointer-Liaison

XPointer-Information Set Liaison Statement, ed. Steven J. DeRose. 24 February 1999. Available at `http://www.w3.org/TR/NOTE-xptr-infoset-liaison`.

Appendix A: XML 1.0 Reporting Requirements (informative)

Although the XML 1.0 Recommendation *[XML]* is primarily concerned with XML syntax, it also includes some specific reporting requirements for XML processors.

The reporting requirements include errors, which are outside the scope of this specification, and document information; all of the XML 1.0 requirements for document information reporting have been integrated into the XML information set specification (numbers in parentheses refer to sections of the Recommendation):

1. An XML processor must always provide all characters in a document that are not part of markup to the application (2.10). We have interpreted this requirement to refer only to characters within the document element.

2. A validating XML processor must inform the application which of the character data in a document is whitespace appearing within element content (2.10).

3. An XML processor must pass a single LF character in place of CR or CR-LF characters appearing in its input (2.5).

4. An XML processor must normalize the value of attributes according to the rules in clause 3.3 before passing them to the application. This implies that the value of attributes after normalization are passed to the application (3.3).

5. An XML processor must pass the names and external identifiers (system identifiers, public identifiers or both) of declared notations to the application (4.7).

6. When the name of an unparsed entity appears as the explicit or default value of an ENTITY or ENTITIES attribute, an XML processor must provide the names, system identifiers, and (if present) public identifiers of both the entity and its notation to the application (4.6, 4.7).

7. An XML processor must pass processing instructions to the application. (2.6)

8. An XML processor (necessarily a non-validating one) that does not include the replacement text of an external parsed entity in place of an entity reference must notify the application that it recognized but did not read the entity (4.4.3).

9. A validating XML processor must include the replacement text of an entity in place of an entity reference. (5.2)

10. A validating XML processor must supply the default value of attributes declared in the DTD for a given element type but not appearing in the element's start tag (5.2).

Appendix B: RDF Schema (informative)

The following RDF Schema provides a formal characterization of the Infoset. In case of disagreement between this schema and the prose in this document, the prose should be taken as normative.

```
<?xml version='1.0'standalone='yes'?>
<rdf:RDF xmlns:rdf='http://www.w3.org/1999/02/22-rdf-syntax-ns#'
  xmlns:rdfs='http://www.w3.org/TR/1999/PR-rdf-schema-19990303#'
  xmlns='http://www.w3.org/1999/WD-infoset-19991201#'>


<!--Enumeration classes and their members-->


<rdfs:Class id='AttrType'/>
<AttrType id='AttrType.ID'/>
<AttrType id='AttrType.IDREF'/>
<AttrType id='AttrType.IDREFS'/>
<AttrType id='AttrType.ENTITY'/>
<AttrType id='AttrType.ENTITIES'/>
<AttrType id='AttrType.NMTOKEN'/>
<AttrType id='AttrType.NMTOKENS'/>
<AttrType id='AttrType.NOTATION'/>
<AttrType id='AttrType.CDATA'/>
<AttrType id='AttrType.ENUMERATED'/>


<rdfs:Class id='Boolean'/>
<Boolean id='Boolean.true'/>
<Boolean id='Boolean.false'/>


<rdfs:Class id='EntityType'/>
<EntityType id=EntityType.InternalGeneral'/>
<EntityType id=EntityType.ExternalGeneral'/>
<EntityType id=EntityType.Unparsed'/>
<EntityType id=EntityType.DocumentEntity'/>
<EntityType id=EntityType.ExternalDTDSubset'/>
```

```
<rdfs:Class id='Integer'
 rdfs:subClassOf='http://www.w3.org/TR/1999/
                  PR-rdf-schema-19990303#Literal'/>

<rdfs:Class id='StandaloneType'/>
<StandaloneType id='StandaloneType.yes'/>
<StandaloneType id='StandaloneType.no'/>
<StandaloneType id='StandaloneType.notSpecified'/>

<!--Info item classes in document order-->

<rdfs:Class id='InfoItem'/>

<rdfs:Class id='Document'rdfs:subClassOf='#InfoItem'/>

<rdfs:Class id='Element'rdfs:subClassOf='#InfoItem'/>

<rdfs:Class id='Attribute'rdfs:subClassOf='#InfoItem'/>

<rdfs:Class id='ProcessingInstruction'rdfs:
            subClassOf='#InfoItem'/>

<rdfs:Class id='Character'rdfs:subClassOf='#InfoItem'/>

<rdfs:Class id='ReferenceToSkippedEntity'rdfs:
            subClassOf='#InfoItem'/>

<rdfs:Class id='Comment'rdfs:subClassOf='#InfoItem'/>

<rdfs:Class id='DocumentTypeDeclaration'rdfs:
            subClassOf='#InfoItem'/>

<rdfs:Class id='Entity'rdfs:subClassOf='#InfoItem'/>

<rdfs:Class id='Notation'rdfs:subClassOf='#InfoItem'/>

<rdfs:Class id='EntityStartMarker'rdfs:
            subClassOf='#InfoItem'/>

<rdfs:Class id='EntityEndMarker'rdfs:subClassOf='#InfoItem'/>
```

```
<rdfs:Class id='CDATAStartMarker'rdfs:
            subClassOf='#InfoItem'/>

<rdfs:Class id='CDATAEndMarker'rdfs:subClassOf='#InfoItem'/>

<rdfs:Class id='Namespace'rdfs:subClassOf='#InfoItem'/>\

<!--Set containers-->

<rdfs:Class id='InfoItemSet'
  rdfs:subClassOf='http://www.w3.org/1999/02/
                  22-rdf-syntax-ns#Bag'/>

<rdfs:Class id='AttributeSet'rdfs:subClassOf='#InfoItemSet'/>

<rdfs:Class id='EntitySet'rdfs:subClassOf='#InfoItemSet'/>

<rdfs:Class id='NamespaceSet'rdfs:subClassOf='#InfoItemSet'/>

<rdfs:Class id='NotationSet'rdfs:subClassOf='#InfoItemSet'/>

<!--Sequence container-->

<rdfs:Class id='InfoItemSeq'
 rdfs:subClassOf='http://www.w3.org/1999/02/
                  22-rdf-syntax-ns#Seq'/>

<!--Info item properties-->

<rdfs:Property id='attributes'>
  <rdfs:domain resource='#Element'/>
  <rdfs:range resource='#AttributeSet'/>
</rdfs:Property>

<rdfs:Property id='attributeType'>
  <rdfs:domain resource='#Attribute'/>
  <rdfs:range resource='#AttrType'/>
</rdfs:Property>

<rdfs:Property id='baseURI'>
  <rdfs:domain resource='#Document'/>
```

```
      <rdfs:domain resource='#Element'/>
      <rdfs:domain resource='#ProcessingInstruction'/>
      <rdfs:domain resource='#Entity'/>
      <rdfs:domain resource='#Notation'/>
      <rdfs:range resource='http://www.w3.org/TR/1999/
                            PR-rdf-schema-19990303#Literal'/>
    </rdfs:Property>

    <rdfs:Property id='characterCode'>
      <rdfs:domain resource='#Character'/>
      <rdfs:range resource='#Integer'/>
    </rdfs:Property>

    <rdfs:Property id='charset'>
      <rdfs:domain resource='#Entity'/>
      <rdfs:range resource='http://www.w3.org/TR/1999/
                            PR-rdf-schema-19990303#Literal'/>
    </rdfs:Property>

    <rdfs:Property id='children'>
      <rdfs:domain resource='#Document'/>
      <rdfs:domain resource='#Element'/>
      <rdfs:domain resource='#Attribute'/>
      <rdfs:domain resource='#DocumentTypeDeclaration'/>
      <rdfs:domain resource='#Namespace'/>
      <rdfs:range resource='#InfoItemSeq'/>
    </rdfs:Property>

    <rdfs:Property id='content'>
      <rdfs:domain resource='#ProcessingInstruction'/>
      <rdfs:domain resource='#Comment'/>
      <rdfs:domain resource='#Entity'/>
      <rdfs:range resource='http://www.w3.org/TR/1999/
                            PR-rdf-schema-19990303#Literal'/>
    </rdfs:Property>

    <rdfs:Property id='declaredNamespaces'>
      <rdfs:domain resource='#Element'/>
      <rdfs:range resource='#NamespaceSet'/>
    </rdfs:Property>
```

```
<rdfs:Property id='default'>
  <rdfs:domain resource='#Attribute'/>
  <rdfs:range resource='#Boolean'/>
</rdfs:Property>


<rdfs:Property id='elementContentWhitespace'>
  <rdfs:domain resource='#Character'/>
  <rdfs:range resource='#Boolean'/>
</rdfs:Property>


<rdfs:Property id='entity'>
  <rdfs:domain resource='#EntityStartMarker'/>
  <rdfs:domain resource='#EntityEndMarker'/>
  <rdfs:range resource='#Entity'/>
</rdfs:Property>


<rdfs:Property id='entities'>
  <rdfs:domain resource='#Document'/>
  <rdfs:range resource='#EntitySet'/>
</rdfs:Property>


<rdfs:Property id='entityType'>
  <rdfs:domain resource='#Attribute'/>
  <rdfs:range resource='#AttrType'/>
</rdfs:Property>


<rdfs:Property id='externalDTD'>
  <rdfs:domain resource='#DocumentTypeDeclaration'/>
  <rdfs:range resource='#Entity'/>
</rdfs:Property>


<rdfs:Property id='inScopeNamespaces'>
  <rdfs:domain resource='#Element'/>
  <rdfs:range resource='#NamespaceSet'/>
</rdfs:Property>


<rdfs:Property id='localName'>
  <rdfs:domain resource='#Element'/>
  <rdfs:domain resource='#Attribute'/>
```

```
      <rdfs:range resource='http://www.w3.org/TR/1999/
                       PR-rdf-schema-19990303#Literal'/>
</rdfs:Property>

<rdfs:Property id='name'>
  <rdfs:domain resource='#ReferenceToSkippedEntity'/>
  <rdfs:domain resource='#Entity'/>
  <rdfs:domain resource='#Notation'/>
  <rdfs:range resource='http://www.w3.org/TR/1999/
                       PR-rdf-schema-19990303#Literal'/>
</rdfs:Property>

<rdfs:Property id='namespaceURI'>
  <rdfs:domain resource='#Element'/>
  <rdfs:domain resource='#Attribute'/>
  <rdfs:domain resource='#Namespace'/>
  <rdfs:range resource='http://www.w3.org/TR/1999/
                       PR-rdf-schema-19990303#Literal'/>
</rdfs:Property>

<rdfs:Property id='notation'>
  <rdfs:domain resource='#Entity'/>
  <rdfs:range resource='#Notation'/>
</rdfs:Property>

<rdfs:Property id='notations'>
  <rdfs:domain resource='#Document'/>
  <rdfs:range resource='#NotationSet'/>
</rdfs:Property>

<rdfs:Property id='predefinedEntity'>
  <rdfs:domain resource='#Character'/>
  <rdfs:range resource='#Boolean'/>
</rdfs:Property>

<rdfs:Property id='prefix'>
  <rdfs:domain resource='#Namespace'/>
  <rdfs:range resource='http://www.w3.org/TR/1999/
                       PR-rdf-schema-19990303#Literal'/>
</rdfs:Property>
```

```
<rdfs:Property id='publicIdentifier'>
  <rdfs:domain resource='#Entity'/>
  <rdfs:domain resource='#Notation'/>
  <rdfs:range resource='http://www.w3.org/TR/1999/PR-rdf-
schema-19990303#Literal'/>
</rdfs:Property>

<rdfs:Property id='referent'>
  <rdfs:domain resource='#ReferenceToSkippedEntity'/>
  <rdfs:range resource='#Entity'/>
</rdfs:Property>

<rdfs:Property id='specified'>
  <rdfs:domain resource='#Attribute'/>
  <rdfs:range resource='#Boolean'/>
</rdfs:Property>

<rdfs:Property id='standalone'>
  <rdfs:domain resource='#Entity'/>
  <rdfs:range resource='#StandaloneType'/>
</rdfs:Property>

<rdfs:Property id='systemIdentifier'>
  <rdfs:domain resource='#Entity'/>
  <rdfs:domain resource='#Notation'/>
  <rdfs:range resource='http://www.w3.org/TR/1999/PR-rdf-
schema-19990303#Literal'/>
</rdfs:Property>

<rdfs:Property id='target'>
  <rdfs:domain resource='#ProcessingInstruction'/>
  <rdfs:range resource='http://www.w3.org/TR/1999/PR-rdf-
schema-19990303#Literal'/>
</rdfs:Property>

</rdf:RDF>
```

Appendix B

XML Productions

The following productions come from the Extensible Markup Language 1.0 and Namespaces in XML specifications (xml and xmlns respectively) and are provided in this summarized format for convenience.

Sorted by production number

Number	Name	Production
xml-1	document	`prolog element Misc*`
xml-2	Char	`#x9 | #xA | #xD | [#x20-#xD7FF] | [#xE000-#xFFFD] |` `   [#x10000-#x10FFFF]`
xml-3	S	`(#x20 | #x9 | #xD | #xA)+`
xml-4	NameChar	`Letter | Digit | '.' | '-' | '_' | ':' |` `   CombiningChar | Extender`
xml-5	Name	`(Letter | '_' | ':') (NameChar)*`
xml-6	Names	`Name (S Name)*`
xml-7	Nmtoken	`(NameChar)+`
xml-8	Nmtokens	`Nmtoken (S Nmtoken)*`
xml-9	EntityValue	`'"' ([^&"] | PEReference | Reference)* '"' | "'"` `([^&'] | PEReference | Reference)* "'"`
xml-10	AttValue	`'"' ([^<&"] | Reference)* '"' | "'" ([^<&'] |` `   Reference)* "'"`
xml-11	SystemLiteral	`('"' [^"]* '"') | ("'" [^']* "'")`
xml-12	PubidLiteral	`'"' PubidChar* '"' | "'" (PubidChar - "'")* "'"`
xml-13	PubidChar	`#x20 | #xD | #xA | [a-zA-Z0-9] |` `   [-'()+,./:=?;!*#@$_]`
xml-14	CharData	`[^<&]* - ([^<&]* ']]>' [^<&]*)`
xml-15	Comment	`'<!--' ((Char - '-') | ('-' (Char - '-')))* '-->'`
xml-16	PI	`'<?' PITarget (S (Char* - (Char* '?>' Char*)))?` `   '?>'`
xml-17	PITarget	`Name - (('X' | 'x') ('M' | 'm') ('L' | 'l'))`

xml-18	CDSect	CDStart CData CDEnd
xml-19	CDStart	'<![CDATA['
xml-20	CData	(Char* - (Char* ']]>' Char*))
xml-21	CDEnd	']]>'
xml-22	prolog	XMLDecl? Misc* (doctypedecl Misc*)?
xml-23	XMLDecl	'<?xml' VersionInfo EncodingDecl? SDDecl? S? '?>'
xml-24	VersionInfo	S 'version' Eq (' VersionNum ' | " VersionNum ")
xml-25 v	Eq	S? '=' S?
xml-26	VersionNum	([a-zA-Z0-9_.:] | '-')+
xml-27	Misc	Comment | PI | S
xml-28	doctypedecl (superseded by [xmlns-13])	'<!DOCTYPE' S Name (S ExternalID)? S? ('[' (markupdecl | PEReference | S)* ']' S?)? '>' [VC: Root Element Type]
xml-29	markupdecl	elementdecl | AttlistDecl | EntityDecl | NotationDecl | PI | Comment
xml-30	extSubset	TextDecl? extSubsetDecl
xml-31	extSubsetDecl	(markupdecl | conditionalSect | PEReference | S)*
xml-32	SDDecl	S 'standalone' Eq (("'" ('yes' | 'no') "'") | ('"' ('yes' | 'no') '"'))
xml-33	LanguageID	Langcode ('-' Subcode)*
xml-34	Langcode	ISO639Code | IanaCode | UserCode
xml-35	ISO	639Code([a-z] | [A-Z]) ([a-z] | [A-Z])
xml-36	IanaCode	('i' | 'I') '-' ([a-z] | [A-Z])+
xml-37	UserCode	('x' | 'X') '-' ([a-z] | [A-Z])+
xml-38	Subcode	([a-z] | [A-Z])+
xml-39	element	EmptyElemTag | STag content ETag
xml-40	STag (superseded by [xmlns-9])	'<' Name (S Attribute)* S? '>' [WFC: Unique Att Spec]
xml-41	Attribute (superseded by [xmlns-12])	Name Eq AttValue
xml-42	ETag (superseded by [xmlns-10])	'</' Name S? '>'
xml-43	content	(element | CharData | Reference | CDSect | PI | Comment)*
xml-44	EmptyElemTag (superseded by [xmlns-11])	'<' Name (S Attribute)* S? '/>'
xml-45	elementdecl	'<!ELEMENT' S Name S contentspec S? '>'

	(superseded by	[VC: Unique Element Type Declaration]
	[xmlns-14])	
xml-46	contentspec	'EMPTY' | 'ANY' | Mixed | children
xml-47	children	(choice | seq) ('?' | '*' | '+')?
xml-48	cp	(Name | choice | seq) ('?' | '*' | '+')?
	(superseded by	
	[xmlns-15])	
xml-49	choice	'(' S? cp (S? '|' S? cp)* S? ')'
		<production><spec>xml</spec><prodno>50
		</prodno><prodname>seq</prodname><rhs>
		<![CDATA['(' S? cp (S? ',' S? cp)* S? ')'
xml-50	seq	'(' S? cp (S? ',' S? cp)* S? ')'
xml-51	Mixed	'(' S? '#PCDATA' (S? '|' S? Name)* S? ')*' |
	(superseded by	'(' S? '#PCDATA' S? ')'
	[xmlns-16])	
xml-52	AttlistDecl	'<!ATTLIST' S Name AttDef* S? '>'
	(superseded by	
	[xmlns-17])	
xml-53	AttDef	S Name S AttType S DefaultDecl
	(superseded by	
	[xmlns-18])	
xml-54	AttType	StringType | TokenizedType | EnumeratedType
xml-55	StringType	'CDATA'
xml-56	TokenizedType	'ID' | 'IDREF' | 'IDREFS' | 'ENTITY' | 'ENTITIES' |
		'NMTOKEN' | 'NMTOKENS'
xml-57	EnumeratedType	NotationType | Enumeration
xml-58	NotationType	'NOTATION' S '(' S? Name (S? '|' S? Name)* S? ')'
		[VC: Notation Attributes]
xml-59	Enumeration	'(' S? Nmtoken (S? '|' S? Nmtoken)* S? ')'
xml-60	DefaultDecl	'#REQUIRED' | '#IMPLIED' | (('#FIXED' S)? AttValue)
xml-61	conditionalSect	includeSect | ignoreSect
xml-62	includeSect	'<![' S? 'INCLUDE' S? '[' extSubsetDecl ']]>'
xml-63	ignoreSect	'<![' S? 'IGNORE' S? '[' ignoreSectContents* ']]>'
xml-64	ignoreSect	Ignore ('<![' ignoreSectContents ']]>' Ignore)*
	Contents	
xml-65	Ignore	Char* - (Char* ('<![' | ']]>') Char*)
xml-66	CharRef	'&#' [0-9]+ ';' | '&#x' [0-9a-fA-F]+ ';'
xml-67	Reference	EntityRef | CharRef
xml-68	EntityRef	'&' Name ';' [WFC: Entity Declared]
xml-69	PEReference	'' Name ';'
xml-70	EntityDecl	GEDecl | PEDecl

xml-71	GEDecl	'<!ENTITY' S Name S EntityDef S? '>'
xml-72	PEDecl	'<!ENTITY' S '' S Name S PEDef S? '>'
xml-73	EntityDef	EntityValue | (ExternalID NDataDecl?)
xml-74	PEDef	EntityValue | ExternalID
xml-75	ExternalID	'SYSTEM' S SystemLiteral | 'PUBLIC' S PubidLiteral S SystemLiteral
xml-76	NDataDecl	S 'NDATA' S Name
xml-77	TextDecl	'<?xml' VersionInfo? EncodingDecl S? '?>'
xml-78	extParsedEnt	TextDecl? content
xml-79	extPE	TextDecl? extSubsetDecl
xml-80	EncodingDecl	S 'encoding' Eq ('"' EncName '"' | "'" EncName "'")
xml-81	EncName	[A-Za-z] ([A-Za-z0-9._] | '-')*
xml-82	NotationDecl	'<!NOTATION' S Name S (ExternalID | PublicID) S? '>'
xml-83	PublicID	'PUBLIC' S PubidLiteral
xml-84	Letter	BaseChar | Ideographic
xml-85	BaseChar	See Character Tables
xml-86	Ideographic	See Character Tables
xml-87	CombiningChar	See Character Tables
xml-88	Digit	See Character Tables
xml-89	Extender	See Character Tables
xmlns-1	NSAttName	PrefixedAttName | DefaultAttName
xmlns-2	PrefixedAttName	'xmlns:' NCName
xmlns-3	DefaultAttName	'xmlns'
xmlns-4	NCName	(Letter | '_') (NCNameChar)*
xmlns-5	NCNameChar	Letter | Digit | '.' | '-' | '_' | CombiningChar | Extender
xmlns-6	QName	(Prefix ':')? LocalPart
xmlns-7	Prefix	NCName
xmlns-8	LocalPart	NCName
xmlns-9	STag (supersedes [xml-40])	'<' QName (S Attribute)* S? '>'
xmlns-10	ETag (supersedes [xml-42])	'</' QName S? '>'
xmlns-11	EmptyElemTag (supersedes [xml-44])	'<' QName (S Attribute)* S? '/>'
xmlns-12	Attribute (supersedes [xml-41])	NSAttName Eq AttValue | QName Eq AttValue
xmlns-13	doctypedecl	'<!DOCTYPE' S QName (S ExternalID)? S?

ESSENTIAL XML: BEYOND MARKUP

```
            (supersedes     ('[' (markupdecl | PEReference | S)* ']' S?)? '>'
            [xml-28])
xmlns-14    elementdecl     '<!ELEMENT' S QName S contentspec S? '>'
            (supersedes
            [xml-45])
xmlns-15    cp (supersedes  (QName | choice | seq) ('?' | '*' | '+')?
            [xml-48])
xmlns-16    Mixed           '(' S? '#PCDATA' (S? '|' S? QName)* S? ')*' |
            (supersedes     '(' S? '#PCDATA' S? ')'
            [xml-51])
xmlns-17    AttlistDecl     '<!ATTLIST' S QName AttDef* S? '>'
            (supersedes
            [xml-52])
xmlns-18    AttDef          S (QName | NSAttName) S AttType S DefaultDecl
            (supersedes
            (supersedes [xml-53]) [xml-53])
```

Sorted by name

Name	Number	Production
AttDef (supersedes [xml-53])	xmlns-18	`S (QName | NSAttName) S AttType S DefaultDecl`
AttDef (superseded by [xmlns-18])	xml-53	`S Name S AttType S DefaultDecl`
AttlistDecl (supersedes [xml-52])	xmlns-17	`'<!ATTLIST' S QName AttDef* S? '>'`
AttlistDecl (superseded by [xmlns-17])	xml-52	`'<!ATTLIST' S Name AttDef* S? '>'`
Attribute (supersedes [xml-41])	xmlns-12	`NSAttName Eq AttValue	QName Eq AttValue`
Attribute (superseded by [xmlns-12])	xml-41	`Name Eq AttValue`
AttType	xml-54	`StringType	TokenizedType	EnumeratedType`
AttValue	xml-10	`'"' ([^<&"]	Reference)* '"'	"'" ([^<&']	Reference)* "'"`

BaseChar	xml-85	See Character Tables
CData	xml-20	`(Char* - (Char* ']]>' Char*))`
CDEnd	xml-21	`']]>'`
CDSect	xml-18	`CDStart CData CDEnd`
CDStart	xml-19	`'<![CDATA['`
Char	xml-2	`#x9	#xA	#xD	[#x20-#xD7FF]	[#xE000-#xFFFD] |` `[#x10000-#x10FFFF]`
CharData	xml-14	`[^<&]* - ([^<&]* ']]>' [^<&]*)`
CharRef	xml-66	`'&#' [0-9]+ ';'	'&#x' [0-9a-fA-F]+ ';'`
children	xml-47	`(choice | seq) ('?' | '*' | '+')?`

choice	xml-49	`'(' S? cp ( S? '|' S? cp )* S? ')'`
		`<production><spec>xml</spec><prodno>50</prodno>`
		`<prodname>seq</prodname><rhs>`
		`<![CDAA['(' S? cp ( S? '|' S? cp )* S? ')'`

CombiningChar	xml-87	See Character Tables
Comment	xml-15	`'<!—' ((Char - '-')	('-' (Char - '-')))* '—>'`
conditionalSect	xml-61	`includeSect	ignoreSect`
content	xml-43	`(element | CharData | Reference | CDSect | PI |` `Comment)*`
contentspec	xml-46	`'EMPTY'	'ANY'	Mixed	children`
cp (supersedes [xml-48])	xmlns-15	`(QName | choice | seq) ('?' | '*' | '+')?`
cp (superseded by [xmlns-15])	xml-48	`(Name | choice | seq) ('?' | '*' | '+')?`
DefaultAttName	xmlns-3	`'xmlns'`
DefaultDecl	xml-60	`'#REQUIRED'	'#IMPLIED'	(('#FIXED' S)? AttValue)`
Digit	xml-88	See Character Tables
doctypedecl (supersedes [xml-28])	xmlns-13	`'<!DOCTYPE' S QName (S ExternalID)? S?` `('[' (markupdecl | PEReference | S)* ']' S?)? '>'`

doctypedecl (superseded by [xmlns-13])	xml-28	`'<!DOCTYPE' S Name (S ExternalID)? S?`
		`('[' (markupdecl | PEReference | S)* ']' S?)? '>'`
		`[ VC: Root Element Type ]`

document	xml-1	`prolog element Misc*`
element	xml-39	`EmptyElemTag	STag content ETag`
elementdecl (supersedes [xml-45])	xmlns-14	`'<!ELEMENT' S QName S contentspec S? '>'`
elementdecl (superseded by [xmlns-14])	xml-45	`'<!ELEMENT' S Name S contentspec S? '>'` `[ VC: Unique Element Type Declaration ]`

ESSENTIAL XML: BEYOND MARKUP

EmptyElemTag (supersedes [xml-44])	xmlns-11	`'<' QName (S Attribute)* S? '/>'`
EmptyElemTag (superseded by [xmlns-11])	xml-44	`'<' Name (S Attribute)* S? '/>'`
EncName	xml-81	`[A-Za-z] ([A-Za-z0-9._] | '-')*`
EncodingDecl	xml-80	`S 'encoding' Eq ('"' EncName '"' | "'" EncName "'" )`
EntityDecl	xml-70	`GEDecl	PEDecl`
EntityDef	xml-73	`EntityValue	(ExternalID NDataDecl?)`
EntityRef	xml-68	`'&' Name ';' [ WFC: Entity Declared ]`
EntityValue	xml-9	`'"' ([^&"] | PEReference | Reference)* '"'	"'"` `([^&'] | PEReference | Reference)* "'"`
EnumeratedType	xml-57	`NotationType	Enumeration`
Enumeration	xml-59	`'(' S? Nmtoken (S? '|' S? Nmtoken)* S? ')'`
Eq	xml-25	`S? '=' S?`
ETag (supersedes [xml-42])	xmlns-10	`'</' QName S? '>'`
ETag (superseded by [xmlns-10])	xml-42	`'</' Name S? '>'`
Extender	xml-89	See Character Tables
ExternalID	xml-75	`'SYSTEM' S SystemLiteral	'PUBLIC' S PubidLiteral` `S SystemLiteral`
extParsedEnt	xml-78	`TextDecl? content`
extPE	xml-79	`TextDecl? extSubsetDecl`
extSubset	xml-30	`TextDecl? extSubsetDecl`
extSubsetDecl	xml-31	`( markupdecl | conditionalSect | PEReference | S )*`
GEDecl	xml-71	`'<!ENTITY' S Name S EntityDef S? '>'`
IanaCode	xml-36	`('i' | 'I') '-' ([a-z] | [A-Z])+`
Ideographic	xml-86	See Character Tables
Ignore	xml-65	`Char* - (Char* ('<![' | ']]>') Char*)`
ignoreSect	xml-63	`'<![' S? 'IGNORE' S? '[' ignoreSectContents* ']]>'`
ignoreSect Contents	xml-64	`Ignore ('<![' ignoreSectContents ']]>' Ignore)*`
includeSect	xml-62	`'<![' S? 'INCLUDE' S? '[' extSubsetDecl ']]>'`
ISO	xml-35	`639Code([a-z] | [A-Z]) ([a-z] | [A-Z])`
Langcode	xml-34	`ISO639Code	IanaCode	UserCode`
LanguageID	xml-33	`Langcode ('-' Subcode)*`
Letter	xml-84	`BaseChar	Ideographic`

LocalPart	xmlns-8	NCName
markupdecl	xml-29	elementdecl | AttlistDecl | EntityDecl | NotationDecl | PI | Comment
Misc	xml-27	Comment | PI | S
Mixed (supersedes [xml-51])	xmlns-16	'(' S? '#PCDATA' (S? '|' S? QName)* S? ')*' | '(' S? '#PCDATA' S? ')'
Mixed (superseded by [xmlns-16])	xml-51	'(' S? '#PCDATA' (S? '|' S? Name)* S? ')*' | '(' S? '#PCDATA' S? ')'
Name	xml-5	(Letter | '_' | ':') (NameChar)*
NameChar	xml-4	Letter | Digit | '.' | '-' | '_' | ':' | CombiningChar | Extender
Names	xml-6	Name (S Name)*
NCName	xmlns-4	(Letter | '_') (NCNameChar)*
NCNameChar	xmlns-5	Letter | Digit | '.' | '-' | '_' | CombiningChar | Extender
NDataDecl	xml-76	S 'NDATA' S Name
Nmtoken	xml-7	(NameChar)+
Nmtokens	xml-8	Nmtoken (S Nmtoken)*
NotationDecl	xml-82	'<!NOTATION' S Name S (ExternalID | PublicID) S? '>'
NotationType	xml-58	'NOTATION' S '(' S? Name (S? '|' S? Name)* S? ')' [VC: Notation Attributes]
NSAttName	xmlns-1	PrefixedAttName | DefaultAttName
PEDecl	xml-72	'<!ENTITY' S '' S Name S PEDef S? '>'
PEDef	xml-74	EntityValue | ExternalID
PEReference	xml-69	'' Name ';'
PI	xml-16	'<?' PITarget (S (Char* - (Char* '?>' Char*)))? '?>'
PITarget	xml-17	Name - (('X' | 'x') ('M' | 'm') ('L' | 'l'))
Prefix	xmlns-7	NCName
PrefixedAttName	xmlns-2	'xmlns:' NCName
prolog	xml-22	XMLDecl? Misc* (doctypedecl Misc*)?
PubidChar	xml-13	#x20 | #xD | #xA | [a-zA-Z0-9] | [-'()+,./:=?;!*#@$_]
PubidLiteral	xml-12	'"' PubidChar* '"' | "'" (PubidChar - "'")* "'"
PublicID	xml-83	'PUBLIC' S PubidLiteral
QName	xmlns-6	(Prefix ':')? LocalPart
Reference	xml-67	EntityRef | CharRef
S	xml-3	(#x20 | #x9 | #xD | #xA)+
SDDecl	xml-32	S 'standalone' Eq (("'" ('yes' | 'no') "'") | ('"' ('yes' | 'no') '"'))

STag (supersedes [xml-40])	xmlns-9	`'<' QName (S Attribute)* S? '>'`
STag (superseded by [xmlns-9])	xml-40	`'<' Name (S Attribute)* S? '>' [ WFC: Unique Att Spec ]`
StringType	xml-55	`'CDATA'`
Subcode	xml-38	`([a-z] | [A-Z])+`
SystemLiteral	xml-11	`('"' [^"]* '"')	("'" [^']* "'")`
TextDecl	xml-77	`'<?xml' VersionInfo? EncodingDecl S? '?>'`
TokenizedType	xml-56	`'ID'	'IDREF'	'IDREFS'	'ENTITY'	'ENTITIES'	'NMTOKEN'	'NMTOKENS'`
UserCode	xml-37	`('x' | 'X') '-' ([a-z] | [A-Z])+`
VersionInfo	xml-24	`S 'version' Eq (' VersionNum ' | " VersionNum ")`
VersionNum	xml-26	`([a-zA-Z0-9_.:] | '-')+`
XMLDecl	xml-23	`'<?xml' VersionInfo EncodingDecl? SDDecl? S? '?>'`

Character Tables

Number	Name	Production
xml-85	BaseChar	`[#x0041-#x005A]	[#x0061-#x007A]	[#x00C0-#x00D6]	[#x00D8-#x00F6]	[#x00F8-#x00FF]	[#x0100-#x0131]	[#x0134-#x013E]	[#x0141-#x0148]	[#x014A-#x017E]	[#x0180-#x01C3]	[#x01CD-#x01F0]	[#x01F4-#x01F5]	[#x01FA-#x0217]	[#x0250-#x02A8]	[#x02BB-#x02C1]	#x0386	[#x0388-#x038A]	#x038C	[#x038E-#x03A1]	[#x03A3-#x03CE]	[#x03D0-#x03D6]	#x03DA	#x03DC	#x03DE	#x03E0	[#x03E2-#x03F3]	[#x0401-#x040C]	[#x040E-#x044F]	[#x0451-#x045C]	[#x045E-#x0481]	[#x0490-#x04C4]	[#x04C7-#x04C8]	[#x04CB-#x04CC]	[#x04D0-#x04EB]	[#x04EE-#x04F5]	[#x04F8-#x04F9]	[#x0531-#x0556]	#x0559	[#x0561-#x0586]	[#x05D0-#x05EA]	[#x05F0-#x05F2]	[#x0621-#x063A]	[#x0641-#x064A]	[#x0671-#x06B7]	[#x06BA-#x06BE]	[#x06C0-#x06CE]	[#x06D0-#x06D3]	#x06D5	[#x06E5-#x06E6] |`

```
[#x0905-#x0939] | #x093D | [#x0958-#x0961] |
[#x0985-#x098C] | [#x098F-#x0990] |
[#x0993-#x09A8] | [#x09AA-#x09B0] | #x09B2 |
[#x09B6-#x09B9] | [#x09DC-#x09DD] |
[#x09DF-#x09E1] | [#x09F0-#x09F1] |
[#x0A05-#x0A0A] | [#x0A0F-#x0A10] |
[#x0A13-#x0A28] | [#x0A2A-#x0A30] |
[#x0A32-#x0A33] | [#x0A35-#x0A36] |
[#x0A38-#x0A39] | [#x0A59-#x0A5C] | #x0A5E |
[#x0A72-#x0A74] | [#x0A85-#x0A8B] | #x0A8D |
[#x0A8F-#x0A91] | [#x0A93-#x0AA8] |
[#x0AAA-#x0AB0] | [#x0AB2-#x0AB3] |
[#x0AB5-#x0AB9] | #x0ABD | #x0AE0 |
[#x0B05-#x0B0C] | [#x0B0F-#x0B10] |
[#x0B13-#x0B28] | [#x0B2A-#x0B30] |
[#x0B32-#x0B33] | [#x0B36-#x0B39] |
#x0B3D | [#x0B5C-#x0B5D] | [#x0B5F-#x0B61] |
[#x0B85-#x0B8A] | [#x0B8E-#x0B90] |
[#x0B92-#x0B95] | [#x0B99-#x0B9A] | #x0B9C |
[#x0B9E-#x0B9F] | [#x0BA3-#x0BA4] |
[#x0BA8-#x0BAA] | [#x0BAE-#x0BB5] |
[#x0BB7-#x0BB9] | [#x0C05-#x0C0C] |
[#x0C0E-#x0C10] | [#x0C12-#x0C28] |
[#x0C2A-#x0C33] | [#x0C35-#x0C39] |
[#x0C60-#x0C61] | [#x0C85-#x0C8C] |
[#x0C8E-#x0C90] | [#x0C92-#x0CA8] |
[#x0CAA-#x0CB3] | [#x0CB5-#x0CB9] | #x0CDE |
[#x0CE0-#x0CE1] | [#x0D05-#x0D0C] |
[#x0D0E-#x0D10] | [#x0D12-#x0D28] |
[#x0D2A-#x0D39] | [#x0D60-#x0D61] |
[#x0E01-#x0E2E] | #x0E30 | [#x0E32-#x0E33] |
[#x0E40-#x0E45] | [#x0E81-#x0E82] | #x0E84 |
[#x0E87-#x0E88] | #x0E8A | #x0E8D |
[#x0E94-#x0E97] | [#x0E99-#x0E9F] |
[#x0EA1-#x0EA3] | #x0EA5 | #x0EA7 |
[#x0EAA-#x0EAB] | [#x0EAD-#x0EAE] | #x0EB0 |
[#x0EB2-#x0EB3] | #x0EBD | [#x0EC0-#x0EC4] |
[#x0F40-#x0F47] | [#x0F49-#x0F69] |
[#x10A0-#x10C5] | [#x10D0-#x10F6] | #x1100 |
[#x1102-#x1103] | [#x1105-#x1107] | #x1109 |
[#x110B-#x110C] | [#x110E-#x1112] | #x113C |
```

```
#x113E | #x1140 | #x114C | #x114E | #x1150 |
[#x1154-#x1155] | #x1159 | [#x115F-#x1161] |
#x1163 | #x1165 | #x1167 | #x1169 |
[#x116D-#x116E] | [#x1172-#x1173] | #x1175 |
#x119E | #x11A8 | #x11AB | [#x11AE-#x11AF] |
[#x11B7-#x11B8] | #x11BA | [#x11BC-#x11C2] |
#x11EB | #x11F0 | #x11F9 | [#x1E00-#x1E9B] |
[#x1EA0-#x1EF9] | [#x1F00-#x1F15] |
[#x1F18-#x1F1D] | [#x1F20-#x1F45] |
[#x1F48-#x1F4D] | [#x1F50-#x1F57] | #x1F59 |
#x1F5B | #x1F5D | [#x1F5F-#x1F7D] |
[#x1F80-#x1FB4] | [#x1FB6-#x1FBC] | #x1FBE |
[#x1FC2-#x1FC4] | [#x1FC6-#x1FCC] |
[#x1FD0-#x1FD3] | [#x1FD6-#x1FDB] |
[#x1FE0-#x1FEC] | [#x1FF2-#x1FF4] |
[#x1FF6-#x1FFC] | #x2126 | [#x212A-#x212B] |
#x212E | [#x2180-#x2182] | [#x3041-#x3094] |
[#x30A1-#x30FA] | [#x3105-#x312C] |
[#xAC00-#xD7A3]
```
```
xml-86    Ideographic      [#x4E00-#x9FA5] | #x3007 | [#x3021-#x3029]
xml-87    CombiningChar    [#x0300-#x0345] | [#x0360-#x0361] |
                           [#x0483-#x0486] | [#x0591-#x05A1] |
                           [#x05A3-#x05B9] | [#x05BB-#x05BD] | #x05BF |
                           [#x05C1-#x05C2] | #x05C4 | [#x064B-#x0652] |
                           #x0670 | [#x06D6-#x06DC] | [#x06DD-#x06DF] |
                           [#x06E0-#x06E4] | [#x06E7-#x06E8] |
                           [#x06EA-#x06ED] | [#x0901-#x0903] | #x093C |
                           [#x093E-#x094C] | #x094D | [#x0951-#x0954] |
                           [#x0962-#x0963] | [#x0981-#x0983] | #x09BC |
                           #x09BE | #x09BF | [#x09C0-#x09C4] |
                           [#x09C7-#x09C8] | [#x09CB-#x09CD] | #x09D7 |
                           [#x09E2-#x09E3] | #x0A02 | #x0A3C | #x0A3E |
                           #x0A3F | [#x0A40-#x0A42] | [#x0A47-#x0A48] |
                           [#x0A4B-#x0A4D] | [#x0A70-#x0A71] |
                           [#x0A81-#x0A83] | #x0ABC | [#x0ABE-#x0AC5] |
                           [#x0AC7-#x0AC9] | [#x0ACB-#x0ACD] |
                           [#x0B01-#x0B03] | #x0B3C | [#x0B3E-#x0B43] |
                           [#x0B47-#x0B48] | [#x0B4B-#x0B4D] |
                           [#x0B56-#x0B57] | [#x0B82-#x0B83] |
                           [#x0BBE-#x0BC2] | [#x0BC6-#x0BC8] |
                           [#x0BCA-#x0BCD] | #x0BD7 | [#x0C01-#x0C03] |
```

```
                              [#x0C3E-#x0C44] | [#x0C46-#x0C48] |
                              [#x0C4A-#x0C4D] | [#x0C55-#x0C56] |
                              [#x0C82-#x0C83] | [#x0CBE-#x0CC4] |
                              [#x0CC6-#x0CC8] | [#x0CCA-#x0CCD] |
                              [#x0CD5-#x0CD6] | [#x0D02-#x0D03] |
                              [#x0D3E-#x0D43] | [#x0D46-#x0D48] |
                              [#x0D4A-#x0D4D] | #x0D57 | #x0E31 |
                              [#x0E34-#x0E3A] | [#x0E47-#x0E4E] | #x0EB1 |
                              [#x0EB4-#x0EB9] | [#x0EBB-#x0EBC] |
                              [#x0EC8-#x0ECD] | [#x0F18-#x0F19] | #x0F35 |
                              #x0F37 | #x0F39 | #x0F3E | #x0F3F |
                              [#x0F71-#x0F84] | [#x0F86-#x0F8B] |
                              [#x0F90-#x0F95] | #x0F97 | [#x0F99-#x0FAD] |
                              [#x0FB1-#x0FB7] | #x0FB9 | [#x20D0-#x20DC] |
                              #x20E1 | [#x302A-#x302F] | #x3099 | #x309A
xml-88    Digit               [#x0030-#x0039] | [#x0660-#x0669] |
                              [#x06F0-#x06F9] | [#x0966-#x096F] |
                              [#x09E6-#x09EF] | [#x0A66-#x0A6F] |
                              [#x0AE6-#x0AEF] | [#x0B66-#x0B6F] |
                              [#x0BE7-#x0BEF] | [#x0C66-#x0C6F] |
                              [#x0CE6-#x0CEF] | [#x0D66-#x0D6F] |
                              [#x0E50-#x0E59] | [#x0ED0-#x0ED9] |
                              [#x0F20-#x0F29]
xml-89    Extender            #x00B7 | #x02D0 | #x02D1 | #x0387 | #x0640 |
                              #x0E46 | #x0EC6 | #x3005 | [#x3031-#x3035] |
                              [#x309D-#x309E] | [#x30FC-#x30FE]
```

Appendix C

Example Gallery

See Aaron. See Aaron Code.

Anonymous, 2000

This appendix contains complete examples in source form. These programs are presented here to provide context for many of the topics discussed throughout the book. The complete source code and build scripts for these examples can be found at `http://www.develop.com/books/essentialxml`.

SAX/DOM Examples

Generating a Document Programmatically

The following two examples illustrate how to generate an XML document, using the SAX2 and DOM Level 2 APIs. The following XML document contains most of the *core* information items defined by the Infoset (including elements, attributes, characters, processing instructions, and namespace declarations), as well as a *peripheral* item, in this case a comment.

```
<?xml version="1.0"?>
<?order alpha ascending?>
<art xmlns='urn:art-org:art'>
  <period name="Renaissance"
        xmlns:a='urn:art-org:artists'>
    <a:artist>Leonardo da Vinci</a:artist>
    <a:artist>Michelangelo</a:artist>
```

```
      <a:artist>Donatello</a:artist>
   </period>
   <!-- insert period here -->
</art>
```

SAX2 Example

The following sample Java code illustrates how to generate the preceding document, using the ContentHandler and LexicalHandler SAX2 interfaces.

```
import org.xml.sax.ContentHandler;
import org.xml.sax.ext.LexicalHandler;
import org.xml.sax.Attributes;
import org.xml.sax.helpers.AttributesImpl;
import org.xml.sax.SAXException;

public void generateArtDocumentSAX(ContentHandler ch,
                                   LexicalHandler lh)
                      throws SAXException {
// create an AttributesImpl class for holding the
// attributes of each element
   AttributesImpl atts = new AttributesImpl();
// declare a String for use with characters method
   String buf;
   ch.startDocument();
// emit [children] of document information item
   ch.processingInstruction("order", "alpha ascending");
   ch.startPrefixMapping("", "urn:art-org:art");
   ch.startElement("urn:art-org:art", "art", "art", atts);
// emit [children] of art element information item
      ch.startPrefixMapping("a", "urn:art-org:artists");
      atts.addAttribute("", "name", "name", "CDATA",
                        "Renaissance");
      ch.startElement("urn:art-org:art", "period",
                      "period", atts);
// emit [children] of period element information item
// clear the Attributes collection for future use
         atts.clear();
         ch.startElement("urn:art-org:artist", "artist",
                      "a:artist", atts);
```

```
// emit [children] of artist element information item
        buf = "Leonardo da Vinci";
        ch.characters(buf.toCharArray(), 0, buf.length());
      ch.endElement("urn:art-org:artist", "artist",
                    "a:artist");
      ch.startElement("urn:art-org:artist", "artist",
                      "a:artist", atts);
// emit [children] of artist element information item
        buf = "Michelangelo";
        ch.characters(buf.toCharArray(), 0, buf.length());
      ch.endElement("urn:art-org:artist", "artist",
                    "a:artist");
      ch.startElement("urn:art-org:artist", "artist",
                      "a:artist", atts);
// emit [children] of artist element information item
        buf = "Donatello";
        ch.characters(buf.toCharArray(), 0, buf.length());
      ch.endElement("urn:art-org:artist", "artist",
                    "a:artist");
    ch.endElement("urn:art-org:art", "period", "period");
    ch.endPrefixMapping("a");
    buf = " insert period here ";
    lh.comment(buf.toCharArray(), 0, buf.length());
  ch.endElement("urn:art-org:art", "art", "art");
  ch.endPrefixMapping("");
  ch.endDocument();
}
```

DOM Level 2 Example

The following sample Java code illustrates how to generate the preceding document, using the DOM Level 2 API.

```
public Document
generateArtDocumentDOM(DOMImplementation domImpl) {
  Document doc = domImpl.createDocument("urn:art-org:art",
                                        "art", null);
// get art element node
  Element art = doc.getDocumentElement();
```

```
    // create the processing instruction node and
    // append to Document node
      ProcessingInstruction pi =
          doc.createProcessingInstruction( "order",
                                           "alpha ascending");
      doc.insertBefore(pi, art);
    // create period element node and append to art node
      Element period = doc.createElementNS("urn:art-org:art",
                                           "period");
    // add name attribute to period element
      period.setAttribute("name", "Renaissance");
      art.appendChild(period);
    // create artist element nodes & underlying text nodes
      Element artist = doc.createElementNS("urn:art-org:artist",
                                           "a:artist");
      Node txt = doc.createTextNode("Leonardo da Vinci");
      artist.appendChild(txt);
      period.appendChild(artist);
      artist = doc.createElementNS("urn:art-org:artist",
                                   "a:artist");
      txt = doc.createTextNode("Michelangelo");
      artist.appendChild(txt);
      period.appendChild(artist);

      artist = doc.createElementNS("urn:art-org:artist",
                                   "a:artist");
      txt = doc.createTextNode("Donatello");
      artist.appendChild(txt);
      period.appendChild(artist);
    // create comment node and append to art element
      Comment comment = doc.createComment(
                                " insert period here ");
      art.appendChild(comment);
      return doc;
    }
```

Building a DOM Tree with SAX2

The following sample Java code illustrates how to build the appropriate DOM tree when processing a document using the SAX2 API:

```java
import org.xml.sax.ContentHandler;
import org.xml.sax.ext.LexicalHandler;
import org.w3c.dom.*;

public class SAX2DOM implements ContentHandler,
                                LexicalHandler
{
    Document m_doc;
    Node m_contextNode;

    public Document getDocument() {
        return m_doc;
    }

    public void startDocument()
    {
        m_doc = new DocumentImpl();
        m_contextNode = m_doc;
    }

    public void endDocument()
    {
    }

    public void startElement(String uri, String local,
        String qname, org.xml.sax.Attributes atts)
    {
        Element e = m_doc.createElementNS(uri, qname);
        m_contextNode.appendChild(e);
        for (int i=0; i<atts.getLength(); i++) {
            e.setAttributeNS(atts.getURI(i),
                    atts.getQName(i), atts.getValue(i));
          }
        m_contextNode = e;
    }

    public void endElement(String uri, String local,
        String qname)
    {
        m_contextNode = m_contextNode.getParentNode();
    }
```

```java
public void characters(char[] buf, int start, int len)
{
    String strText = new String(buf, start, len);
    Node n = m_doc.createTextNode(strText);
    m_contextNode.appendChild(n);
}

public void ignorableWhitespace(char[] buf, int start,
    int len)
{
    // ignore whitespace
}

public void processingInstruction(String target,
    String data)
{
    ProcessingInstruction pi =
        m_doc.createProcessingInstruction(target, data);
    m_contextNode.appendChild(pi);
}

public void comment(char[] buf, int start, int len)
{
    String strComment = new String(buf, start, len);
    Comment t = m_doc.createComment(strComment);
    m_contextNode.appendChild(t);
}

// the rest of the ContentHandler & LexicalHandler
// methods omitted for clarity
// ...
}
```

Pushing a DOM Tree Through SAX2

The following sample Java code illustrates how to traverse a standard DOM tree and emit the appropriate SAX2 events. This makes it possible to push the information in the DOM through a SAX2 consumer.

```java
import org.xml.sax.ContentHandler;
import org.xml.sax.ext.LexicalHandler;
```

```
import org.xml.sax.helpers.AttributesImpl;
import org.xml.sax.SAXException;
import org.w3c.dom.*;

public class DOM2SAX
{
  AttributesImpl atts = new AttributesImpl();


  public void
  traverseDOMviaSAX(Node node,
                    ContentHandler ch,
                    LexicalHandler lh)
      throws SAXException {
    switch (node.getNodeType()) {
    case node.DOCUMENT_NODE:
      ch.startDocument();
      break;
    case node.ELEMENT_NODE:
      atts.clear();
      NamedNodeMap natts = node.getAttributes();
      for (int i=0; i<natts.getLength();i++) {
        Attr a = (Attr)natts.item(i);
        atts.addAttribute(a.getNamespaceURI(),
                          a.getLocalName(),
                          a.getName(), "CDATA",
                          a.getNodeValue());
      }
      ch.startElement(node.getNamespaceURI(),
                      node.getLocalName(),
                      node.getNodeName(), atts);
      break;
    case node.COMMENT_NODE:
      lh.comment(node.getNodeValue().toCharArray(), 0,
                 node.getNodeValue().length());
      break;
    case node.PROCESSING_INSTRUCTION_NODE:
      ch.processingInstruction(node.getNodeName(),
                               node.getNodeValue());
      break;
    case node.TEXT_NODE:
      ch.characters(node.getNodeValue().toCharArray(), 0,
```

```
                        node.getNodeValue().length());
        break;
      default:
        break;
      }
    // process child nodes recursively
      NodeList children = node.getChildNodes();
      for (int i=0; i < children.getLength(); i++)
        traverseDOMviaSAX(children.item(i), ch, lh);
  // emit any endXXX methods
      if (node.ELEMENT_NODE == node.getNodeType())
        ch.endElement(node.getNamespaceURI(),
                      node.getLocalName(),
                      node.getNodeName());
      else if (node.DOCUMENT_NODE == node.getNodeType())
        ch.endDocument();
    }
  }
```

XPath Expressions

The XPath language is capable of building sophisticated expressions that aren't always completely obvious. This section provides some examples of the more esoteric XPath expressions.

```
/guitars/guitar[model]
```

Identifies all guitar element nodes (under the root guitars element node) that have a child model element node.

```
//guitar[@type and @topic]
```

Identifies all guitar element nodes anywhere in the document that have both a type and topic attribute node.

```
guitar[(sum(*/rating) div count(*/rating)) > 4.0]
```

This expression identifies all guitar element nodes that are children of the context node and that have a rating average (average value of rating grandchildren element nodes) greater then 4.0.

```
//guitar[/featured-model = model[1]]
```

Identifies all guitar element nodes anywhere in the document whose first model child element node has the same `string-value` *as the featured-model element node under the root node in the same document.*

```
/guitars//guitar//model
```

Identifies all the model element nodes that are anywhere at or under the `guitar` *element nodes that are anywhere at or under the root guitars element node.*

```
.//text()
```

Identifies all the text nodes that are anywhere at or under the context node.

```
..//text()
```

Identifies all the text nodes that are anywhere at or under the context node's parent node

```
//guitar/*[self::type or self::model][last()]
```

uses a boolean predicate expression to identify the last child element node (of all `guitar` *elements) that is either a type or model element.*

```
guitar/@*[.='foo']
```

Identifies all of the attribute nodes of the context node's guitar child nodes that have a value of 'foo'.

```
*/*/*
```

Identifies all of the context node's great-great-grandchildren element nodes.

```
following::model[position() = 1]
```

Identifies the first model element node that follows the context node in the document structure (excluding descendant nodes).

```
preceding::guitar[contains(@topic, 'XML')]
```

Identifies all of the guitar element nodes that come before the context node in the document structure (excluding ancestor nodes) and whose topic attribute node contains 'XML'.

```
/descendant-or-self::model[1]
```

This expression identifies the first model element node in document order.

```
//model[1]
```

This expression identifies all of the model element nodes that are the first child of their parent nodes. While at first this expression seems the same as the previous example, it expands to the following expression, which (hopefully) explains the difference in behavior:

```
/descendant-or-self::node()/child::model[position() = 1]
```

Programming XPath

The following examples illustrate how to use XPath with two commonly used XML processors.

XPath and MSXML 2.6 (and Above)

The following Javascript code executes and XPath expression against the MSXML DOM implementation and displays the results:

```
// make sure arguments are correct
if (WScript.Arguments.length != 2)
{
        WScript.echo("usage: xpath fname xpath:xpathExpr");
        WScript.Quit(1);
}
// get XML file name and xpath expression string
var fname = WScript.Arguments.Item(0);
var xpe = WScript.Arguments.Item(1);
// echo expression
WScript.echo(xpe);
```

```
// create DOM for input document
var dom = new ActiveXObject("MSXML2.DOMDocument");
// set the selection language to XPath, the default for
// MSXML 2.6 and above is XSL Patterns
dom.setProperty("SelectionLanguage", "XPath");

// load the document
if (dom.load(fname))
{
        // execute the XPath expression
        var sel = dom.documentElement.selectNodes(xpe);
        // print the results
        WScript.echo("<selection>");
        for (var i = 0; i < sel.length; i++)
                WScript.echo(sel.item(i).xml);
        WScript.echo("</selection>");
}
else
        WScript.echo("### parse error: " +
            dom.parseError.reason);
```

XPath and Apache.org's Xalan/Xerces

The following Java code illustrates how to execute XPath expressions against the
Xerces DOM implementation, using the XPath classes in the Xalan library:

```
import org.apache.xerces.parsers.DOMParser;
import org.w3c.dom.Node;
import org.w3c.dom.NodeList;
import org.xml.sax.SAXException;
import java.io.IOException;

import org.apache.xalan.xpath.XPathSupport;
import org.apache.xalan.xpath.XPath;
import org.apache.xalan.xpath.XPathProcessorImpl;
import org.apache.xalan.xpath.XObject;
import org.apache.xalan.xpath.xml.XMLParserLiaisonDefault;
import org.apache.xalan.xpath.xml.PrefixResolverDefault;

import org.apache.xalan.xpath.xml.FormatterToXML;
import org.apache.xalan.xpath.xml.TreeWalker;
```

```
public class Class1
{
    public static void main (String[] args)
    {
        // make sure arguments are correct
        if (args.length != 2) {
            System.out.println(
                    "usage: xerxpath filename expression");
            System.exit(1);
        }

        // create the Xerces DOM parser
        DOMParser parser = new DOMParser();

        try {
            // parser the input document
                // & get document element node
            parser.parse(args[0]);
            Node root =
                    parser.getDocument().getDocumentElement();

            // install default XPath support
            XPathSupport xSupport = new
                    XMLParserLiaisonDefault();
            PrefixResolverDefault pr = new
                    PrefixResolverDefault(root);

            // create XPath object
            XPath xp = new XPath();
            // create XPath processor
            XPathProcessorImpl xpp = new
                    XPathProcessorImpl(xSupport);
            // initialize XPath object
            xpp.initXPath(xp, args[1], pr);

            // execute XPath expression
            XObject result = xp.execute(xSupport,
                    root, pr);
            // print the returned node-set
            printSelection(result.nodeset());
        }
```

```
        catch(SAXException e) {
            e.printStackTrace();
        }
        catch(IOException e) {
            e.printStackTrace();
        }
    }


    public static void printSelection(NodeList sel)
    {
        try {
            FormatterToXML ftox = new
                    FormatterToXML(System.out);
            TreeWalker tw =new TreeWalker(ftox);

            System.out.println("<selection>");
            for (int i=0; i<sel.getLength(); i++) {
                tw.traverse(sel.item(i));
                ftox.flush();
                ftox.flushWriter();
                System.out.print('`');
            }
            System.out.println("</selection>");
        }
        catch(Exception e) {
            e.printStackTrace();
        }
    }
}
```

Xalan also provides the following helper class implementation that can be used from the command line for testing purposes: `org.apache.xalan.xpath.Process`. This class can be used in the following fashion:

```
java org.apache.xalan.xpath.Process -in source.xml
    -select /child::foo/@bar
```

XML Schema Examples

The following XML Schema document describes the vocabulary of XSLT:

```
<?xml version="1.0"?>
<schema
  xmlns="http://www.w3.org/1999/XMLSchema"
  targetNamespace="http://www.w3.org/1999/XSL/Transform"
  xmlns:xsl="http://www.w3.org/1999/XSL/Transform"
  elementFormDefault="qualified"
  version="May 11, 2000"
>
  <annotation>
    <documentation>A Schema for XSLT - Don Box
    (http://www.develop.com/dbox)</documentation>
    <documentation>Thanks to Curt Arnold, Henry Thompson and
    Noah Mendelsohn for catching some errors along the
    way.</documentation>
  </annotation>
  <!-- internal types -->
  <simpleType name="avt" base="string">
    <annotation>
      <documentation
        source="http://www.w3.org/TR/xslt#attribute-value-
          templates"/>
    </annotation>
  </simpleType>
  <simpleType name="pattern" base="string">
    <annotation>
      <documentation
        source="http://www.w3.org/TR/xslt#patterns"/>
    </annotation>
  </simpleType>
  <simpleType name="expr" base="string">
    <annotation>
      <documentation
        source="http://www.w3.org/TR/xslt#section-
          Expressions"/>
    </annotation>
  </simpleType>
  <simpleType name="XPathNumber" base="decimal">
    <annotation>
```

ESSENTIAL XML: BEYOND MARKUP

```xml
      <documentation
        source="http://www.w3.org/TR/xpath#NT-Number"/>
    </annotation>
  </simpleType>
  <simpleType name="char" base="string">
    <minLength value="1"/>
    <maxLength value="1"/>
  </simpleType>
  <simpleType name="yesno" base="NMTOKEN">
    <enumeration value="yes"/>
    <enumeration value="no"/>
  </simpleType>
  <simpleType name="single-multiple-any" base="NMTOKEN">
    <enumeration value="single"/>
    <enumeration value="multiple"/>
    <enumeration value="any"/>
  </simpleType>
<!-- space-delimited list of QName -->
  <simpleType name="QNames" base="QName" derivedBy="list"/>
<!-- NCName OR #default -->
  <simpleType name="NCNamePlus"
              base="string" derivedBy="restriction"/>
  <simpleType name="NCNamesPlus"
              base="xsl:NCNamePlus" derivedBy="list"/>


<!-- literal result element attributes -->
  <attribute name="version" type="decimal"/>
  <attribute name="extension-element-prefixes"
   type="xsl:NCNamesPlus"/>
  <attribute name="exclude-result-prefixes" type="xsl:
   NCNamesPlus"/>
  <attribute name="use-attribute-sets" type="xsl:QNames"/>
<!-- exemplars for the equiv classes -->
  <element name="instruction" abstract="true"/>
  <element name="char-instruction" abstract="true"
          equivClass="instruction"/>
<!-- char-template is used for templates that
     produce only character data-->
  <complexType name="char-template" content="mixed">
    <sequence minOccurs='0' maxOccurs='unbounded' >
      <element ref="xsl:char-instruction"/>
```

```
        </sequence>
      </complexType>
  <!-- template is used for templates that produce
       only character data with markup-->
    <complexType name="template" content="mixed">
      <sequence minOccurs='0' maxOccurs='unbounded' >
        <element ref="xsl:instruction"/>
      </sequence>
      <any namespace="##other"/>
    </complexType>
  <!-- named-template is only used for xsl:template -->
    <complexType name="named-template" content="mixed">
      <sequence minOccurs='1' maxOccurs='1' >
        <element ref='xsl:param' minOccurs='0'
                                 maxOccurs='unbounded' />
        <choice minOccurs='0' maxOccurs='unbounded' >
          <element ref="xsl:instruction"/>
          <any namespace="##other"/>
        </choice>
      </sequence>
      <attribute ref="xml:space"/>
      <attribute name="match" type="xsl:pattern"/>
      <attribute name="name" type="QName"/>
      <attribute name="priority" type="xsl:XPathNumber"/>
      <attribute name="mode" type="QName"/>
    </complexType>
  <!-- variable-definition is only used for both param and
   variable -->
    <complexType name="variable-definition"
                 base="xsl:template" derivedBy="extension">
      <attribute name="name" type="QName" use="required"/>
      <attribute name="select" type="xsl:expr"/>
    </complexType>
  <!-- char-template-with-space simply adds the
       xml:space attribute to char-template -->
    <complexType name="char-template-with-space"
                 base="xsl:char-template" derivedBy=
                    "extension">
      <attribute ref="xml:space"/>
    </complexType>
  <!-- template-with-space simply adds the xml:space attribute
   to template -->
```

```
  <complexType name="template-with-space"
               base="xsl:template" derivedBy="extension">
    <attribute ref="xml:space"/>
  </complexType>
<!-- conditional-template is used by both xsl:if and xsl:
  when -->
  <complexType name="conditional-template"
               base="xsl:template-with-space" derivedBy=
                  "extension">
    <attribute name="test" type="xsl:expr"/>
  </complexType>
<!-- import-or-include is used by both xsl:include and
  xsl:import -->
  <complexType name="import-or-include" content="empty">
    <attribute name="href" type="uriReference" use=
      "required"/>
  </complexType>
  <complexType name="sort" content="empty">
    <attribute name="select" type="xsl:expr" value="."
      use="default"/>
    <attribute name="lang" type="xsl:avt"/>
    <attribute name="data-type" type="xsl:avt" value="text"
      use="default"/>
    <attribute name="order" type="xsl:avt" value="ascending"
      use="default"/>
    <attribute name="case-order" type="xsl:avt"/>
  </complexType>
  <complexType name="for-each"
               base="xsl:template-with-space" derivedBy=
                  "extension">
    <sequence minOccurs='1' maxOccurs='1' >
      <element name="sort" type="xsl:sort" minOccurs="0"
        maxOccurs="unbounded"/>
      <choice minOccurs='0' maxOccurs='unbounded' >
        <element ref="xsl:instruction"/>
        <any namespace="##other"/>
      </choice>
    </sequence>
    <attribute ref="xml:space"/>
    <attribute name="select" type="xsl:expr" use="required"/>
  </complexType>
  <complexType name="choose" content="elementOnly">
```

```
    <sequence minOccurs='1' maxOccurs='1' >
      <element name="when" type="xsl:conditional-template"
       maxOccurs="unbounded"/>
      <element name="otherwise" type="xsl:template-with-
       space" minOccurs="0"/>
    </sequence>
  </complexType>
  <complexType name="call-template" content="elementOnly">
    <sequence minOccurs="0" maxOccurs="unbounded" >
      <element name="with-param" type="xsl:variable-
       definition" />
    </sequence>
    <attribute name="name" type="QName" use="required"/>
  </complexType>
  <complexType name="apply-templates" content="elementOnly">
    <choice minOccurs="0" maxOccurs="unbounded">
      <element name="with-param" type="variable-definition"/>
      <element name="sort" type="xsl:sort"/>
    </choice>
    <attribute name="select" type="xsl:expr" value="node()"
     use="default"/>
    <attribute name="mode" type="QName"/>
  </complexType>
  <complexType name="copy" base="xsl:template-with-space"
   derivedBy="extension">
    <attribute name="use-attribute-sets" type="xsl:QNames"/>
  </complexType>
  <complexType name="copy-of" content="empty">
    <attribute name="select" type="xsl:expr" use="required"/>
  </complexType>
  <complexType name="value-of" base="xsl:copy-of" derivedBy=
   "extension">
    <attribute name="disable-output-escaping" type="xsl:
     yesno" use="default" value="no"/>
  </complexType>
  <complexType name="message" base="xsl:template-with-space"
   derivedBy="extension">
    <attribute name="terminate" type="xsl:yesno" value="no"
     use="default"/>
  </complexType>
  <complexType name="apply-imports" content="empty"/>
  <complexType name="number" content="empty">
```

```
  <attribute name="level" type="xsl:single-multiple-any"
   value="single" use="default"/>
  <attribute name="count" type="xsl:pattern"/>
  <attribute name="from" type="xsl:pattern"/>
  <attribute name="value" type="xsl:expr"/>
  <attribute name="format" type="xsl:avt" value="1" use=
   "default"/>
  <attribute name="lang" type="xsl:avt"/>
  <attribute name="letter-value" type="xsl:avt"/>
  <attribute name="grouping-separator" type="xsl:avt"/>
  <attribute name="grouping-size" type="xsl:avt"/>
</complexType>
<complexType name="text" content="textOnly">
  <attribute name="disable-output-escaping" type="xsl:
   yesno" value="no" use="default"/>
</complexType>
<complexType name="processing-instruction" base="xsl:
 char-template-with-space" derivedBy="extension">
  <attribute name="name" type="xsl:avt" use="required"/>
</complexType>
<complexType name="attribute" base="xsl:processing-
 instruction" derivedBy="extension">
  <attribute name="namespace" type="xsl:avt"/>
</complexType>
<complexType name="element" base="xsl:template-with-space"
 derivedBy="extension">
  <attribute name="name" type="xsl:avt" use="required"/>
  <attribute name="namespace" type="xsl:avt"/>
  <attribute name="use-attribute-sets" type="xsl:QNames"/>
</complexType>
<complexType name="preserve-or-strip-space" content=
 "empty">
  <attribute name="elements" type="xsl:QNames" use=
   "required"/>
</complexType>
<complexType name="output" content="empty">
  <attribute name="method" type="QName"/>
  <attribute name="version" type="NMTOKEN"/>
  <attribute name="encoding" type="string"/>
  <attribute name="omit-xml-declaration" type="xsl:yesno"/>
  <attribute name="standalone" type="xsl:yesno"/>
  <attribute name="doctype-public" type="string"/>
```

```
      <attribute name="doctype-system" type="string"/>
      <attribute name="cdata-section-elements" type=
       "xsl:QNames"/>
      <attribute name="indent" type="xsl:yesno"/>
      <attribute name="media-type" type="string"/>
    </complexType>
    <complexType name="key" content="empty">
      <attribute name="name" type="QName" use="required"/>
      <attribute name="match" type="xsl:pattern" use=
       "required"/>
      <attribute name="use" type="xsl:expr" use="required"/>
    </complexType>
    <complexType name="decimal-format" content="empty">
      <attribute name="name" type="QName"/>
      <attribute name="decimal-separator" type="xsl:char"
       value="." use="default"/>
      <attribute name="grouping-separator" type="xsl:char"
       value="," use="default"/>
      <attribute name="infinity" type="string" value="Infinity"
       use="default"/>
      <attribute name="minus-sign" type="xsl:char" value="-"
       use="default"/>
      <attribute name="NaN" type="string" value="NaN" use=
       "default"/>
      <attribute name="percent" type="xsl:char" value="%"
       use="default"/>
      <attribute name="per-mille" type="xsl:char" value=
       "&#x2030;" use="default"/>
      <attribute name="zero-digit" type="xsl:char" value="0"
       use="default"/>
      <attribute name="digit" type="xsl:char" value="#" use=
       "default"/>
      <attribute name="pattern-separator" type="xsl:char"
       value=";" use="default"/>
    </complexType>
    <complexType name="attribute-set" content="elementOnly">
      <sequence minOccurs="0" maxOccurs="unbounded">
        <element ref="xsl:attribute" />
      </sequence>
      <attribute name="name" type="QName" use="required"/>
      <attribute name="use-attribute-sets" type="xsl:QNames"/>
    </complexType>
```

```
  <complexType name="namespace-alias" content="empty">
    <attribute name="stylesheet-prefix" type="xsl:NCNamePlus"
     use="required"/>
    <attribute name="result-prefix" type="xsl:NCNamePlus"
     use="required"/>
  </complexType>
<!-- note that equivClass is used to distinguish char-
 instructions from normal instructions -->
<!-- char-instructions -->
  <element name="apply-templates" type="xsl:apply-templates"
   equivClass="char-instruction"/>
  <element name="call-template" type="xsl:call-template"
   equivClass="char-instruction"/>
  <element name="apply-imports" type="xsl:apply-imports"
   equivClass="char-instruction"/>
  <element name="for-each" type="xsl:for-each" equivClass=
   "char-instruction"/>
  <element name="value-of" type="xsl:value-of" equivClass=
   "char-instruction"/>
  <element name="copy-of" type="xsl:copy-of" equivClass=
   "char-instruction"/>
  <element name="number" type="xsl:number" equivClass=
   "char-instruction"/>
  <element name="choose" type="xsl:choose" equivClass=
   "char-instruction"/>
  <element name="if" type="xsl:conditional-template"
   equivClass="char-instruction"/>
  <element name="text" type="xsl:text" equivClass=
   "char-instruction"/>
  <element name="copy" type="xsl:copy" equivClass=
   "char-instruction"/>
  <element name="variable" type="xsl:variable-definition"
   equivClass="char-instruction"/>
  <element name="message" type="xsl:message" equivClass=
   "char-instruction"/>
  <element name="fallback" type="xsl:template-with-space"
   equivClass="char-instruction"/>
<!-- instructions -->
  <element name="comment" type="xsl:char-template-with-space"
   equivClass="instruction"/>
  <element name="processing-instruction" type="xsl:
   processing-instruction" equivClass="instruction"/>
```

```xml
  <element name="attribute" type="xsl:attribute" equivClass=
    "instruction"/>
  <element name="element" type="xsl:element" equivClass=
    "instruction"/>

<!-- note that local element declarations are used for
 non-instruction elements -->
  <complexType name="stylesheet" content="elementOnly">
    <sequence minOccurs='1' maxOccurs='1' >
      <element name="import" type="xsl:import-or-include"
        minOccurs="0" maxOccurs="unbounded"/>
      <choice minOccurs="0" maxOccurs="unbounded">
        <element name="include" type="xsl:import-or-
          include"/>
        <element name="strip-space" type="xsl:preserve-or-
          strip-space"/>
        <element name="preserve-space" type="xsl:preserve-or-
          strip-space"/>
        <element name="output" type="xsl:output"/>
        <element name="key" type="xsl:key"/>
        <element name="decimal-format" type="xsl:decimal-
          format"/>
        <element name="attribute-set" type="xsl:attribute-
          set"/>
        <element name="variable" type="variable-definition"/>
        <element name="param" type="variable-definition"/>
        <element name="template" type="xsl:named-template"/>
        <element name="namespace-alias" type="xsl:namespace-
          alias"/>
        <any namespace="##other"/>
      </choice>
    </sequence>
    <attribute name="version" type="decimal" use="required"/>
    <attribute name="extension-element-prefixes" type="xsl:
      NCNamesPlus"/>
    <attribute name="exclude-result-prefixes" type="xsl:
      NCNamesPlus"/>
    <attribute name="use-attribute-sets" type="xsl:QNames"/>
  </complexType>
  <element name="stylesheet" type="xsl:stylesheet"/>
  <element name="transform" type="xsl:stylesheet"/>
</schema>
```

XSLT Examples

In this section, we will consider some nontrivial XSLT programs to show combinations of the principles of XSLT in practice. The first example demonstrates how to convert documents between element and attribute-normal forms. It illustrates quite effectively the power of recursive transformations. The second example demonstrates how to convert a large set of XML elements into a series of pages that can be viewed by an XHTML browser. It demonstrates the utility of conditional expressions and the following-sibling XPath axis. The final example demonstrates how you can transform an attribute-normal-form ADO recordset document that is missing some attributes into an XHTML table that accounts for the missing attributes. It demonstrates how you can use information from nodes in one part of the source document to affect the transformation of nodes in another part of the source document.

Example 1: Converting between element-normal and attribute-normal forms

This example illustrates the power of recursive transformations using XSLT. There are two general ways that hierarchical XML information can be represented: element-normal and attribute-normal forms. The following document is an example of element-normal-form XML:

```
<people>
  <person>
    <firstName>Juliet</firstName>
    <lastName>Shakespeare</lastName>
  </person>
  <person>
    <firstName>Francis</firstName>
    <lastName>Allbright</lastName>
  </person>
</person>
```

The following document contains the same information as above but rendered in attribute-normal-form:

```
<people>
  <person firstName="Juliet" lastName="Shakespeare"/>
  <person firstName="Francis" lastName="Allbright"/>
</people>
```

Two important observations about the structure of the preceding two XML documents allow us to write an extremely compact XSLT program to perform the desired transformations. The first observation is that *all leaf elements in element-normal-form documents are eligible for conversion to attributes*. A leaf element is defined as any element that does not have any child elements. In our sample document, <firstName> and <lastName> are leaf elements, whereas <person> is not. The second observation is that *any nonleaf element nodes must be copied to the result tree*. In our sample document, the <people> and <person> element nodes are copied to the result tree.

Listing 52 shows a program that recursively converts an element-normal form document to attribute-normal form. It uses two XPath expressions that allow us to distinguish between leaf elements and nonleaf elements. Assuming that we are evaluating an XPath expression relative to an element node, we need to detect whether it contains any child leaf elements. The XPath expression that allows us to detect child leaf elements is *[count(child::*) = 0]. This expression selects child elements that do not contain any child elements themselves. We also need an XPath expression that allows us to detect child nonleaf elements: *[count(child::*) > 0]. This expression selects child elements that contain at least one child element themselves.

```xml
<?xml version="1.0"?>
<xsl:stylesheet
    xmlns:xsl="http://www.w3.org/1999/XSL/Transform"
    version="1.0">
    <xsl:template match="*">
        <xsl:copy>
            <xsl:for-each select="*[ count( child::* ) = 0 ]">
                <xsl:attribute name="{name()}">
                    <xsl:value-of select="."/>
                </xsl:attribute>
            </xsl:for-each>
            <xsl:apply-templates select="*[ count( ./* ) > 0 ]"/>
        </xsl:copy>
    </xsl:template>
</xsl:stylesheet>
```

This program contains a single template rule that matches all elements in the source document. When it encounters an element node in the source document, it copies it to the result tree fragment. It then checks to see if that element contains any child leaf elements. If it finds any, it will convert these child leaf elements to attributes. Next it recursively calls itself for any child nonleaf elements.

The template converts child leaf elements to attributes, using an `<xsl:for-each>` instruction. This instruction uses the `*[ count( child::* ) = 0 ]` XPath expression to create a node-set containing all of the current element's leaf elements. It then proceeds to traverse this node-set, converting each child element into an attribute node.

The template declared by the `<xsl:for-each>` instruction is instantiated for each element in the node-set. Its `<xsl:attribute>` instruction creates a new attribute node. It uses the XPath `name()` function to retrieve the name of the current leaf element and assigns it to the attribute node's name. It converts the current leaf element node to a string, using the `<xsl:value-of select="."/>` instruction and assigns it to the attribute node's value.

The recursive behavior of the template rule is initiated by the `<xsl:apply-templates select="*[ count( ./* ) > 0 ]"/>` instruction. It instructs the XSLT processor to create a node-set containing all of the nonleaf child elements. If this node-set contains one or more elements, the XSLT processor will call the program's one and only template rule for each of those nonleaf child elements. Otherwise, the instruction does nothing, and control is returned to the template instance that called the template rule.

The following XSLT stylesheet converts from attribute-normal to element-normal form. This single template-rule program is conceptually much easier to understand; it recursively traverses all element nodes in the source document. This recursive traversal is accomplished by using the `<xsl:apply-templates select="*"/>` instruction.

For each element that it encounters, it simply copies it to the result tree fragment. It then walks the attribute node axis of that element, looking for attribute nodes that it can convert to child element nodes. For each attribute node that it encounters, it creates a new child element using the `<xsl:element>` instruction. The attribute value template `{name()}` assigns the name of the attribute node as the name of the element. The content of the `<xsl:element>` instruction contains an `<xsl:value-of>` instruction that converts the attribute node's value to a text node and copies it to the result tree fragment.

```xml
<?xml version="1.0"?>
<xsl:stylesheet
  xmlns:xsl="http://www.w3.org/1999/XSL/Transform"
  version="1.0">
  <xsl:template match="*">
    <xsl:copy>
      <xsl:for-each select="@*">
        <xsl:element name="{name()} ">
          <xsl:value-of select="."/>
        </xsl:element>
      </xsl:for-each>
      <xsl:apply-templates select="*"/>
    </xsl:copy>
  </xsl:template>
</xsl:stylesheet>
```

Example 2: Paginated data

Our next example[1] illustrates an XSLT program that renders a long list of XML data for display. Typically, long lists of data are broken up into a paginated form (similar to result lists from search engines). The user would see the list of data broken up into a series of pages and can navigate between those pages using standard "Prev" and "Next" buttons that would appear at the top of each page.

Our goal is to write an XSLT program that will generate an XHTML page that will display the paginated data. The idea is that the list of data would be read by the page and transformed into the desired paginated form by the XSLT program on the client. JavaScript code within the XHTML page will show and hide various `<div>` elements within the page that define the individual data pages that will be shown to the user.[2]

---

[1] This example is modeled on a similar problem presented during a series of discussions on the XSL-List mailing list. `xsl-list@mulberrytech.com`. Nikolai Grigoriev, Michael Kay, and Steve Muench contributed insightful solutions to this problem.

[2] The goal of this chapter is not to provide you with a tutorial on DHTML. See *Dynamic HTML in Action* by William Pardi and *Dynamic HTML* by Danny Goodman for excellent discussions on DHTML.

The following is a skeleton XHTML page that would suit this purpose. Our goal is to write the XSLT program that will generate the contents of the <div> element whose ID is `divContainer`. The rest of this page contains event handling code that will allow various <div> elements to be displayed and hidden on the page.

```
<html>
 <head>
  <title>Sample multi-page DHTML</title>
   <link rel="stylesheet" type="text/css"
       href="global.css"></link>
 </head>
 <body>
  <h2>An example of a multi-page set of tabular data</h2>
    <script>
    function onBtnClick() {
      var targetSection = parseInt(
                    event.srcElement.value );
      var thisSection =
          event.srcElement.parentElement.parentElement;


      thisSection.style.display = "none";
      divContainer.children.item(
            targetSection ).style.display = "block";
    }
    function onInitialize() {
      divContainer.children.item( 0 ).style.display
                                        = "block";
    }
    window.onload = onInitialize;
    </script>
    <div class="container" id="divContainer"
        onclick="return onBtnClick()">
      <div class="section">
        <div class="navbar">
          <span value="1">Next</span>
        </div>
        Section 1
      </div>
      <div class="section">
```

```
        <div class="navbar">
            <span value="0">Prev</span>
            <span value="2"></span>
        </div>
        Section 2
    </div>
    <div class="section">
        <div class="navbar">
            <span value="1">Prev</span>
        </div>
        Section 3
    </div>
  </div>
 </body>
</html>
```

Navigation between pages is controlled by the Prev and Next buttons. These buttons are declared by the `</span>` elements on the page. Each `</span>` element's value attribute declares which page to display when the user clicks on that button. Note that the set of pages that will be displayed by this code is 0-indexed.

Our program must accomplish three primary goals. It must break up the elements in the source document into groups of a specific size. It must ensure that the value attributes are correctly generated for the Prev and Next buttons. Finally, it must ensure that the first page only has a Next button and that the last page only has a Prev button. Consider the following source document shown below:

```
<?xml version="1.0"?>
<list>
  <item>Wilkins</item>
  <item>Bryant</item>
  <item>Carter</item>
  <item>McGrady</item>
  <item>Jordan</item>
  <item>Barry</item>
</list>
```

The following XSLT stylesheet breaks up the list of `<item>` elements into groups of a specific size. It accepts a SIZE parameter that the user can set to control the number of elements in each page. This parameter is declared by the `<xsl:param>` instruction, which sets its default value to 2.

```
<?xml version="1.0"?>
<xsl:stylesheet
  xmlns:xsl="http://www.w3.org/1999/XSL/Transform"
  version="1.0">

<!-- Page size input parameter -->
<xsl:param name="SIZE" select="2"/>

<xsl:template match="item">
  <xsl:param name="PAGES"/>

  <!-- Generate a section -->
  <div class="section">

    <!-- Generate navigation bars -->
    <div class="navBar">
      <xsl:variable name="PAGE" select="position() - 1"/>

      <xsl:choose>
        <xsl:when test="$PAGE = 0">
          <span value="{$PAGE + 1} "></span>
        </xsl:when>
        <xsl:when test="$PAGE = $PAGES">
          <span value="{$PAGE - 1} "></span>
        </xsl:when>
        <xsl:otherwise>
          <span value="{$PAGE - 1} "></span>
          <span value="{$PAGE + 1} ">Next</span>
        </xsl:otherwise>
      </xsl:choose>
    </div>

    <!-- Generate data -->
    <xsl:for-each select="self::item |
        following-sibling::item[ position() &lt; $SIZE ]">
```

```
        <div><xsl:value-of select="."/></div>
      </xsl:for-each>
    </div>
  </xsl:template>

  <xsl:template match="list">
    <xsl:apply-templates
      select="item[ position() mod $SIZE = 1 ]">

      <!-- Calculate the number of pages that we
           need to display -->
      <xsl:with-param name="PAGES"
        select="floor( count( item ) div $SIZE ) - 1"/>
    </xsl:apply-templates>
  </xsl:template>
</xsl:stylesheet>
```

The following XPath expression allows us to break a list of *n* elements into groups that each contains a maximum of SIZE elements:

```
item[ position() mod $SIZE = 1 ]
```

If we assume that this expression is using the default value of 2 for the SIZE parameter, it will select <item> elements 1, 3, and 5 from our sample document. This expression generates a node-set that when traversed will form the main loop of our program.

The template rule that matches the <list> element of the source document is the entry-point into our program. Its template contains an <xsl:apply-templates> instruction that forms the main loop of our program by iterating over the node-set that was generated by the XPath expression that we discussed before. Since this node-set consists exclusively of <item> elements, the XSLT processor will call the template rule that matches all <item> elements for each node within the node-set.

The template rule that matches <item> elements creates a <div> element that contains SIZE <item> elements. Recall that this template rule is only called for <item> elements 1, 3, and 5. To complete the generation of a page, it needs to retrieve the next SIZE - 1 items from the source document. The following XPath expression selects the current context node (which is, of course, an `<item>` element) as well as the next `SIZE - 1` `<item>` elements that immediately follow it:

```
self::item | following-sibling::item[ position() < $SIZE ]
```

The expression generates a node-set that is traversed by the `<xsl:for-each>` instruction. The `<xsl:for-each>` instruction contains a template that is responsible for generating the result tree fragment that contains `SIZE` `<item>` elements.

The `<xsl:for-each>` instruction's template converts each `<item>` element that it encounters into a `<div>` element in the result tree fragment. It uses an `<xsl:value-of>` instruction to create the child text node of the `<div>` element. This instruction converts the current context node into a string and assigns it to the value of the text node that it creates, thereby completing the transformation.

Now that we have successfully partitioned the source document into a set of pages that each contains a maximum of `SIZE` `<item>` elements, we need to generate the data that will be used to navigate between these pages. Page navigation is accomplished through the use of page numbers.

A page number identifies the page that will be displayed when the user clicks on the Next and Prev buttons. Recall that each of these buttons is represented by a `<span>` element. Each `<span>` element's value attribute identifies the page that will be displayed when the button is clicked. When the `<span>` element is clicked, the following JavaScript code executes:

```
var targetSection = parseInt( event.srcElement.value );
var thisSection =
          event.srcElement.parentElement.parentElement;
thisSection.style.display = "none";
divContainer.children.item(
          targetSection ).style.display = "block";
```

This code hides the current page by setting its parent `<div>` element's display property to none. It obtains the page number of the target page by retrieving the `<span>` element's `value` attribute. Since the `<span>` element that was clicked on is the *source* of the event, it can be referenced by using the `event.srcElement` `object`. We use the page number to select the correct child `<div>` element of the divContainer `<div>` element and make it visible by setting its display property to block.

Page numbers are calculated at runtime. Each time that the template rule that matches `<item>` elements is called, it generates a new page. Therefore, we can calculate the current page number using the XPath `position()` function. Since our page numbers are 0-based, we must subtract 1 from the result of the XPath `position()` function. We assign the page number to a temporary constant called PAGE using the following instruction:

```
<xsl:variable name="PAGE" select="position() - 1"/>
```

Page numbers are assigned to the `<span>` elements at creation time. The `<span>` element is created using a literal result element, and we use an attribute value template to calculate the value of its target attribute. For any given page, a Prev button will always select the previous page, so it can be created using the following literal result element:

```
<span value="{$PAGE - 1} ">Prev</span>
```

Similarly, for any given page, a Next button can be created using the following literal result element:

```
<span value="{$PAGE + 1} ">Next</span>
```

However, not all pages will contain both buttons. The first page will only contain a Next button, and the last page will only contain a Prev button. We must write some code that allows us to distinguish between the first and the last page of our document. Therefore, we must calculate ahead of time the number of pages that will be generated. The following XPath expression performs this calculation:

```
floor( count( item ) div $SIZE ) - 1
```

We pass this value to our `<item>` template rule as a named parameter called PAGES.

The template that generates the Next and Prev buttons uses an `<xsl:choose>` instruction to conditionally generate different sets of buttons based on the current page number. It generates only a Next button if $PAGE = 0. It generates only a Prev button if $PAGE = $PAGES. For any other value of PAGE, it generates a Next and a Prev button.

This sample discussed a solution to a common problem in XSLT transformations. XSLT transformations will commonly be used to transform XML data into XHTML documents either on the client or on the server. Since users are used to seeing result sets returned in a paginated form, this transformation allows the data to be rendered for display in the browser without the overhead of returning to the server to generate each successive page of data.

Example 3: Dealing with missing attributes

Our final example illustrates a problem that is encountered when dealing with source documents that are stored in attribute-normal-form: missing attributes. One such class of documents is the serialized form of Microsoft Active Data Object (ADO) recordsets. A simplified ADO recordset document is shown here.

```
<?xml version="1.0"?>
<xml xmlns:s="uuid:BDC6E3F0-6DA3-11d1-A2A3-00AA00C14882"
     xmlns:dt="uuid:C2F41010-65B3-11d1-A29F-00AA00C14882"
     xmlns:rs="urn:schemas-microsoft-com:rowset"
     xmlns:z="#RowsetSchema">
  <s:Schema id="RowsetSchema">
    <s:ElementType ...>
      <s:AttributeType name="title_id" ...> ...
      <s:AttributeType name="title" ...> ...
      <s:AttributeType name="type" ...> ...
      ...
    </s:ElementType>
  </s:Schema>
  <rs:data>
    <z:row title_id=" ... " title=" ... " type=" ... " .../>
    <z:row title_id=" ... " title=" ... " type=" ... " .../>
    ...
  </rs:data>
</xml>
```

An ADO recordset object represents a row-column set of data. Such data can easily be represented in attribute-normal-form, which allows for a more compact representation of the data. Each row of the recordset is represented by a `<z:row>` element, where `z` is a namespace prefix that references an embedded XML-Data Reduced (XDR) schema. Each column of a given row is represented by an attribute node on its associated `<z:row>` element. The name of the attribute node is the name of the column, and the value of the attribute node is the value of the column.

What makes ADO recordset documents tricky to parse is that SQL NULLs are not represented by attributes. That is, if a column of a given row is a SQL NULL, no attribute is generated for that column. This makes it difficult to process the document based on the assumption that (1) all attributes are always present and (2) all attributes are arranged in the same order. If we were able to make this assumption, then we could easily transform an ADO recordset document into an XHTML table using the following XSLT stylesheet:

```
<?xml version="1.0"?>
<xsl:stylesheet
  xmlns:xsl="http://www.w3.org/1999/XSL/Transform"
  xmlns:s="uuid:BDC6E3F0-6DA3-11d1-A2A3-00AA00C14882"
  xmlns:rs="urn:schemas-microsoft-com:rowset"
  xmlns:z="#RowsetSchema"
  version="1.0">

<xsl:template match="@*">
 <td><xsl:value-of select="."/></td>
</xsl:template>

<xsl:template match="z:row">
  <tr><xsl:apply-templates select="@*"/></tr>
</xsl:template>

<xsl:template match="xml">
  <table><xsl:apply-templates
          select="rs:data/z:row"/></table>
</xsl:template>
</xsl:stylesheet>
```

In this program, the template rule that matches the `<xml>` element in the source document creates the `<table>` node in the result tree fragment. The XSLT processor then traverses all of the `<z:row>` elements, using the `<xsl:apply-templates select="rs:data/z:row"/>` instruction. The template rule that matches `<z:row>` elements in the source document creates a `<tr>` node in the result tree fragment, which represents a row in an XHTML table. The XSLT processor then traverses all of the attributes of the current `<z:row>` element, using the `<xsl:apply-templates select="@*"/>` instruction. The template rule that matches attributes in the source document creates a `<td>` node in the result tree fragment, which represents a cell within a row in an XHTML table. The XSLT processor then converts the current node (which is an attribute) to a text node in the result tree fragment, using the `<xsl:value-of select="."/>` instruction.

However, this program would fail in a scenario where attributes are missing because it assumes that all attributes will be present for any given row in the document. To solve this problem, we need to use the information within the XDR schema that is embedded within the document.

The XDR schema identifies all of the attributes that *may* exist for a given `<z:row>` element. Each attribute is represented by an `<s:AttributeType>` element in the XDR schema. The `<s:AttributeType>` element's name attribute identifies the name of an attribute of a `<z:row>` element in the source document. We can use this information to traverse the attributes in a `<z:row>` element instead of relying on the attributes being returned in document order as is the case with the `@*` XPath expression that we used earlier.

The program in Listing 57 uses the XDR schema to account for missing attributes. The core of the program is contained in the template rule that matches all `<z:row>` elements in the source document. It uses the XPath expression

```
/xml/s:Schema/s:ElementType/s:AttributeType/@name
```

to generate a node-set that contains all possible attribute names as declared the XDR schema. It then proceeds to iterate over this node-set, using an

`<xsl:for-each>` instruction. Each time through the loop, the template declared by the `<xsl:for-each>` instruction creates a new `<td>` element in the result tree fragment. If the attribute exists in the source document, the `<td>` element will contain a child text node whose value is the value of that attribute. If the attribute does not exist, the `<td>` element will not contain a child text node; but the `<td>` element still exists.

The key idea in this template is to retrieve an attribute, using a parameterized name. To do so, we will use the following XPath expression:

```
$NODE/@*[ name() = $ATT ]
```

The $NODE constant refers to the current `<z:row>` element, and the $ATT constant refers to the name of the attribute that we would like to retrieve. We use an `<xsl:value-of>` instruction to convert the result of this expression (which is a node-set) into a text node in the result tree fragment. However, we first need to discuss how we calculated the NODE and ATT constants.

The NODE and ATT constants are declared in two different places. Prior to entering the `<xsl:for-each>` loop, the current context node (a `<z:row>` element) is saved in a temporary constant called NODE. The reason for this is that the `<xsl:for-each>` instruction will change the current context node as it iterates over its node-set. Once inside the `<xsl:for-each>` loop, the current attribute name is saved in another temporary constant called ATT. Once we have declared these two constants, we are ready to evaluate our XPath expression.

The `<xsl:value-of>` instruction evaluates the `$NODE/@*[ name() = $ATT ]` XPath expression. When evaluating this expression, the `$NODE` constant refers to a node-set, and is treated as a location step by the XSLT processor. The `@*` location step refers to all attributes of the element identified by the `$NODE` constant. We use a predicate expression to retrieve the attribute whose name matches the string `$ATT`. If this expression evaluates to a node, the `<xsl:value-of>` instruction creates a text node in the result tree fragment whose value is the value of the attribute node. If this expression does not evaluate to a node, the `<xsl:value-of>` instruction does nothing.

Following is a program that uses XDR schema information to account for missing attributes in an ADO recordset document

```xml
<?xml version="1.0"?>
<xsl:stylesheet
  xmlns:xsl="http://www.w3.org/1999/XSL/Transform"
  xmlns:s="uuid:BDC6E3F0-6DA3-11d1-A2A3-00AA00C14882"
  xmlns:rs="urn:schemas-microsoft-com:rowset"
  xmlns:z="#RowsetSchema"
  version="1.0">

  <xsl:template match="z:row">
    <tr>
      <xsl:variable name="NODE" select="."/>
      <xsl:for-each select=
          "/xml/s:Schema/s:ElementType/s:AttributeType/@name">
        <xsl:variable name="ATT" select="string( . )"/>
        <td>
         <xsl:value-of
          select="$NODE/@*[ name() = $ATT ]"/>
        </td>
      </xsl:for-each>
    </tr>
  </xsl:template>

  <xsl:template match="xml">
    <table>
      <xsl:apply-templates select="rs:data/z:row"/>
    </table>
  </xsl:template>
</xsl:stylesheet>
```

Programming XSLT

Each XSLT processor has its own proprietary API for invoking XSLT programs. The following examples show how the Microsoft and Apache processors are used.

XSLT and MSXML

MSXML 2.x (and above) provides the `transformNode` function for performing an XSLT transformation against an in-memory DOM. The following Javascript code illustrates how to use `transformNode`:

```
// make sure parameters are correct
if (WScript.Arguments.length != 2 && WScript.Arguments.
    length != 3)
{
        WScript.echo("usage: xslt source stylesheet");
        WScript.Quit(1);
}
var source = WScript.Arguments.Item(0);
var stylesheet = WScript.Arguments.Item(1);

// create DOM document for source & stylesheet docs
var xmlSource = new ActiveXObject("MSXML2.DOMDocument");
var xmlStylesheet = new ActiveXObject("MSXML2.DOMDocument");

// set the selection language to XPath 1.0 - the default
// for MSXML 2.6 and above is XSL Patterns
xmlSource.setProperty("SelectionLanguage", "XPath");

// load the source document
if (xmlSource.load(source))
{
   // load the stylesheet document
   if (xmlStylesheet.load(stylesheet))
   {
       try {
          var output = xmlSource.transformNode(
             xmlStylesheet.documentElement);
          WScript.echo(output);
       }
       catch(e) {
       WScript.echo("### tranform error: " + e.description);
       }
   }
   else WScript.echo("### parse error: " +
      xmlStylesheet.parseError.reason);
}
else WScript.echo("### parse error: " +
   xmlSource.parseError.reason);
```

`transformNode` simply returns a string containing the result of the transformation. MSXML 2.x also provides the `transformNodeToObject` method for

ESSENTIAL XML: BEYOND MARKUP

returning the result as an in-memory DOM. The problem with both of these methods is that they don't provide a mechanism for passing in parameters to the stylesheet. MSXML 2.6 introduced a new set of interfaces that improves the overall efficiency of the processor and makes it possible to feed in parameters. The following example illustrates how these new interfaces are used:

```
if (WScript.Arguments.length != 2 &&
    WScript.Arguments.length != 3)
{
        WScript.echo(
            "usage: xslt source stylesheet [params]");
        WScript.Quit(1);
}
var source = WScript.Arguments.Item(0);
var stylesheet = WScript.Arguments.Item(1);

// params should look like this "foo1=bar foo2=baz ..."
var params = "";
if (WScript.Arguments.length == 3)
   params = WScript.Arguments.Item(2);

// create the template object for caching compiled XSL
// templates
var xslTemplate = new ActiveXObject("MSXML2.XSLTemplate");

// create a free-threaded DOM document for the source,
// output, and stylesheet documents
var xmlSource = new
   ActiveXObject("MSXML2.FreeThreadedDOMDocument");
var xmlOutput = new
   ActiveXObject("MSXML2.FreeThreadedDOMDocument");
var xmlStylesheet = new
   ActiveXObject("MSXML2.FreeThreadedDOMDocument");

// declare a reference to the XSLProcessor for performing
// transformations against compiled stylesheets
var xslProcessor = null;

// set the selection language to XPath 1.0
xmlSource.setProperty("SelectionLanguage", "XPath");
```

```
        // load the source document
        if (xmlSource.load(source))
        {
            // load the stylesheet document
            if (xmlStylesheet.load(stylesheet))
            {
                try {
                    // associate the stylesheet with the template
                    xslTemplate.stylesheet = xmlStylesheet;
                    // create the XSLProcessor for this transformation
                    xslProcessor = xslTemplate.createProcessor();
                    // specify the input and output DOMs
                    xslProcessor.input = xmlSource;
                    xslProcessor.output = xmlOutput;


                    // break apart the parameter string "foo1=bar
                    // foo2=baz ... and add each name/value pair to
                    // the processor
                    if (params != "") {
                        var parr = params.split(" ");
                        for (i=0; i<parr.length; i++) {
                            var p = parr[i];
                            var pair = p.split("=");
                            xslProcessor.addParameter(pair[0],
                                pair[1]);
                            xslProcessor.addParameter(pair[0],
                            pair[1]);
                        }
                    }
                    // call transform
                    b = xslProcessor.transform();
                    // echo the output to the console
                    WScript.echo(xmlOutput.xml);
                }
                catch(e) {
                WScript.echo("### tranform error: " + e.description);
                }
            }
            else WScript.echo("### parse error: " +
                xmlStylesheet.parseError.reason);
        }
```

```
      else WScript.echo("### parse error: " +
         xmlSource.parseError.reason);
```

XSLT and Xalan

The Xalan XSLT implementation from Apache.org also makes it possible to pro-
grammatically perform transformations, using parameters if desired. The following Java example demonstrates how this is done:

```
import org.xml.sax.SAXException;
import org.apache.xalan.xslt.XSLTProcessorFactory;
import org.apache.xalan.xslt.XSLTInputSource;
import org.apache.xalan.xslt.XSLTResultTarget;
import org.apache.xalan.xslt.XSLTProcessor;
import org.apache.xalan.xpath.XString;

public class Class1
{
    public static void main(String[] args)
    throws java.io.IOException,
           java.net.MalformedURLException,
           org.xml.sax.SAXException
    {
        // make sure there are enough parameters
        if (args.length < 2) {
            System.out.println(
                    "usage: xalanxslt source stylesheet" +
                    " [param1=value1 param2=value2 ...]");
            System.exit(1);
        }
        // Have the XSLTProcessorFactory obtain a
          // interface to a new XSLTProcessor object.
        XSLTProcessor processor =
              XSLTProcessorFactory.getProcessor();

        // pass command-line parameters to XSLT processor
        for (int i=2; i<args.length; i++) {
            String name, value;
            name = args[i].substring(0,
                    args[i].indexOf("="));
            value = args[i].substring(
```

```
                    args[i].indexOf("=")+1);
              processor.setStylesheetParam(name,
                    processor.createXString(value));
        }

        // Have the XSLTProcessor processor object perform
        // transformation using the specified files
        processor.process(new XSLTInputSource(args[0]),
                    new XSLTInputSource(args[1]),
                    new XSLTResultTarget(System.out));
      }
    }
```

Xalan also provides the following helper class implementation that can be used from the command line for testing purposes: `org.apache.xalan.xslt.Process`. This class can be used in the following fashion:

```
java org.apache.xalan.xslt.Process -IN %1 -XSL %2
```

Where `%1` is the URL of the source document and `%2` is the URL of the stylesheet document.

Index

Plus signs (+) in XPath, 122
Point locations, 140
Points, 140–141
Polymorphism
    in interface design, 247
    in messaging, 267
popContext method, 40–41
position function
    for axes, 114
    for paginated data, 342
    in XPath, 123–125, 134–135
POST method, 262
Pound signs (#)
    for character reference serialization, 26
    for URIs, 137
Precedence in XSLT patterns, 235
preceding axes, 112–114
preceding-sibling axes, 112–114
[predefined entity] property, 280
Predicates
    in location steps, 107
    in node tests, 119–123
prefix attribute, 72
[prefix] property, 285
Prefixed QNames, 150
Prefixes, 11–12
preserve-space directive, 243
Primary sort keys, 217
Primitive data types in SOAP, 260
printStackTrace method, 94
Priority in XSLT patterns, 235–236
Private drafts of Infoset specifications, 271
processContent attribute, 176
Processing instruction information items
    in document type declaration information items, 281
    in Infoset specification, 278
processing-instruction instruction
    for filtering, 118–119
    in XSLT, 208, 225–226
Processing instruction nodes
    in DOM, 63, 66, 73
    for filtering, 118–119
    in template-based patterns, 239
    in XPath, 103–104, 106

Processing instructions (PIs), 3, 13–15
    in documents, 5
    in XSLT, 226
processingInstruction method
    in ContentHandler, 34, 42–43
    in SAX2DOM, 316
Productions
    sorted by name, 303–307
    sorted by number, 299–303
Programming, 31–32
    DOM. See DOM (Document Object Model)
    SAX, 32–44
        auxiliary interfaces for, 44–50
        error handling in, 53–56
        and I/O, 50–53
        XMLReader interface in, 56–61
    XPath. See XPath programming
prohibited attributes, 173
Protocols, interfaces as, 247
[public identifier] property
    in entity information items, 91, 282
    in notation information items, 91, 283
Public identifiers, 16–17
pushContext method, 40–41

QName production, 11–12
QNames in schemas, 150
Qualified elements, 158
&quot entity, 27, 241
Quotation-marks (") in character serialization, 26

Range feature, 96
range function, 140
range-inside function, 140
Ranges in XPointer, 139–140
RDF Schema, 291–297
Read-only properties, 74
Recordset documents, 343–344
ref attribute, 161
refer attribute, 192
Reference constraints, 190–197
References
    entity, 17–18
    in Infoset specification, 289

Addison-Wesley Professional

How to Register Your Book

Register this Book

Visit: **http://www.aw.com/cseng/register**

Enter the ISBN*

Then you will receive:

- Notices and reminders about upcoming author appearances, tradeshows, and online chats with special guests
- Advanced notice of forthcoming editions of your book
- Book recommendations
- Notification about special contests and promotions throughout the year

*The ISBN can be found on the copyright page of the book

Visit our Web site

http://www.aw.com/cseng

When you think you've read enough, there's always more content for you at Addison-Wesley's web site. Our web site contains a directory of complete product information including:

- Chapters
- Exclusive author interviews
- Links to authors' pages
- Tables of contents
- Source code

You can also discover what tradeshows and conferences Addison-Wesley will be attending, read what others are saying about our titles, and find out where and when you can meet our authors and have them sign your book.

We encourage you to patronize the many fine retailers who stock Addison-Wesley titles. Visit our online directory to find stores near you.

Contact Us via Email

cepubprof@awl.com

Ask general questions about our books.
Sign up for our electronic mailing lists.
Submit corrections for our web site.

cepubeditors@awl.com

Submit a book proposal.
Send errata for a book.

cepubpublicity@awl.com

Request a review copy for a member of the media interested in reviewing new titles.

registration@awl.com

Request information about book registration.

Addison-Wesley Professional
One Jacob Way, Reading, Massachusetts 01867 USA
TEL 781-944-3700 • FAX 781-942-3076